MARCEL PRONOVOST · JOHNNY WILSON · METRO PRYSTAI · V

UCE MACGREGOR · BILL GADSBY · DOUG BARK

DANNY GRANT · DENNIS POLONICH · REED LARSON · VACLAV

EDDIE MIO · SHAWN BURR · HARRY NEALE · JACQUES DEMERS

NICKLAS LIDSTROM · MARK HOWE · SCOTTY BOWMAN · KRIS

MAS HOLMSTROM · LARRY MURPHY · BRENDAN SHANAHAN · KE

LUC ROBITAILLE · HENRIK ZETTERBERG · TED LINDSAY · LEO

HNNY WILSON · METRO PRYSTAI · VIC STASIUK · BENNY WOIT ·

SBY · DOUG BARKLEY · PAUL HENDERSON · PETE MAHOVLICH ·

S POLONICH · REED LARSON · VACLAV NEDOMANSKY · PAUL WO

BURR · HARRY NEALE · JACQUES DEMERS · DAVE LEWIS · JIM NIL

MARK HOWE · SCOTTY BOWMAN · KRIS DRAPER · CHRIS OSC

LARRY MURPHY · BRENDAN SHANAHAN · KEN HOLLAND · CHR

HENRIK ZETTERBERG · TED LINDSAY · LEO REISE · RED KELLY

METRO PRYSTAI · VIC STASIUK · BENNY WOIT · LARRY ZEIDEL ·

RKLEY · PAUL HENDERSON · PETE MAHOVLICH · BRYAN WATSON

ED LARSON · VACLAV NEDOMANSKY · PAUL WOODS · STEVE YZ

ALE · JACQUES DEMERS · DAVE LEWIS · JIM NILL · TIM CHEVELDAE

TTY BOWMAN · KRIS DRAPER · CHRIS OSGOOD · DOUG BROWN

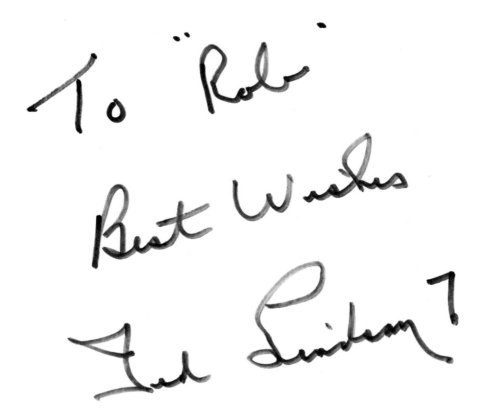

To "Rob"

Best Wishes

Ted Lindsay?

WHAT IT MEANS TO BE A RED WING

DETROIT'S GREATEST PLAYERS
TALK ABOUT DETROIT HOCKEY

FOREWORD BY STEVE YZERMAN

KEVIN ALLEN AND ART REGNER

TRIUMPH
BOOKS
CHICAGO

Library of Congress Cataloging-in-Publication Data

Allen, Kevin, 1956–
What it means to be a Red Wing / Kevin Allen and Art Regner.
    p. cm.
ISBN-13: 978-1-57243-885-9
ISBN-10: 1-57243-885-1
    1. Detroit Red Wings (Hockey team)—History. 2. Hockey players—Michigan—Detroit—Biography. I. Regner, Art, 1957– II. Title.

GV848.D47A45 2006
796.962'640977434—dc22

                                                                2006012301

This book is available in quantity at special discounts for your group or organization. For further information, contact:

Triumph Books
542 South Dearborn Street
Suite 750
Chicago, Illinois 60605
(312) 939-3330
Fax (312) 663-3557

Printed in U.S.A.
ISBN-13: 978-1-57243-885-9
ISBN-10: 1-57243-885-1

All photos courtesy of the Detroit Red Wings, except where indicated otherwise. Jersey shot courtesy of Peter Kuehl.
Design by Nick Panos. Editorial and page production by Prologue Publishing Services, LLC, Oak Park, Illinois.

CONTENTS

FOREWORD

What It Means to Be a Red Wing

If I could write a script about my Red Wings career, could I have written a better one? Sure, I suppose. I probably wouldn't have written in it for me to wait 14 years before I won a Stanley Cup! But things have worked out pretty well for me along the way. I came here when I was 18 years old, and over the years I've grown up and changed. I've learned a lot over the course of my career: about the game, about leadership, about the things that need to be done to make a team sport successful. You learn that by experiencing some of the defeats that we had along the way.

It goes without saying—I've been very fortunate to be able to play my entire career in Detroit. Detroit is an Original Six team with a great history of winning. I've had quite a few very successful years here and a lot of that is luck and timing. Going back to my very first year, I've been lucky to play with some Hall of Fame players. When you look back on this team in 10 years, some of the players I'm playing with now will also be in the Hall of Fame.

Right after I was drafted by the Red Wings, I was given a hat, jersey, and Red Wings media guide. I read through all the names of the great Red Wings players who had played for the team and immediately became excited about being a part of the organization. Every player who gets drafted has the initial dream that it's going to work out for him—that he's going to win games on his new team and eventually win the Stanley Cup. That was my dream—along with every other hockey player. You have so much optimism at that time.

When I looked at the Red Wings media guide, it was pretty impressive. Detroit had so many of the great players of the 1950s and 1960s play for them that it really stuck out to me. Players such as Gordie Howe, Alex Delvecchio,

Detroit captain Steve Yzerman generated six goals and 18 assists for 24 points to lead the Red Wings to the 1998 Stanley Cup championship. He has been the Red Wings' captain since 1986, making him the longest-tenured captain in NHL history.

Ted Lindsay, and Terry Sawchuk; the list seemed to go on and on. The uniforms hadn't changed much over the years, and it was special to be a part of an organization with such an illustrious tradition. Talking to Jimmy Devellano at the time or Mr. and Mrs. Ilitch, they had a lot of excitement toward the team. You fed off of the talk of winning; when we won there was excitement and when we lost there was a lot of emotion spent. That kind of feeling carried down to the players because of the passion of the organization.

Of course our fan base has also been a key to our success. When we play on the road and see their arena filled with a large portion of Red Wings fans, it's that sort of enthusiasm that is a great motivator. We share in the joy when we win and the disappointment when we lose. The dedication and strength of our fans to be able to keep coming back and cheering us on is a significant contribution to the player's determination to go through it all again; we all feed off of one another.

Very few guys in the NHL, or any sport, are fortunate enough to go through their careers without some type of major injury. For me, the two bad ones are my knee and my neck; those two have really taken their toll on me in terms of debilitating injuries. Everything else, I don't think has really affected what I can do on the ice in the long term. Some guys get hurt more than others, and I don't know that there's a reason for it. I look at my injuries as things that really forced me to train harder, and prepare to work harder; so in some ways they were good for me. But on the other side of that, unfortunately, they've had some permanent effects on what I can and cannot do.

I've stated this before: when you looked at our team, I didn't feel like I was "the centerpiece." Since Nick Lidstrom arrived, we've had tremendous talent in Detroit. Since then, people have debated, "Who's the best player on the Red Wings?" and despite popular belief, most of our players have been drafted by the organization. We've brought in Shanahan, Chelios, and Hasek to help, but our core has been homegrown. I've always felt that I'm just playing my role—nothing more than Lidstrom, Fedorov, or Shanahan have done. We've really become a team since 1995, and it's been about good players meshing together more than any one in particular standing out. I never felt like I was who this team is built around because I was just one of several good players that make up a good team.

Between 1992 and 1996 our team was full of guys who could score, but we were never a solid defensive team. Our way of winning was to score more goals than you could; it was a wide-open style of play. If it was 0–0 in the third period, we were going to try and force it to score. But once Scotty Bowman came to our team, a 0–0 game meant that we were going to sit back and wait for them to make a mistake. We weren't really comfortable with that at the beginning.

In 1995 our team's philosophy started to change dramatically because Scotty told us that we were going to become a good defensive hockey club. I played on quite a few different line combinations over the next few seasons. At that point in time, I wanted to play on a good team—a team that was a winner. I wasn't about to complain about lines or anything else. For years I had said, "I'll do whatever I have to do to win." If Scotty told me, "This is the role you're going to play," whatever the reason was, I was going to accept it. It helped me and I became a better defensive hockey player because of it. Scotty wanted to change our team and told me what I needed to do, saying, "This is how I'm going to play you and this is what I expect from you." At center we had Igor Larionov, Sergei Fedorov, and Kris Draper—plus a lot of offense on the team at that time. I agreed that we had to be a better defensive club, and we all stressed it, from the head coach to the assistant coaches to our entire lineup—and as a result we won two Stanley Cups in a row.

With each game that we won in the 1997 Stanley Cup Finals vs. Philadelphia, we got more nervous. In Game 4, we were up 3–0 in the series, and that was the most nervous I felt going into a game. I kept thinking, "The Stanley Cup is right there. We have to win!" It was very nerve-racking, so it was a great relief after the game ended and we finally won. I wasn't focused on the 42-year drought in Red Wing Stanley Cups, I was just glad to be in a position to win that series and I didn't want to mess it up! That's all I was thinking about at the time and afterward it was more, "Oh, God—what a relief!"

I've seen the Stanley Cup raised so many times, so it was the biggest highlight of my entire career to be able to lift that Stanley Cup in front of everyone at Joe Louis Arena! I could have stood there at center ice forever. Holding that Stanley Cup is an irreplaceable moment in my life.

I had never thought about who I would hand the Stanley Cup to the first time we won it. I just wanted to win it; I couldn't think about the actual act of what would happen once we did. In 1998 we didn't plan what we would do with the Cup when it was awarded to us either because we didn't want to jinx it, but Vladdy just happened to be sitting there on the ice with us. Things happen for a reason, and we were able to share it with him at that moment.

With our third Stanley Cup in 2002, they brought all of the families out onto the ice; my daughter Isabella was standing next to me when Commissioner Gary Bettman started to make the presentation. I turned to her and said, "Let's go get it!" It was just a coincidence to have her next to me. It's funny because she was shy and didn't really want to be in the spotlight with me, but I told her to raise her hands up when I lifted the Cup. Whichever photographer snapped the picture of the two of us with hands raised had perfect timing because Isabella only raised her hands up for a split-second—but it made for a great moment.

It was an honor for me to win the Conn Smythe Trophy in 1998. Over the course of my years as a hockey player, I hadn't won a lot of individual awards and I really didn't care, but that's as important of an award that you can ever win. Winning three Stanley Cups and winning the Conn Smythe Trophy makes for three very special years. If you look at the names of the players who have won that trophy—wow!

★   ★   ★

Those were the moments in a career that players dream about. Winning a Stanley Cup with the Detroit Red Wings was my dream when I was drafted by the team as an 18-year-old kid who had no idea that his dreams would be realized. When we won the Cup in 1997, at that moment in time I felt that we had finally arrived.

I've played with a lot of great players over the course of my career and under a lot of great coaches whom I learned a lot from. If I were to point out one player, it would be Gerard Gallant. He was a great player with a great heart who was loved by everyone. He was an awesome teammate, my roommate, and my best friend while he was here. I really wish that he could have been here when we won the Stanley Cup. He was a great teammate and linemate and deserved to be on a Stanley Cup winner. It's one of the few disappointments that I have in hockey that Gerard Gallant and I didn't get to win the Stanley Cup together.

Some years I did have things to say to try and motivate the team. Sometimes it appeared to work and sometimes it didn't. I honestly believe the whole "impact of a speech" is all Hollywood stuff. I don't think any speech I've ever given has had a huge effect on the outcome of a game or series. The attitude of the players is what makes or breaks it. What is said in meetings or in the room gets exaggerated as far more important than it really deserves. As long as the guys on the team have a positive attitude, and the leaders on the team go out there and show that they want to win, everyone will follow along.

I was the captain of the Red Wings for so long that there was only so much that I could say. We had the same core of players for a long time; I'm sure they probably knew what was coming out of my mouth before I could even say it in those situations. In the last few years, I've said less and less. I think it's the same way around the league because the players all have pretty good attitudes and they work harder now. They are all very conscientious and professional. There is very little that needs to be said. You don't need to tell guys that they need to get in shape or work harder now. The most important thing a leader on a team can do is make sure everyone is on the same page and that they all have the best interest of the team as their number-one goal. You just have to make sure that no one is sidetracked by what they want individually. Just make sure that everyone is a key part—because that is what leaders on a team do. Our team has done this, so there hasn't been a lot of work for the captain to have to go and straighten things out.

Being a Detroit Red Wing to me is being a part of an organization that has a history that goes way back. Some of the greatest players in the National Hockey League have played for the Red Wings. For me, I feel like I have a responsibility of getting or keeping the organization at a level that players like Gordie Howe, Terry Sawchuk, Alex Delvecchio, Ted Lindsay, and Sid Abel brought it to. Being a Red Wing is having an obligation to play and conduct yourself in the same manner and with the same expectations that those players had. The level of play and level of professionalism should always meet that of the Red Wings greats that came before you.

If you don't have a love and passion for the sport that you play then you won't be successful in the long haul. Money isn't the motivator in sports; you have to have the will to win and a drive to be the best. You have to want to be good, to want to win. You have to have the pride in yourself, the pride in your team to succeed.

As you read these Red Wings player's stories, you'll find that regardless of their era, or their success or failure on the ice, we all share the common bond of not only a love and passion for hockey, but the commitment to uphold the tradition of a team—our team—the Detroit Red Wings.

—Steve Yzerman

ACKNOWLEDGMENTS

A SMALL BLACK-AND-WHITE TELEVISION with a snowy picture was my intro-duction to the Detroit Red Wings. My mother and Uncle Jack were the hockey fans in the family, and it seems like just yesterday that the three of us were glued to the tube watching the men that donned the winged wheel. The Red Wings have been a part of my life since I was a child and without my mom and Uncle Jack this book could have never been written. Thanks, Ma and Uncle Jack.

There are so many people that I would like to offer my gratitude to for either giving me their time or giving me my space to complete this project. My colleagues at WXYT, especially my radio partner Doug Karsch, my niece Jessica, along with my good friends Sally and Simon Coan were all extremely supportive and always willing to listen to my constant ramblings about this book. A special thanks to Sarah Zientarski for her transcription: you came through again. But most of all, I would like to single out Michelle Depue. Michelle is my inspiration. You're the best.

Finally, to all the players who shared their stories for this book—thank you. And thanks to Triumph Books for giving us the opportunity to write about one of hockey's most storied teams.

I dedicate this book to my father and my sister, Mary. I miss them, but I know that once this book reaches heaven's library, they'll be the first two in line.

—Art Regner

★　★　★

THIS BOOK IS DEDICATED TO John Reinhart and the late Paul Morrow for nurturing my love of sports and for supporting the idea that I could turn my passion into a profession.

—Kevin Allen

INTRODUCTION

WE APPRECIATED DETROIT RED WINGS tradition and history long before we purchased the franchise in 1982. We grew up in the Detroit area and witnessed the team's glory seasons of the 1950s. We were hockey fans before we were owners, having learned to appreciate the energy and beauty of the sport through the efforts of Hall of Famers such as Gordie Howe, Ted Lindsay, Red Kelly, Marcel Pronovost, and a host of others.

When we opened our first Little Caesars store in Garden City, Michigan, on May 8, 1959, Gordie was hockey's king. He would win his fifth Hart Trophy the following season. Gordie was a remarkable player and person. It's simply unfathomable that he was still playing in the NHL at age 52. We have known Gordie and his lovely wife, Colleen, for more than 40 years. The Howes have always been about family and commitment.

In those days, as today, Little Caesars would sponsor amateur youth teams around the Detroit metropolitan area. It was our tradition to celebrate championships at Little Caesars, and we would invite Gordie to attend. He never turned us down. Gordie has always had time for young people. He would come in and congratulate our players, encourage them, and make everyone feel special.

We still laugh today about the time years ago when our daughter, Lisa, then just starting elementary school, asked Gordie for his autograph. Wanting to personalize it for her, Gordie asked Lisa what specifically she wanted him to write on paper.

"Your name," she said.

Before we bought the Red Wings, we supported the team as fans and sponsors. When the opportunity to purchase the team presented itself, we jumped in with both feet. The team structure was in disarray when the sale was complete, and everyone in our family pitched in to restore fans' faith in the team. Past and current season ticket holders all received phone calls from a member of the Ilitch family asking them to support the team.

We were as aggressive as we could be in our rebuilding efforts. We gave away a car at every game, and we brought in name free agents at a time when free agency was almost nonexistent in the National Hockey League. However, it still took us longer than we expected to bring the Stanley Cup back home to Detroit. Coach Jacques Demers showed us how to win in the late 1980s, and then Scotty Bowman transformed us into an elite-level team in the 1990s. Fifteen years after we bought the team, the Steve Yzerman–led Red Wings won the Stanley Cup.

As happy as we are about the three Stanley Cup championships the team won from 1997 to 2002, the real satisfaction about owning this team comes from seeing how Detroit is now known as "Hockeytown."

We have always believed in downtown Detroit. We moved our Little Caesars offices to Detroit, and we bought the Detroit Tigers, and now we have beautiful Comerica Park located across the street from the Fox Theater. The Detroit Lions moved back here. There is excitement in this city, and we are proud that the Red Wings played a role in renovating the pride of Detroit.

xiii

Ten years ago you didn't see the traffic downtown to support restaurants and entertainment because everyone went home after 5:00 P.M. Now that we have two downtown stadiums, the corporations, the residential lofts, and other entertainment, the city is really alive.

It's a shame that Gordie Howe didn't start and finish his career in a Red Wings uniform. That's why we feel honored that we were able to watch Steve Yzerman start and finish his career wearing the winged wheel on his chest. It's difficult to find the right words to describe what he has meant to our franchise. He has essentially been with the team as long as we have. He is part of our family. Remember when Jacques Demers had the audacity to make this 20-year-old kid the team's captain? As we look back, it was the best move this franchise could have made. He gave us the leadership we needed to find success. Like many fans, we consider Steve one of the greatest athletes in Detroit history.

Loyalty has always been important to us; it's gratifying to have watched Nick Lidstrom's transformation from a young prospect to one of the league's all-time great defensemen. When we became owners, our plan was not only to find great players, but to also keep them. One reason why the Red Wings have stayed at, or near, the top for many years is that players have stayed with us. They have pride in wearing the Detroit sweater.

We have been blessed with so many elite athletes during our ownership, and it makes us extremely happy that players feel good about playing in Detroit. Thanks to the efforts of people like Jimmy Devellano and Ken Holland, among many others, the team has had a consistency of success for many years.

If you ask us what it means to be a Red Wing, we would say that it means that everyone in the organization strives for success while conducting himself or herself in a classy and professional manner. It's about pride. Little Caesars is a family business. And the Detroit Red Wings are a family organization. Pride has played an important role in the success of each venture.

—Mike and Marian Ilitch

The FORTIES

TED LINDSAY

LEFT WING

1944–1957 ★ 1964–1965

SID ABEL WAS THE PERFECT CENTER for Gordie Howe and me when we were young: Gordie had to be pumped up, and I had to be calmed down. And Sid could do that. He was a father figure. We spent a lot of time at his house. His wife, Gloria, was a wonderful Italian lady, and she used to make good pasta meals for a couple of hungry hockey players.

A lot of people said anybody could play hockey with those two guys. One day they put a rocking chair at center ice, and Gordie and I stood on each side of Sid in the rocking chair. We all had a good laugh. Sid was the catalyst that kept us together.

We had great players with great talent on those Red Wings teams in the 1950s. We won four Stanley Cup championships, and we would have won more if General Manager Jack Adams hadn't torn apart the team.

After we won in 1955, Adams traded away eight players from our team. In those days, 18 players made up a roster: you had one goaltender, five defensemen, three forward lines, and two extra players. Adams traded away almost half of our team. He didn't want to trade Terry Sawchuk to Montreal because he thought he would make the Canadiens too strong, so he traded him to Boston. He traded other players to Chicago. We ended up with some guys who were good hockey players, but they weren't winners. We lost our chemistry. We were a machine that was running efficiently, and Adams disrupted everything. The only weakness we could see is that Bob Goldham would

Pound per pound, the 163-pound Ted Lindsay was considered one of the toughest players in NHL history. "Terrible Teddy" boasted the proper blend of skill and grit. He still shares the Detroit record for goals in a playoff game. He netted four against Montreal in 1955.

probably be retiring in two more years. And we could have received a dog-gone good defenseman from Montreal for Sawchuk, if Adams would have been willing to trade Sawchuk there.

Maybe Montreal may have given up Tom Johnson or even Doug Harvey for Sawchuk at that point in their careers.

I still believe to this day that the five Stanley Cups that Montreal won [from 1956 to 1960] should have been ours. At worst, we should have won three of the five. We had the team. We had the talent. We had the chemistry.

Although I know I was the first one to lift the Stanley Cup over my head, I'm the wrong guy to ask when it was. I didn't plan it. I just did it for the fans.

My feelings were that the fans paid my salary, not the management. We didn't have glass or screens back then. The only place we had chicken wire was at the end of the rink where the high glass is now. Along the boards, the people who had season tickets had their elbows up there when you came by. They would move back when we went down into the corner. They would have to put their head out to see what's going on in the corner.

I just decided to show it to the fans who were just as important as the players. I'm sure when I picked up the Stanley Cup, Adams must have said, "What's the idiot Lindsay gonna do now?"

But that's what I did. I can't say whether it was 1955 or before then.

When I was traded to Chicago by Adams, my heart was still with the Red Wings. That's why I retired in 1960 [at 34]. I was still a Red Wing. I had it tattooed on my chest, and on my forehead, and on my backside. That's why I quit. I didn't quit because I believed I was finished. I quit because I was just existing. I wasn't living.

I stayed retired until Sid Abel took over the Red Wings and talked me out of retirement. I wanted to become the color analyst on television. I just wanted to end up a Red Wing. Then Sid changed things up.

"I think you can help us if you come back and play," he said.

After I decided to do it, NHL President Clarence Campbell said it was "the blackest day in the history of hockey" because a 39-year-old player thought he could play after being retired for four years. He called it a disgrace to hockey.

That season I scored 14 goals. In the six-team NHL, a 15-goal scorer was like being a .315 to .325 hitter in baseball. That was before expansion.

Two months into the season, Campbell apologized about what he said about my comeback.

Ted Lindsay's Career Highlights

* Leading all scorers with five goals and seven points to help the Red Wings win the 1952 Stanley Cup championship.

* Winning the 1949–1950 Art Ross trophy as NHL scoring champion with league-leading 78 points. He and Nels Stewart are the only players in NHL history to have led the league in scoring and in penalty minutes during their careers.

* Being selected eight times as a first-team NHL All-Star.

* Serving as captain of the 1954 and 1955 Red Wings Stanley Cup championship squads. The consensus seems to be that Lindsay raised the Cup for fans in 1955.

* Being able to still play organized men's league hockey into his late seventies. "That's the wonderful thing about hockey," he said. "Many of the players will continue to play into their fifties, sixties, even their seventies. You can go into Canada and find players in their eighties."

LEO REISE
DEFENSEMAN
1946–1952

WHEN I SCORED TWO OVERTIME GOALS in the 1950 semifinals against Toronto, I'm sure I shot the puck so fast that goaltender Turk Broda couldn't see it. I was renowned for a hard shot.

I'm being facetious.

I didn't do too much shooting. All I did on those goals was shoot the puck from the blue line. I backhanded one, and the other one I forehanded. The first one in Toronto [scored 38 seconds into the second overtime] hit someone in front and went in. I don't think Broda saw it. [The goal gave Detroit a 2–1 win and evened the best-of-seven series at 2–2.]

In the seventh game, I took a shot that missed everyone and went into the corner at 8:39 of overtime to give us a 1–0 win.

Why did I seem to score more in the playoffs than I did in the regular season? In the months prior to the playoffs, I would say, *Okay, I have to make sure I'm in real good shape.* I made an effort in the last couple of weeks of the season to push myself harder. When the playoffs came, I was flying.

I don't have a favorite individual memory of being with the Red Wings. The memory I have is the camaraderie. Scoring goals and making the plays—that's all incidental. It's the fellowship of the Red Wings that I remember. The Red Wings were about being a team, not making individual plays. We could skate with any team in the league. We could outhit the other teams and

Defenseman Leo Reise is one of only six Red Wings ever to score two overtime goals in a single playoff year. Mud Bruneteau, Syd Howe, Ted Lindsay, Vyacheslav Kozlov, and Brendan Shanahan are the others.

we could outscore everyone. We shot the puck, passed the puck, and then got back where we belonged.

In 1951–1952 we had a powerhouse team. We only lost 14 games in the regular season and we won the Stanley Cup in eight straight games. Nobody could touch us. We just had a great team. It was the definition of what a team should be. When we went out after a game, we all went together. It was like a family. There was no bitching. No one was unhappy with each other. When you have a team like that, you can take a feeling of fellowship a long way.

I got along with everyone, including Adams. One time he said he was going to send me to the farm team in Indianapolis. "You aren't going to send me anywhere," I said. "I don't have to play hockey." I wouldn't let them push me around, and that was the end of that.

When you reached a certain salary level, they didn't want to keep you around too long if they could find a substitute. I believe I was moved out because I was among the team's highest paid players. In 1951–1952, Marcel Pronovost and Red Kelly were carrying the puck a lot, and I let them go ahead. I played back. I wasn't too effective from the scoring end. Maybe that was one of the reasons why they traded me. But at the time, I was one of the best defenseman in the country. So it was a bit of a shock to be traded.

After the 1952 playoffs, we were coming home on a train from Montreal, and I sat by Jack Adams and the team's publicity man, Fred Huber.

"I'm thinking about taking out my [immigration] papers and moving to the States," I said to them at one point. Huber and Adams each looked at each other. I thought, *Uh-oh, I had better not do that because they are going to trade me.*

Later in the summer I read in the newspaper that I had been traded to the New York Rangers for Reg Sinclair and John Morrison.

I go to American Hockey League Hamilton Bulldogs games now, and people there know that I played in the NHL. One guy came up to me and said, "You don't think of yourself as a New York Ranger, do you?"

When you consider how close we all were back then, it's hard not to think of myself as a Red Wing.

Leo Reise's Career Highlights

* Playing for two Stanley Cup championship teams in Detroit and scoring the two OT goals in 1950.

* Being named as second-team NHL All-Star in 1950 and 1951.

* Although not known as an offensive defenseman, stepping up his scoring in the playoffs. In 494 regular-season games, he netted 28 goals for an average of one goal every 17.6 games. In 52 playoff games, he scored eight goals for an average of one goal every 6.5 games.

* Having five points in six games in the 1951 NHL playoffs.

* Playing in the NHL with his father, Leo Sr., as one of the first father-son combinations. Lester Patrick had played one game for the New York Rangers as an emergency goalie in the 1928 Stanley Cup Finals. His sons, Lynn and Muzz, both were regulars for the New York Rangers in the mid- to late-1930s. Bert Lindsay and his son, Ted, were also ahead of the Reises. Bert Lindsay was a goalie for the Montreal Wanderers and Toronto Arenas from 1917 to 1919. Ted Lindsay came to the NHL in 1944, two seasons before Reise. The elder Reise had played for the Hamilton Tigers, New York Americans, and New York Rangers, in a career that lasted from 1920 to 1930. "For a long time I thought I was the first son of a former NHL regular to play in the NHL," Reise said. "It was even written up that way."

RED KELLY

DEFENSEMAN

1947–1960

WHEN YOU WERE A MEMBER OF THE Detroit Red Wings in the 1950s, you played at Olympia Stadium and you lived at Ma Shaw's rooming house.

Ma Shaw's place was about two blocks from Olympia Stadium. She had four rooms, and four players lived there at a time. Defenseman Jack Stewart stayed there before my time, along with Bill Quackenbush and Harry Lumley. Then the rooms were filled by Gordie Howe, Ted Lindsay, Marty Pavelich, and myself. After Lindsay was married, Metro Prystai moved in. Ma Shaw was a widow. We didn't have our meals there, but we had the run of the house. She had a piano, and we would fiddle around on that. When we went out, we took Ma Shaw with us, almost like a chaperone.

NHL scheduling was different in those days, too. Usually we'd play Saturday and Sunday night, and maybe Wednesday. We'd be off on Monday and Tuesday, and when we would be off, we'd all go out to dinner and one of the clubs might stay open for us because we liked to dance. We would go to the Grande or Graystone ballrooms or Baker's Lounge. Everyone would bring their wives, girlfriends, or dates, and we would all dance with everyone. It was usually all mixed up. Gordie, Marty, and I used to love to dance. But Ted wasn't so active on the dance floor.

If we weren't dancing, we would be bowling at the Lucky Strike or over at someone's house. But we were usually all together, and that probably had a lot to do with our success. We were a close-knit team.

Considered one of the NHL's best handling defenseman in the 1950s, Red Kelly was a first- or second-team All-Star seven times in his 13-season career in Detroit. Few players in the league skated as well as Kelly did in that era.

Probably the best team I played for was the 1951–1952 team. We had good teams throughout the years, and some were stronger in some areas than others and maybe weaker in other departments. But they all had that winning attitude. The '52 Detroit team was certainly one of the best of all time. No question. We were all about winning in those days. Everyone on that team lived and breathed hockey.

Tommy Ivan was a good coach. Jack Adams had a tendency to get down on players, and Tommy would build them up. He played me a lot of minutes. Guys used to say, "Tommy is going to wear you out." But it never worked out that way. Even as a defenseman, I carried the puck often. But I wouldn't hang around in the other end. I was in great shape. The only words I heard from Tommy about my style was, "Don't get caught. Don't hang around up there. You're not a forward." I'd make the offensive play and then get back in my defensive position.

I loved to play with Benny Woit. He wasn't necessarily the fastest or the best skater in the world, but he could skate and he could hit. And when Benny would hit them, they knew they were hit. He delivered solid checks. I would be carrying the puck, and Benny would be hitting, and we'd work well together. Benny always had a great attitude, but Jack Adams liked to ride him all of the time.

Jack always liked to pick on somebody one way or another, and Benny was a favorite target. After a game, Jack would come into the dressing room and head straight to Benny. Pigeon-toed Adams would stand in front of Benny chewing him out for something real or imagined. After this happened a few times, Benny figured out what to do. He would rush in, grab an orange or two, and then he would toss the peels on the floor. Now Jack would come flying toward Benny, and he would slip on the peels and forget what he was saying. Benny was quite a jokester.

Defenseman Bob Goldham was a great shot-blocker on our team. He wasn't the fastest skater, but he could weave. He was a good stick-handler.

The line of Lindsay, Sid Abel, and Howe was a great line, although Sid, or "Old Boot Nose" as we called him, had to remind Howe and Lindsay from time to time that he was on their line. Gordie and Ted were so close to each other, on and off the ice, that they would get in the habit of passing the puck across to each other.

"Hey," Sid would yell, "do I look like a statue out here?"

Sid was a great captain. Ted was feisty and he wanted to win. He was a great Red Wing and he wouldn't back off from anybody. He could score goals and was good around the net. He had great determination. Of course Gordie was a big, strong guy. He was always supportive of Lindsay. And of course Gordie could score goals; he was a solid skater and had hockey sense. He had a great elbow.

I had played against Terry Sawchuk when we were in junior hockey. I was at St. Mike's and he was at Galt. We beat him in the playoffs, but it was nip and tuck. Then I played with Sawchuk when I came up to Detroit, and I played against him when he was traded Boston. I played with him again in Detroit when he was traded back. I played with him in Toronto and I coached him in Los Angeles. I can say Ukey was a great goaltender. He had the crouch. He could be up on his feet and be crouching. I think it was the shape of his body. He was wide-bodied. And when he was in the net, you didn't see too much.

Lumley's nickname was "Apple Cheeks" because when he got scored on, his cheeks would get red. He was a good goaltender. I know that some players weren't as happy with Lum because they thought he blamed them for goals. I was a young guy playing defense, and he never blamed me for a goal. And I would apologize to him if I let a guy get away.

I enjoyed my time in Detroit. There were many heroes on that team, but you can't win unless you have a team. And we had that. I played there 13 seasons until an article by *Toronto Globe and Mail* writer Trent Frayne caused me to be traded to the New York Rangers on February 5, 1960.

There were several different stories about why I wouldn't report to the New York Rangers when I was traded there in 1960. It wasn't because my mother-in-law lived in New York, it was because they were saying we didn't make the playoffs for the first time in the 1958–1959 season because Kelly had a bad year.

Frayne had interviewed me at the Royal York Hotel, and he started asking me questions centered around the idea that I was playing better than I had the previous season.

"There were reports that your legs are going, and that you're on your way out," he said. "But you are having a better year. Why is that?"

"Well, I don't know, it's just one if those things, I guess," I said. "You have your ups and downs."

"Aw, c'mon," Frayne said. "There's got to be a reason."

Finally, I told him the truth. "There's no harm in telling you now, but I spent all summer running barefoot on the beach and using a tennis ball to try and get my ankle back into shape because I broke the ankle last year and the team was struggling a bit," I said. "We lost four games in a row on the road, and they came and asked if I could take the cast off and tape it up and if I could play, help the team out. And I said, 'I can try.'"

I told him the whole story. The first game was in Chicago. Of course the ankle wasn't bendable; it was stiff. Bobby Hull was going down the ice and I couldn't turn to the left. I couldn't turn that ankle, so I had to move over and force Bubby Hull to cut over on the right side so I could turn and stay with him. I did what I could to play with the injury. So that's what I told him and he wrote the story. He wrote it for a weekend magazine.

Then we went back to Detroit because we had a game the next day. Lindsay's wife, Pat, called my wife and said, "Do you have your bags packed?"

My wife didn't know what she was talking about. "Haven't you seen the newspaper?" Pat asked. "Go read it and then pack."

My wife went to a newsstand and bought the *Detroit Free Press*. The headline was: "Was Red Kelly forced to play on a broken foot?"

I read the story, and what was in the paper didn't come close to matching what the headline said. I thought the story didn't say much, and I went out and played that night against the New York Rangers like everything would be fine. My wife was in the stands, and she heard midway through the game that I had been traded.

When Adams told me I had been traded with Billy McNeill for Bill Gadsby and Eddie Shack, I said, "I'll think about it."

"What do you mean you will think about it," Adams said. "You'll be there."

But I went home and thought about it. At that point, the Rangers were unable to make the playoffs no matter what they did the rest of the season. I decided to call the place I worked in the summer—a tool company—and asked if I could start work there "tomorrow morning." I was told that I could, and that's what did. I began to work at the tool company.

I called and told Adams, "I'm retiring, and it has nothing to do with New York."

I didn't think I owed the Red Wings anything. I always signed one-year contracts and I didn't break the bank.

The next phone call came from NHL president Clarence Campbell. "Jack Adams wants you suspended, but I'm holding off because I want you to have more time to think about it," Campbell said.

"Well, thank you, Mr. Campbell," I said, "but I'm not changing my mind. I've given everything I have to hockey since I've been knee high to a grasshopper, and if you want to suspend me, go ahead."

"If we suspend you," Campbell said, "it means you can't play. You can't referee. You can't coach. You can't do anything that involves hockey."

"Go ahead," I said again, "because I'm not reporting to New York."

That's the way it went. The trade was nullified, and Shack and Gadsby went back to New York. Five days later, I was with the Toronto Maple Leafs. The Boston Bruins had called me as well. [On May 10, Kelly's suspension was rescinded after the Maple Leafs and Red Wings agreed to a trade that sent Kelly to Toronto for Marc Reaume.]

Recently my wife was going through old papers upstairs in our home and found a letter from Frayne. In the letter, he had explained what had happened. He had been working on a biography of Jack Adams for years, and he tried to call Adams and explain the situation. He finally called the Detroit publicity man, but Adams still wouldn't talk to him. The PR guy told Frayne that Adams was no longer going to help Frayne with the bio. He said Adams hadn't seen Frayne's magazine piece, he had only seen the *Free Press* article. Frayne's story never said anything about me being forced to play with a broken foot. Adams wouldn't talk to him after that.

That's the story of why I wouldn't report to New York. I broke the bone just below my ankle bone and played on it because players always did that back then. We didn't tell anyone about it because we didn't want anyone taking a swing on it. When Detroit blamed me for missing the playoffs, it made me mad. That's the story.

Red Kelly's Career Highlights

* Winning four more Stanley Cups with Toronto to go with the four he won with Detroit. Only four other players—Henri Richard, Jean Beliveau, Yvan Cournoyer, and Claude Provost—have won more.

* Being elected to the Hall of Fame in 1969.

* Playing forward for the Red Wings. "Whenever they ran into trouble offensively, I'd get moved up," Kelly said. "I didn't mind. I didn't even mind missing out on the first All-Star team as long as I was helping the team." In seasons when Kelly played frequently at forward, sportswriters sometimes didn't know whether he would be selected at defense or forward so he wouldn't get all the votes he should receive. That explains why he was voted a NHL second-team All-Star, instead of first-team for some seasons.

* Winning the Norris Trophy in 1954 as the NHL's top defenseman. He had 16 goals and 33 assists that season.

* Scoring the tying goal in Detroit's 2–1 overtime triumph against Montreal in the 1954 Stanley Cup Finals.

MAX McNAB

CENTER

1947–1950

WHEN I CAME UP WITH THE RED WINGS in 1947–1948, the practices were tougher than the games. We used to run drills over and over and over because Coach Tommy Ivan could only allow us to scrimmage for 20 minutes. If we went any longer, it would get mean out there. This was the most competitive bunch of guys I've seen. I figured if I could just hold my own in practice, I could compete against any other team in the league.

It was an honor to play with the Red Wings because it seemed as if they had the best organization. They had the best farm system. They had working agreements with Indianapolis and Omaha, plus affiliations with more junior teams than other National Hockey League teams. I felt they had good management.

I came to the Red Wings as a scorer, having scored 44 goals in 44 games at Omaha in the United States Hockey League. But when I saw the caliber of players in Detroit, I knew immediately that I had to be defensive-minded. Ivan seemed determined that I would be a forechecking center. I would stay after practice and work with him alone on the ice. I wasn't worried about scoring because we already had enough scoring. The other three centers on the team—George Gee, Jim McFadden, and Sid Abel—were all good producers. George was a fluid stick handler and skater. McFadden scored 24 goals and was named the league's rookie of the year in 1948. And Sid was the perfect guy to play with Gordie Howe and Ted Lindsay. When I came up, Gordie was 19 and Ted was 22. Sid was 30.

Back then, guys would have done almost anything not to reach 30 because that seemed like the kiss of death. Teams wanted to trade you when you hit 30. But I learned from watching Abel. Sid never blew his own horn, but he always knew what was happening on the ice. He took those two kids and turned them into a unit. Sid couldn't skate with Lindsay and Howe, but he was the engineer. He directed traffic. He knew where to go and how to get there.

After I came up, Sid was going to retire the following season, but then I got hurt at the start of next year and he came back. Then he ended up playing four more seasons.

I played on a line with Lindsay and Howe when I first arrived in Detroit. I played 12 games and totaled two goals and two assists. I think Howe and Lindsay had a point per game in that span. Howe and Lindsay just showed up at training camp in such excellent shape. They would be ready for the season to start after about 48 hours of practice. They could play for a minute and a half. Sid would play for about a minute, and then I would go out and clean up the last 20 or 25 seconds of his shift. Basically, I watched the puck go across my nose between Lindsay and Howe. They were excellent playing with each other. The record book shows how efficient that combination was. Ted was a rah, rah, fiery guy. He was outspoken. If he didn't think you were playing 110 percent, he would say it to you.

Lindsay and Howe had the corners of Olympia Stadium figured out. I don't know how many goals they would score each year just from understanding the bounces along those Olympia boards, but I bet it was six or seven. The boards were oval-shaped, and the puck reacted differently than in any other arena. Lindsay would come down the left wing and rap the puck against the boards. A young defenseman just didn't know that the puck was going to bounce from the boards across the crease toward Howe cutting in.

When I came to the Red Wings I already knew Gordie. When I played for the Saskatoon Quakers in the Saskatchewan Junior Hockey League, Gordie was our stick boy. We were all 16 and 17, and he was 13. Gordie used to practice with us, but I can remember that our captain, Bob Dawes, went to the coach and said, "We don't think the stick boy should work out with us anymore because he is going to hurt someone."

Everyone knew about Gordie in Saskatchewan. When Gordie was going to public school, coaches passed the Howe Rule. The rule was that Gordie could only play as a goalkeeper in the school games. Otherwise, the coaches wouldn't allow their teams to play against Gordie's school because, when Gordie played forward or defense, it was like a man against boys.

When I played with Gordie in Detroit, he was Mr. Relaxed. In the dressing room, between periods, he was so relaxed that it almost seemed like he was meditating. On the ice, Gordie never went looking for trouble, but players would only get too close to Gordie one time. He had a long memory. He accepted the responsibility of breaking up the fights. And when he joined in, the fights stopped abruptly.

The Red Wings had many talented players. I had great respect for "Black Jack" Stewart. Jack didn't say much, but when he did, everyone listened. He was the strongest voice in the Red Wings' dressing room. He said less and had more effect than anyone I ever saw. To me, Stewart seemed indestructible. It seemed like he had been carved out of rock.

The night before a big playoff game, I remember Stewart telling the young players, "I don't want any of you fooling around tonight or the first guy you will be meeting when you come back in the dressing room will be me." We took that warning seriously because he was the toughest son-of-a-gun you will ever meet.

Defenseman Red Kelly was also a superstar. There wasn't anything that Red couldn't do on the ice.

In my checking role, I did penalty killing with Marty Pavelich, who was a terrific player. Back then, there was no Frank Selke Trophy for the best defensive forward. If the trophy had existed, Marty Pavelich would have been in line for it several years in a row.

My respect for Ivan was high because he had respect for the role players. After a game, when Tommy had praise, it was usually about the third-line players. He never said much about Lindsay, Howe, Abel, Stewart, or Bill Quackenbush. He knew those guys were getting enough publicity and attention. Sometimes he would even sit and play bridge with the third-line players.

A lot of people knocked Jack Adams, but I believe you can only judge a man by how he treats you. Adams treated me well. I don't know what happened after, though I've heard all the stories about how Adams didn't handle himself in a gentlemanly fashion.

Considered one of the true gentlemen of the hockey world, Max McNab was a 6'2", 170-pound center who played 25 playoff games for the Red Wings from 1947 to 1951.

In my years there I had no complaints, even after they traded me. I think I just didn't measure up to Adams's standards for players. To be honest, I wasn't a player who played with tremendous confidence. As I was playing my first game in Omaha, I remember thinking they would probably send me home the next day because everyone seemed to be moving faster than I was. But by the end of the season, it was funny to me that everyone seemed like they had slowed down. Obviously I had adjusted to the speed.

But while I was in Detroit, I thought the organization was well managed. Adams certainly knew how to select players. When you look at his record, what comes through is the string of good goaltenders he brought to the team. Certainly Adams could be tough. I can remember in 1950 Adams coming in after a loss and threatening to send us all to the minors.

He would say, "[Alex] Delvecchio and [Lou] Jankowski are going good in Oshawa. They are going to be ready."

I remember when I was going to the minors, Adams had asked whether I had gotten married over the summer. "I want to know because we are paying single guys $4,000 if they get sent down, $4,500 if they are married." I guess he was happy to save the $500 with me.

In 1949–1950, I made $6,500 and I thought I was rich. The average working guy was making $3,000. I was making more than my dad, who was the postmaster of Saskatchewan. I figured I was doing well because Gordie Howe was only making $10,000. The amazing thing is that when we won the Cup, I received a bonus of $3,500. That's why qualifying for the playoffs was such a big deal for players back then. Can you imagine today if a player could make 50 percent of his salary for winning the Stanley Cup? I do think that budgets were stretched thin back then. I think Olympia only held 11,000 people, and I remember tickets for the 1950 Finals were $2.50 each.

If the playoffs had been televised back then like they are today, our playoff run might have been considered the most exciting of all time. In the first playoff game against Toronto, on March 28, 1950, Gordie Howe suffered a serious head injury. He went into the boards face-first after being checked by Teeder Kennedy. It was scary. We all knew this was life-threatening. But from what I could see, Teeder didn't do anything illegal. The Red Wings used to put us up in a hotel in Toledo during the playoffs, and we went down there, but we couldn't sleep. We were sick with worry. One of the radio stations sent a reporter down to the hospital, and we listened to the radio reports every half-hour. At 6:00 A.M., we all came down to coffee because we hadn't been to sleep.

Fortunately, Gordie recovered. But we had to play without him the rest of the way. This was a serious injury. The Maple Leafs had beat us 5–0 in that first game. But we ended up going seven games and beating them 1–0 in overtime on Leo Reise's goal to win the semifinals and reach the Stanley Cup Finals to play the Rangers. The Rangers were really playing well. They had defeated the Montreal Canadiens in five games. But we went to seven games in that series as well, and Pete Babando scored at 8:31 in the second overtime to win the Cup for us.

Babando was a good, solid player. He was a shy guy, and he would have much preferred that anybody but him would have scored that goal. Pete was a handsome bugger. He was also the most meticulous dresser I've ever seen. We always had our suits made in Montreal from the same guy. The Canadian prices were attractive. And you would go in and get measured up, and next time you would come in the tailor would have the suit ready. But Pete's suits were never right. There was always something wrong with the shoulder or neck or sleeve. He would say, "I'll come in the next time," then it would be the next time. It's a good thing we had seven games every year season against Montreal.

Harry Lumley played well for us in those playoffs, and Red Kelly was very good. But a guy I remember playing a big part was Joe Carveth. He hadn't played much for us that year, but with Gordie out, he played like a champ at right wing.

The championship party wasn't planned particularly well. We were all beer drinkers, but when we got there, there was only champagne. It seemed like there were one thousand bottles of champagne. No beer. Every player was totally fatigued and dehydrated and we just couldn't quench our thirst with champagne. Guys were popping champagne. Many guys got sick. The party just about wiped out the whole organization. I remember a Red Wings scout named Carson Cooper was sitting at a table, making fun of the players. He said, "These young guys don't know how to drink." He sat at the table for a long time and didn't get up. When he did get up, he just hit the deck. He was out like a light. That was a night to remember and to forget.

The break-up party a couple of days later was an emotional event. Every team had five superstars and the rest of the spots went to the players who worked the hardest. Some of us knew we might not be back on the team. When you are with a team, it was like being in the service. You get close, then you say your good-byes, and there are some tears.

The next year I was back in Indianapolis and came up for a couple of play-off games. Then Adams traded me to Chicago and I hurt my back. I was in the hospital for six weeks, and the doctor couldn't come up with a diagnosis. He said that maybe it was the damp weather.

I was finally released and went to Detroit to pick up my car. While I was there, I went to a game. As I waited outside the dressing room to see some of the guys, Adams saw me and came over and asked how I was doing. "Not so good," I said and told him what had happened.

He immediately took me in to see the Red Wings' team doctor. He told me he had an idea and to come and see him in his office. I went to the hospital on Friday and had surgery on Monday for a chipped disc. I never had another problem. I also never had a bill. Even though I wasn't with the Red Wings anymore, Adams took care of it. I remember the entire time I was in the hospital in Chicago, Blackhawks GM Bill Tobin never came to see me. When I got out, he said, "I was just coming up to see you today and they told me you checked out." Jack Adams and Tommy Ivan came to see me three times a week when I was in the hospital in Detroit.

Back when we won the Stanley Cup, players didn't receive championship rings. But my son David organized my family to have a special Stanley Cup ring created for me. It's like the rings the players receive today. They gave it to me as a present. It has the scores of the games from the 1950 playoffs. After I had it, I ran into Tommy Ivan. He said he liked my ring, and asked if it was a college ring.

"No, it's my Red Wings championship ring," I said. "Didn't you get one?"

Max McNab's Career Highlights

* Scoring in the third overtime to give Detroit a 2–1 win against the Montreal Canadiens in the 1949 playoffs.

* Winning the Lester Patrick Trophy for service to hockey in the United States in 1998.

* Serving as general manager of both the Washington Capitals and New Jersey Devils.

* Watching his son Peter enjoy a noteworthy NHL career and his son David become the assistant general manager of the Mighty Ducks of Anaheim. Today, Peter is a television analyst for NBC.

* Scoring two goals against the Rangers and being selected as the number one star of the game. He received a wallet for that honor. "Funny what you remember," he said.

MARTY PAVELICH
LEFT WING
1947–1957

For 10 years I checked Rocket Richard. My job was to stop him. He tried to kill me one night. Other than that, it was a good role.

He was coming around the net, and I hit him. And I cut him. It wasn't on purpose. It was an accident. But he was madder than hell. He wanted to clobber me. Then he came after me, and he was the one who ended up getting the penalty. In those days, when Detroit played Montreal, we used to verbally give it to the other players. So I called him a "Dumb Frenchman" for taking the penalty. Back then, that was just part of the game.

When his penalty was just about expired, I jumped onto to the ice because I had to check him. One of our defensemen, Bob Goldham, was throwing the puck up from the corner to me when I heard him yell, "Look out."

Rocket was coming right after me, and he just scraped the top of my head with his stick. And I remember thinking, "Oh, my goodness gracious, this has to change."

Right then I decided I was going to get him laughing now and then. And that's what I did. Every once in while I would score a goal, and I would say, "I'm hot tonight, you'd better check me," and he would start laughing. And from that time on, we became the best of friends. I checked him hard. But if he would have me lined up for a big hit, sometimes he would just make a left turn.

When I played junior hockey I scored goals—22 in 28 games in my last season in Galt, Ontario. But when I came to the Red Wings, Coach Tommy

Ivan had started the idea of a checking line, and that became my role. Tommy also started using the box formation for killing penalties. He was an outstanding coach. We got to the Finals five times in seven years. What I liked most about him is that he would protect his players.

If Jack Adams happened to be mad at me, Tommy would take care of me. We'd go on the road, and Tommy would talk to Jack after the game and say, "Marty Pavelich played fantastic." Adams couldn't wait to see me play when I got back.

If someone was having a tough time out there, we would all work with him. The chemistry on this team was great. The guys hung out together. When we were on the road, we were together. At home, every couple of weeks, we would have a party, and the guys would bring their wives and girlfriends.

We even had our own bowling league at the Lucky Strike bowling alley near Olympia. Fred Wolf and Andy Varipapa were the big bowlers in the city, and they would come out and bowl with us sometimes. The top Stroh's bowlers would all come out. We weren't that good, most of us averaged 160 or 170. But we played every week. We even had bowling shirts.

The chemistry on this team helped it be successful. But we also had talented players. I sat next to Terry Sawchuk, and he was the greatest. He had a fantastic pair of hands. This was a guy who could really catch the puck. He was a moody guy, but we just let him do his thing. He was over 200 pounds when I met him, but he got mononucleosis and lost a lot of weight. That changed him.

Benny Woit was a good, steady defenseman. If he caught you on the right railroad track, you couldn't get out of it. Oh, he could hurt you. He could really bodycheck. Red Kelly and Marcel Pronovost were both good skaters. Marcel was choppier and quicker. Red was smoother. Teddy Lindsay was the sparkplug of the team. Bob Goldham and Al Arbour were, by far, the best shot blockers we had. And there was another guy we had, Lee Fogolin, who could block shots.

But Adams broke up our team. He got mad at Sawchuk first. And he traded Johnny Bucyk. He was 190 pounds, and Adams and Jimmy Skinner thought he should be thinner. Adams traded away both of my linemates, Tony Leswick and Glen Skov. It was a truckload trade. Adams sent over Cadillacs and got back Chevettes.

Just before the 1957–1958 season, Adams got rid of me.

Marty Pavelich was revered for his checking ability against the opposition's top lines. But he also contributed some clutch goals during his career. He scored nine goals in the Red Wings' four Stanley Cup marches in the 1950s.

"I tried to trade you, but no one wanted you," Adams told me. "I'm going to send you to the minors."

"You aren't sending me anywhere, because I quit," I told him.

He was mad then because he wasn't getting anything for me. Then, three weeks later, three clubs wanted to know if I was interested in playing, but I decided I was done.

I have great memories of those Detroit teams. Born and raised in Sault Ste. Marie, Ontario, Detroit was always my favorite team. As Canadians, most kids from there liked Toronto or Montreal, but I liked the Red Wings. So to be picked by the Red Wings and to play for them, I couldn't ask for anything more.

What I've always said is that if we ever lost two games in a row, I felt sorry for the team that had to play us next. And the 1951–1952 team was special. Sid Abel played with Gordie Howe and Ted Lindsay. I was with Leswick and Skov; and Johnny Wilson, Metro Prystai, and Alex Delvecchio were on the third line. We won eight straight in the playoffs, and Sawchuk didn't give up a goal in Detroit. We could have played all summer and not been beat.

The Red Wings were in first place for seven years in a row, from the 1948–1949 season to 1954–1955, and we won four Stanley Cups in 1950, 1952, 1954, and 1955. When people ask me what it was like to play 10 years in Detroit, I always say, "It was great because we were winning every year."

Marty Pavelich's Career Highlights

* Playing for four Stanley Cup championship teams. In his 10 Detroit seasons, the Red Wings captured first place in the regular season eight times.

* Scoring the game-winning shorthanded goal in Game 1 of the 1955 Stanley Cup Finals. "I had been watching Boom Boom Geoffrion and Doug Harvey for years as the point men on the Montreal power play," Pavelich said. "They would fake the shot and pass it across. I would always think, *I'm going to catch you some night.* Howe was in the penalty box with less than four minutes left in the game. I threw my body toward Harvey and threw my stick the other way. Sure enough, Harvey passed the puck. I hit it flush and the puck went out to center ice. I was in full stride and buried it."

* Scoring against Chicago in his first shift wearing a Red Wings sweater.

* Seeing his brother Matt become a Hall of Fame NHL linesman.

* Playing his entire NHL career with the Red Wings and appearing in 91 playoff games. He had 13 playoff goals.

The
FIFTIES

MARCEL PRONOVOST

DEFENSEMAN

1949–1965

WHEN GORDIE HOWE SUFFERED the head injury in the 1950 playoffs, I had my ticket to the NHL. Coach Tommy Ivan moved Red Kelly up to forward, and I was brought up from Omaha to play defense with Leo Reise.

I made my NHL debut in the playoffs. We were down 3–2 going into the sixth game of the Stanley Cup Finals against the New York Rangers, and I remember Black Jack Stewart trying to convince us that we needed a better effort.

"If I have to hit players on both teams, I will," Stewart told us. "If you don't play any better, you will have to face me."

Stewart even went after our captain, Sid Abel. Stewart was unhappy that Don Raleigh had scored back-to-back overtime goals against us.

"That bag of bones Don Raleigh is making an ass of you," Stewart said.

Stewart had a back problem, and he would rub hot liniment oil all over himself. That stuff would burn, but he splashed it on like aftershave. He was one tough son of a bitch.

Abel ended up with two third-period goals in the sixth game, and we won 5–4. Then we won the seventh game in overtime.

I was on cloud nine when we won. I was only 19 years old at the time. But all my Stanley Cup championships were special.

This was a very close team. When I joined the Red Wings organization in 1947, we all went to training camp together in Sault Ste. Marie. Even the

Smooth-skating defenseman Marcel Pronovost only missed the playoffs twice in his 16-year Red Wings' career. He was a four-time NHL All-Star and was equally respected for his offensive and defensive ability.
Photo courtesy of AP/Wide World Photos.

juniors went. At that time, general manager Jack Adams promoted the idea that keeping the team helped build closeness. The old man would give Ted Lindsay and Gordie Howe money and tell them to take the junior players to lunch. And when the Red Wings weren't playing, Gordie, Teddy, and Marty Pavelich would come over and watch the Windsor Spitfires play because that was one of Detroit's sponsored teams.

Tommy Ivan was our coach in Detroit and acted as a buffer between Adams and the players. "Little T" was a player's coach. I remember once we lost a game in Boston, and Little T put a curfew on us. By then, all the guys had already made plans to go to a Chinese restaurant. And we were all there, past curfew, when Tommy Ivan came in. He walked in, looked around, and saw everybody was there. And do you know what he did? He paid the bill for everybody.

Ivan was an understanding coach. Adams never realized it wasn't him winning championships, it was the horses he had in front of him.

Adams used to call me his "Flying Frenchman." When Howie Young got there, he called me "Wheels."

I roomed with Terry Sawchuk. He was able to crouch so low that he could see the pucks coming. At that time, the general idea was that you could score much better along the ice than you could at the top of the net. It's the opposite now. He was a competitor and hated to lose. I got along with him because I didn't pay attention to what he was saying. I took what I wanted and I left the rest. He hated for people to pat him on the back. "Those SOBs," he would say, "they're looking for a place to put the knife."

When Sawchuk came down with mononucleosis, it changed him. He didn't know he had it. While he was sick, it affected his head. It affects you mentally and physically.

Red Kelly was a great player. He would practice with the forwards and the defensemen. He was very versatile guy. I always joked that he played with "three sticks." He had one hockey stick and he used his two feet like they were sticks. He was the best guy I had ever seen using his skates to control the puck. He was quite a soccer player at St. Mike's.

Gordie Howe was the best I played with or against. He wasn't the greatest goal-scorer ever. Rocket Richard was. Gordie was the greatest all-around player. The ability that he has over Wayne Gretzky, he was able to take care of himself. In those days everyone had to take care of themselves. There was no place for a bully to take care of the opposition. You had to do it yourself. If you didn't, you were in the minors.

I was there when Gordie Howe fought Lou Fontinato. When Gordie was on the ice, Fontinato always had a eye out for him. It all started with Red Kelly and Eddie Shack. When it started, Fontinato started skating from his end, dropping his stick at the half line and gloves at the blue line. He went straight for Gordie. They grabbed each other, but Gordie was so strong. Gordie switched hands and that's when he nailed Fontinato on the nose. You could hear the smack from the bench where I was. Fontinato went splat, splash. His knees buckled. He never recovered.

My years in Detroit were great, especially when we were winning the championships. Even after Adams made a few changes, and the team was struggling, that's when I started making the All-Star teams. I can't complain about that.

Back then, you didn't celebrate a championship the way you do today. When we won the Stanley Cup, do you know where the parade took place? From center ice to the dressing room.

Marcel Pronovost's Career Highlights

* ★ Being elected to the Hall of Fame in 1978.

* ★ Winning four Stanley Cups in Detroit, garnering seven regular-season titles, and being on four consecutive league All-Star teams, including the first team in 1960 and 1961.

* ★ Breaking his nose 14 times during his career.

* ★ Having a goal and two assists in the 1955 Finals against Montreal.

* ★ Starting his career as a high-scoring center but being converted to defense when he moved to the Windsor Spitfires as a junior player.

JOHNNY WILSON
LEFT WING
1949–1955 ★ 1957–1959

THE DETROIT RED WINGS and Toronto Maple Leafs had both scouted me when I was playing high school hockey in Quebec, and the Maple Leafs beat the Red Wings to the punch. They put me on their negotiation list.

Even though I was on that list, I could go play junior anywhere, and I wanted to go to the Red Wings junior team in Windsor to play with my brother and Marcel Pronovost. We had won the juvenile championship of Quebec together. Marcel was our center. The system back then is different than it is today. Each team had three spots on the negotiation list. The player wasn't even notified. Someone from the team would just notify the league that they were putting Johnny Wilson on the negotiation list, and then the team would try to sign you in a hurry because, if all of their negotiation spots were full, they could miss a player. So they wanted to sign you so they could move you to the "reserved list." Once you were on the reserved list, you were there for eternity.

When you joined a junior team, the parent team would give you a pair of skates and, once you signed with an NHL team, you got $500, which was a lot of money in those days.

It was a dogfight for three or four weeks to make the Windsor team because the Red Wings brought in all of their prospects. Most of them were from western Canada. Once I got there, I wanted to be a Red Wing.

My dad was a good hockey fan and happened to mention to Detroit Red Wings scout Marcel Cote that he thought Marcel Pronovost could be a great defenseman. When we came to Windsor, the team needed defensemen, and put Pronovost there. And he turned out to be an All-Star and Hall of Famer at that position.

When I played in Windsor, I got to know Detroit players. Gordie Howe and Ted Lindsay used to come over to watch us play, and that had a big impression on me. I wanted to play with the Red Wings.

But I had a couple of good seasons in juniors, and the Maple Leafs came after me.

Once we played a game in Toronto that I didn't play in because Stafford Smythe was running around the building trying to get me to sign. In the summertime, the Maple Leafs had sent Syl Apps down to try to convince me to go with the Leafs. They wanted me to play with George Armstrong and Danny Lewicki on the Toronto Marlies.

The second year I was playing in Windsor, Red Wings general manager Jack Adams told me to "hang tight because we are going to try to make a deal with Toronto to get your negotiating rights."

What nobody knew is that I had signed a contract with the Red Wings, but Jack Adams had put it in the safe where nobody could see it. Eventually he was able to make a trade with the Maple Leafs. I think the Red Wings traded Dusty Blair to get my rights.

When you trace back over the years to the players who won those Cups in the 1950s, we were all branded by the Red Wings when we were 16 and 17 years old.

Ted Lindsay was a good captain, and he was particularly good with rookies. When I came to the team, he gave me some advice. "Johnny," he said, "you always play hurt up here, because if you are out three or four games, someone will take your place and you will never get it back."

He made himself more clear, saying you only sat out "if you had had a broken bone."

"That's how I got my job," Lindsay told me. "A player got hurt, I jumped in, and he never played in the National Hockey League again."

Adams was a very aggressive general manager. He was running the team his way, and no one told him what to do. He made it clear to the players that their jobs were always in jeopardy. If you had a couple of bad weeks, Adams would send you to the minors. As you got older, you could expect to spend your last two or three years in the minors because the team was going to want to bring up some young kids. Most of us had been goal scorers in junior hockey, but when we came to Detroit, you had better play two-way hockey or you wouldn't be around long. You always ignored some of your offensive skill to help backcheck.

Before the season started, Adams would tell players, "We selected you fellows because we feel you are highly qualified. That's why you will wear a Red Wings uniform. But we won't need any enforcers because we believe you guys can defend yourself and win your own battles."

We would go to training camp in Sault Ste. Marie, and there would be 110 players there because he had to fill all of the farm teams. Adams needed players for Detroit, Indianapolis, and Omaha. Some guys would end up in the Quebec or out west.

After a week of training camp, he would put out that word for everyone to "hang around the hotel, I'm going to start signing players."

He could sign everyone on the team within a week's time. Everyone would get a one-year deal. The whole negotiation would take 10 minutes, and then he would tell you to bring in someone else.

Let's say you were making $12,000 and you had a good year. Adams would call you in and say, "You played well. What kind of money were you looking to make?"

You would say, "Well, Jack, I was thinking that I would like to make $14,000."

He would show you a contract that he already had typed out. He would say, "How about if we give you a $500 raise to play in Detroit. That makes it $12,500 in Detroit. If you go to Indianapolis, it would be $9,500, and if you go to Omaha it will be $7,500."

Then he would pause and say, "Where do you want to play?"

"Give me the pen," you would say. "I'll sign right now for Detroit."

That's the power Jack had in those days. During games, Jack would sit behind our bench in his own box. There was a steel gate there. Just before the period ended, if you heard that gate go "clang," you knew that he was mad and someone was going to get yelled at.

If Metro, Alex, and I had a bad period, we would know that he would be coming after us. He would stand in front us, and we would have our head down, and he would have his fist clenched.

Johnny Wilson (far left) was nicknamed "Iron Man" because he was never out of the lineup. He only had one game of NHL experience when general manager Jack Adams brought him up to play in the 1950s playoffs. He helped the Red Wings win the first of their four Stanley Cups in the 1950s. *Photo courtesy of Bettman/Corbis.*

"I don't know what kind of game you are playing out there," he would say, "But it's not hockey. You had better start playing the game the way it should be played or you won't be around here too long."

Needless to say, the next period we would be flying around the ice, and I don't think the opposition touched the puck.

If the team had lost a game or two, Jack would come down close to the ice surface to watch practice the next day. One time, Metro Prystai was in a bit of a scoring slump, and Jack called Tommy Ivan and all the players over and wanted to see Metro's stick.

Metro liked to doctor his sticks, putting tape on it here and there. Adams took the stick, inspected it, and threw it across the rink.

"That thing looks like it has been out in the rain all summer—it's all warped," Adams yelled. "Go get another stick."

Another time, Billy McNeill was having a tough time scoring. Apparently Jack thought Billy had cut his stick a little bit, and Adams hated when players cut off pieces of their sticks. Some guys would cut an inch or two because they felt more comfortable using a shorter stick.

Adams started going after McNeill. "Son," he said, "why don't you use a man's stick like Gordie Howe."

Just to make his point, Adams grabbed Gordie's stick and put the two together. The problem was that Gordie's stick was shorter than McNeill's stick. We all started to laugh.

Coach Tommy Ivan was a great guy who knew how to handle the players. He didn't put a lot pressure on his players. He wanted you to play your own game. But Adams was completely different. If you played well, and he saw you in the lobby of the hotel, he would pat you on the back and tell you what a good job you had done. If you didn't play well, he wouldn't say "hello," "good-bye," or "how are you?" if he saw you.

I think Tommy became irritated with Jack over time. Adams would come into the room and start talking about what he thought about how the team was playing. Tommy resented that from time to time. Players have respect for their coaches, and they also don't like it if they are getting coaching from upstairs.

During a game, Adams would give messages to Tommy through the trainers on the bench. He would tell them to tell Ivan not to play specific players. In one game, Adams kept sending messages to bench players.

Frustrated, Tommy finally told trainer Lefty Wilson to deliver a message to Adams: "Tell him he has asked me to bench pretty much everyone on the team. Who does he want me to play? There's no one left."

I think that's why Tommy eventually went to the Chicago Blackhawks. He became tired of the interference.

Gordie Howe and Ted Lindsay were a great tandem. What made Gordie such a great player is that he could control the game. He could kill the penalties, play on the power play, and fight the big guys on the other team. With all due respect to Wayne Gretzky and Mario Lemieux, if you said to them, "Hey, that guy on the other team is trying to intimidate us. Go out there and push him around and calm him down," they couldn't really help you.

But Gordie could dish out bodychecks and he could play mean if he wanted to. He could hurt you. "I have to straighten that guy out," he would say, and you knew what that meant.

On the night he fought New York Rangers' tough guy Lou Fontinato, I think Ted must have been hurt because I was up playing with Gordie. Before the game started, Fontinato skated through the circle and said, "If you fool around with Shack, you are going to be dealing with me."

Gordie blinked his eyes and told him where to go.

Then, when Red Kelly was carrying the puck behind the net and Shack crashed him into the boards, they started going at it pretty good. We were all standing around watching the fight. Gordie was, too. Then we saw Lou coming after Gordie, and everyone yelled, "Look out." When Gordie turned around to fight Fontinato, that became the main event. The Kelly vs. Shack preliminary fight was done.

Then Gordie put a couple of good whacks on Lou. Gordie beat him up pretty badly. Lou would be going down, and Gordie would grab him by the back of the sweater and whacked him again. He broke his nose. Supposedly, what I heard later, is that Phil Watson, the coach of the Rangers, grabbed Lou's arm as he was skating off the ice and raised it like he was the champion.

That caused a ruckus with Lou. He supposedly told Watson, "Don't ever raise my arm and embarrass me when I get beat up."

Years later, I played with Lou and we became friends.

"I had to fight Gordie because he was the king," he told me. "If I beat him, I would have been king. I was a half inch from being king until he got a hold of me."

These days, kids have the privilege of being able to watch the top players on TV. They even use videotape to watch themselves and others to play. It's a great development tool. The guys in western Canada had to listen to games on the radio. Back then it was a big event to be able to go over and watch the Red Wings. I was a left wing and I watched Ted Lindsay. I would go back to practice the next day and try to emulate Teddy. I tried to pick up some of Teddy's mannerisms and implemented them into my game.

One of the best fights I saw was Ted against Bill Ezinicki. I was playing junior in Windsor when I saw that fight. They were going at it with their sticks and then they dropped their sticks and went at it. What made it interesting is that they were both about the same size. [At 5′10″, 170 pounds, Ezinicki was actually about two inches taller and maybe 10 pounder heavier than Lindsay.] Neither guy could overpower the other guy. It was going to be the guy who got the last punch in, and Ted ended up knocking Ezi down. It was a great fight.

What I liked about Ted is that if you were down about the mouth, he could get you fired up. One thing about Teddy, he was mild and meek off the ice. He never showed his temper. But on the ice, no one was his friend. Even if you played with him before, he was such a competitor. He hated to lose.

After I was traded to the Blackhawks, I was playing on a line with a couple of kids, Hank Ciesla and Hector Lalande. We were playing against the Red Wings, and I told Lalande, "When you go into the corner, keep your stick up because Teddy will work you over pretty good."

Hector was stubborn and he said, "Don't worry about him. I will take care of myself."

In the second period, they both had their sticks up, and I remember going over toward Teddy.

"Don't bother the kid," I yelled at Teddy. "He's just a rookie—he doesn't know what's going on."

Lindsay turned toward me and said, "Johnny get that head of yours out of here before I cut your ear off."

Most of us still think about Jack Adams breaking up our team. When you knock off nine guys from a Stanley Cup team, you can't expect it to have the same chemistry. I think that's why Adams eventually lost his job. He traded away too many good players, and Norris decided to retire him.

Those were fun years that I played in Detroit. It was a great bunch of guys. We had a lot of respect for each other. We stuck together. And when you are winning, it adds to the glamour of your career. I have so much respect for the organization and the team. It's fun to still live in the area. I still go down to the games and I know the players.

Even though it's been years since I played, fans still remember my efforts. Players like Lindsay, Delvecchio, myself, and others have been with the organization since we were 16. The first NHL sweater I wore was the Red Wings, and it feels like I've never left them.

Johnny Wilson's Career Highlights

* Having two game-winning goals in the eight victories the Red Wings claimed to win the 1952 Stanley Cup championship. He scored the only goal in a 1–0 win against Toronto in the semifinals. He netted the first goal in a 3–0 win against the Maple Leafs.

* In 1954, scoring the game-winning goal in Game 4 of the Stanley Cup Finals when he scored the first goal in a 2–0 win against Montreal. The second goal in that game was an empty netter by Red Kelly.

* Wilson did what Lindsay had told him and earned the nickname "Ironman" after not missing a game for eight consecutive seasons.

* Coaching the Red Wings from 1971 to 1973 and having winning records both years, even though the team didn't make the playoffs. Also coached in the WHA with the Michigan Stags, Baltimore Blades, Cleveland Crusaders, and in the NHL with Pittsburgh and Los Angeles.

* Playing 20 games with his brother, Larry, on the Red Wings. His brother, father of San Jose coach Ron Wilson, also coached the Red Wings briefly.

METRO PRYSTAI
CENTER
1950–1955 ★ 1955–1957

IN 1952–1953 I PLAYED MOST OF THE SEASON with Gordie Howe and Ted Lindsay. I think Coach Tommy Ivan thought there was a fit there. But those guys were hard to play with because they were all over the place. Usually a left winger would go up and down, but Ted Lindsay would cross over. Howe would cross over. They were crossing over all of the time. You had to make adjustments for that.

When Tommy put Alex Delvecchio with them, he fit them like a glove. He was just a helluva passer. He was a tremendous player. He would put that puck right on your stick.

We had a helluva team, particularly in 1951–1952, when we won eight straight games in the playoffs. We just had three well-balanced lines and four great defensemen and some good extra guys. Vic Stasiuk was an extra guy that year, and he was a good player. In 1951–1952 I played with Johnny Wilson, Alex Delvecchio, and Tony Leswick. Marty Pavelich and Leswick also killed a lot of penalties together. Those guys and Glen Skov checked the hell out of Montreal in 1952. Terry Sawchuk only gave up five goals in eight games, and we didn't give up a goal in Detroit during those playoffs. He was a remarkable goaltender. He was a little funny at times. Sometimes, you would block a shot, and he would say, "Get the hell out of my way."

People ask what made the 1952 playoff team better, and I say, "I guess we were just luckier."

The 5'9" Metro Prystai averaged 17 goals per season for the Detroit Red Wings from 1950 to 1954. He also produced 12 goals and 14 assists in 43 playoff games for the Red Wings.

We had a heckuva team in 1951 and 1953. In 1953 we beat Boston 7–0 in the first game and five games later we were out of the playoffs. It was one of those things. We couldn't put the puck in the ocean. We had the puck in their end the whole time, and their goaltender—I can't even remember who it was—was luckier than hell. They would come down against us, and Terry Sawchuk would be cold because the play had been always down at the other end. The Bruins would score.

Our team chemistry was terrific. The guys got along well together. We bowled together. Gordie Howe was a pretty good bowler. But Gordie was good at everything. We went to the dance halls together. We were always together. I was there in the Lucky Strike bowling alley when Gordie met Colleen. He liked her, and the next thing you know they were married.

Hockey was a big deal in Detroit in those days. It didn't matter where we went, they knew us. We would try to find a hiding spot to have a beer, but someone would spot us and send us over a beer. Jack Adams was also always sending us, especially the single guys, to father-son banquets or churches or to the schools to talk to kids.

The train rides would bring us together. We would leave in the afternoon and then be in Montreal or New York the next morning. We would play cards, especially pinochle. Sometimes we would travel with the team we played against the night before. They would be in one car, we would be in another, and the dining car would be in between. When we went into the dining car, they would be at one end of the car and we would be at the other. We would see the Canadiens and someone would just say, "Hi, Rocket."

We all liked Coach Tommy Ivan. He was a quiet man who looked out after his players. Jack Adams was a tough manager.

Adams would always say, "I've got 10 guys in Indianapolis waiting to take your place." He would usually bring that up when you went in to sign your contract and asked for a $500 raise. Then you would want to sign for what you signed the season before.

Frequently, Adams would be in the dressing room to yell at us for something, and when he would leave, Tommy would say to us, "Don't listen to that old bugger. He doesn't know what he's talking about it."

That would really perk up the guys. Adams was a difficult man. One minute he would be mad at you, and then if you got into a fight on the ice a couple of minutes later, he would be a guy who backed you to the end.

At the end of our championship run, he clearly let his personal feelings get the best of him, especially when he got rid of Lindsay and Sawchuk.

But I can't complain because he traded for me twice. When he traded me back to Chicago [on November 9, 1954], it seemed to be out of his hands. It appeared to be ownership making him do it. He called me at Ma Shaw's one day and told me not to answer the phone no matter what. I think he was trying to talk people out of trading me.

The story was that the Chicago franchise was having problems. The problem was that general manager Bill Tobin didn't know a puck from a football. He traded away a lot of talented players, including Bob Goldham and Bert Olmstead. The Blackhawks didn't have anyone left, and all the NHL teams got together and decided to give the Blackhawks some players. They wanted me because I had played pretty well there. Whatever Adams was trying to do, it didn't work. He sent for me, and when I came into his office, he apologized for trading me.

"I didn't want you to go," he said.

He proved that by trading for me again a year later. But I was devastated when I was traded back to Chicago. I was very happy in Detroit. I liked being around the guys. The team had gotten 101 points in 1950–1951 and 100 points in 1951–1952 to become the first NHL team to achieve the 100 points. Think about that. That's the equivalent of 50 wins and we only played 70 games.

At that time, I was probably making $10,000 with bonuses. And I couldn't complain. It was a helluva lot more than I could have made anywhere else. I would have had to be a doctor or a lawyer to make that much in those days.

Honestly, I don't think hockey was as dirty as it is today. I don't think we boarded as much. We had more respect for each other. I wouldn't take a guy into the boards and risk breaking his neck the way they do today.

I remember once that [Toronto Maple Leafs great] George Armstrong grabbed my stick once to prevent me from sliding into the boards with my back. I couldn't stop. I fell, and my stick was in the air, and George grabbed it and gave it a yank. I stopped a foot from the boards. I thanked him and I went on my way. A lot of things like that happened when we played.

People haven't forgotten those of us who played in those years. A week doesn't go by that I don't get a couple of items in the mail to sign. Some even come from Europe and a lot of them come from the Detroit area.

43

Metro Prystai's Career Highlights

* In Game 4 of the 1952 Stanley Cup Finals, being named first star, scoring twice and adding an assist in the Wings' 3–0 win against Montreal at Olympia. His first goal, coming at 6:50 of the first period, was the Stanley Cup–winning goal. He had seven points in eight games of that playoff year.

* In 2005, 51 years after he won his second Cup, being able to bring the Stanley Cup to his hometown of Yorkton, Saskatchewan, to celebrate his accomplishments. He then took the Cup to Wynyard, population 2,000, located about 90 miles west of Yorkton. That's where he raised his family.

* Netting 16 goals and adding a career-high 34 assists in 1952–1953 when he played much of the season with Howe and Lindsay. His 34 assists ranked fifth in the league. Howe, Lindsay, and Delvecchio were all in front of him.

* Scoring 29 goals for Chicago in 1949–1950, ranking him fourth in the NHL. That summer, Jack Adams acquired him from Chicago, along with Jim Henry, Bob Goldham, and Gaye Stewart for Harry Lumley, Jack Stewart, Al Dewsbury, Don Morrison, and Pete Babando.

* In his junior days, playing with the Moose Jaw Canucks of the SJHL between 1944 and 1947, leading his team to three consecutive provincial championships plus a trip to the Memorial Cup Finals. He also twice led his league in scoring.

VIC STASIUK

LEFT WING

1950–1955 ★ 1961–1963

EVERY MONTH, BRONCO HORVATH CALLS ME and doesn't say anything until I finally demand, "Tell me who's calling or I'm going to hang up." Then I hear his voice say, "Don't tell me that Alex Delvecchio is better than I was."

People associate the Uke line of Johnny Bucyk, Horvath, and myself with the Boston Bruins, but we started in the Detroit organization. We were called the Uke line because we all had Ukrainian heritage. Bruins General Manager Lynn Patrick had seen the Uke line play together when I was demoted to the Detroit farm team in Edmonton. Apparently, Patrick said at the time, "Someday I'm going to get those players from Detroit." That's what he eventually did.

But in the 1955 playoffs, I was back up with the Red Wings playing on the third line. We were tied 3–3 with Montreal going into a Game 7 in Detroit. That was the year Maurice Richard was suspended for manhandling a linesman.

In those days, we stayed at a hotel in Toledo during the playoffs. When I stepped off the bus, I was surprised to see Bucyk and Horvath in the lobby.

"What the hell are you guys doing here?" I asked.

"The Uke line is going to play together in the seventh game," Horvath said.

I didn't sleep that night because I was thinking that I was going to have to go back to right wing. That's where I played with the Uke line. With the

A member of three of Detroit's Stanley Cup teams in the 1950s, Vic Stasiuk earned his place on the Red Wings with some strong minor league performances. In 1952, playing for Detroit's farm team in Edmonton, Stasiuk had 37 goals and 43 assists in 48 games.

Red Wings, I played left wing unless they moved Gordie Howe back to the point. Then I took his spot on right wing.

I was pretty excited about playing with Bucyk and Horvath, but when we drove to Olympia and got into the dressing room, their sweaters weren't hanging up. As it turned out, they couldn't play because there were rules that stipulated that they would be ineligible to play for the Edmonton Flyers in the Dominion championship if they played with the Red Wings in that game.

The Uke line never played for the Detroit Red Wings, which is why Bronco always says what he says to me on the phone.

The point is, it was hard to play for the Red Wings in those years, but I kept trying. They had so many good players and they didn't use too many. The Red Wings were a two-line team. We had the power line with Ted Lindsay and Gordie Howe and whomever they were trying with them. They must have tried a dozen players to fill Sid Abel's spot after he went to Chicago. Then we had the checking line of Marty Pavelich, Glen Skov, and Tony Leswick. They would play against the other team's top line. There were four or five us trying to play on the third line, but we seldom got on the ice.

The Red Wings got me from the Chicago Blackhawks in 1950, and I didn't get on the ice for the first 13 games.

Jack Adams would watch us all closely in practice, and I remember thinking, *I'll show you, the old bastard.* At times, Adams would compliment me. There was no sentiment coming from him. That's for sure.

One day, Jack was on the rubdown table and I came by and said, "Good morning, Mr. Adams."

He said, "Do you know why you are with the big club?"

"No," I said

"Mud gave me the word," Adam said.

Who the hell is Mud? I thought.

I had to look it up. It was the former Red Wings player Mud Bruneteau who was the manager in Omaha when I was in Kansas City. I wasn't a scorer in Kansas City, but he must have liked what he saw because he told Jack if he had a chance to get me, he should.

I had a great opportunity to learn from Gordie Howe in practice. He led the two championships with his meanness, I guess he decided: *no one is going to intimidate me. I'm going to do the intimidating.* Most of the intimidating from Howe came when someone was coming to check him. Up came the right elbow and the end of the stick so quickly. You would run into the elbow. Consequently, he got the nickname Mr. Elbows. I don't think they were illegal elbows or high sticking. He came up only on the defensive because everyone was trying to check him. But he was strong. When you thought you had him in the midsection, up would come the elbow.

Howe was a stickler for conditioning. I learned that. Watching him and Red Kelly work, I realized you had to work extra to stay in shape. I had to go get a YMCA membership—just being able to get on the punching bag to protect myself from Andy Bathgate helped. I took him on three times, and he knocked me out three times.

There was one guy in Red Wings training camp named Ching Johnson. If you got called up with the big club, he would ask you, "How is it playing up there? If I could just play one game with Gordie Howe, I would die happy."

There were many good players on that Detroit team. I played against former Moose Jaw player Metro Prystai in juniors, and if there would have been a draft in those days, he would have gone number one. He was that great.

Terry Sawchuk was having a rough marriage and he drank a lot. That was no secret. If you raised the puck in practice, he didn't like. But when it was game time, he was the best, no question.

"Get me a goal, I might get you a point. Give me two goals I guarantee you a point," Sawchuk would say. "If you get me three, I guarantee you a win."

As a junior, I was a hard worker and a back checker—that's what got me into the league, I think. The Red Wings sent me to Indianapolis in 1951–1952, and I played with Delvecchio and scored seven goals in eight games. I got called back up.

The Uke line was put together in training camp one year, and in one game we kicked the hell out of the Red Wings regular team with Gordie Howe, Delvecchio, and others. Then we played another game and we were dominating again. But then Ted Lindsay started a fight and we never finished the game.

Ted is the most spirited little guy you would ever see, and the greatest captain you could ever hope to have. He was a skill guy down that left side. He had that snarl when he talked to you. He always treated me as a Red Wing and always complimented me.

"You've got a good shot, use that goddamned thing," he would say.

Ted and Gordie would always invite us out to dinner. We never turned it down.

The Red Wings sent me to the Edmonton Flyers with the hope I might become a scorer. I almost won a scoring title down there. I dislocated my hip before the end of the season. I played very well down there—so good that Adams decided to give me a full cut of Detroit's 1954 Stanley Cup playoff money shares even though I didn't play in the playoffs. The Flyers went into the Dominion championship and I also received that full cut.

That was one of Ted Lindsay's pet peeves about Adams. He gave the ice-maker a part share, the doorman a part share. It was supposed to be 18 equal shares. Ted talked about that when he was trying to organize the NHL Players Association.

I bragged about that to my teammates when I finally got back to Detroit. Since I also got the minor playoff share, I reminded them, "I made way more money than you guys did."

But I loved playing in Detroit. When I got traded to the Bruins in 1955, I cried. I went to see Ed Bruchet, owner of the Lethbridge Native Sons. He was like a second father to me.

"Vic," he said, "this is the best thing that could happen to you. Look at all the players they have in Detroit."

He took out a copy of the protected list.

"They have hundreds of players, and look at Boston," he said. "They don't have enough even for one team. You'll be playing regularly there." He was right.

That's what happened. Sawchuk also went with me in that deal. The Red Wings wanted Ed Sanford, who had been an All-Star five years in a row. Supposedly, Lynn Patrick said, "Throw in Stasiuk and you have a deal."

But when I got back to Detroit in 1961, Sid Abel and his wife Gloria picked me up. "You should have never gotten traded, Vic," he said. "I'm going to play you on left wing with Gordie Howe and Alex Delvecchio."

If Delvecchio wasn't the best centerman I had been with on the ice, he was damn close to it.

Would history have been different had the Uke line stayed in Detroit? I don't think the Uke line would have stayed together long enough to make the point, the way the Red Wings operated under Adams. You were never going to break up the Howe and Lindsay pairing. And Pavelich and Skov were on the checking line. If you look at Pavelich's minor record, he was actually a goal scorer until he came to Detroit.

It was automatic that the power line would get a couple shifts and the checking line would be out there against the other team's big line before anyone else played. You couldn't do that today, but Howe could do it. And Lindsay was tough enough. He was only 140 or 150 pounds by the end of the season.

Years later, Ken Dryden came to speak at the University of Lethbridge, which is just down the road from me. I listened to him talk, and then I went up and introduced myself and told him I had seen him play a great game against the Bruins.

Dryden then told me he had a story for me. He said he was in a line with former Red Wing Red Kelly, and he had asked him, "What was the reason for the demise of the Red Wings in the 1955–1956 season? Was it the trading of Terry Sawchuk?"

Dryden said that Kelly had told him, "No. It was the trading of Vic Stasiuk."

"Are you kidding me?" I asked. Dryden said that's what Red told him. He said Red said I was there every day, worked hard at practice, and I was on the verge of becoming a key player.

I always had great respect for Red Kelly. Not only did Red not swear, he never even thought about swearing. But he was so strong.

I was with Gordie when he met Colleen. We were at the counter of the Lucky Strike, and Gordie said to the cashier: "I sure like the looks of that girl down the alley there." The guy at the counter said he could arrange for Gordie to meet her, but Gordie said he could do it on his own. And he did.

I built a golf course out here in Lethbridge, Alberta, for one reason: to play one more round of golf with Gordie Howe. We used to always go golfing on Monday, which was our day off.

"Make it nice and green," Gordie would say.

Gordie and I never lost a best ball match. But he has bad knees now. They're like a sack of marbles when he shakes them. It sounds like bone on bone.

Metro Prystai visited me last summer, and we were sitting in the kitchen and he said, "Wasn't Terry Sawchuk fantastic?"

Before I could answer, he said, "We never had to worry about being up ice because if there was a breakaway, you knew Terry would stop it."

What I think about now is that he would be something to watch if we would have had these shootouts back when we were playing. Back then, Terry would only do it if you put a case of beer on the line. Then he would be great. If I got one out of 10, it would be lucky, and if I got two, it would be cause for a celebration.

Vic Stasiuk's Career Highlights

* Winning three Stanley Cup championships with the Detroit Red Wings in 1952, 1954, and 1955.

* In Game 6 of the 1955 Stanley Cup Finals, starting the play that created the first Detroit goal by Alex Delvecchio. "I was backchecking in the first period, and the puck came in my corner. I picked up the puck, went behind Terry Sawchuk, and I was thinking, *Off the boards and out*," Stasiuk recalled. "But I peeked around Sawchuk and saw Delvecchio. He gave me the big fluff of the stick. Montreal came rushing up and I threw up a perfect backhand pass right through the slot, which you should never do. It deflected to him and he went down and scored."

* Having five goals and three assists during the Red Wings' 1955 championship run. He had three goals in the Finals.

* Averaging 24 goals per season for his first five seasons with Boston after Detroit traded him to the Bruins.

* Coaching in the NHL with the Philadelphia Flyers (1969 to 1971), California Golden Seals (1971 to 1972), and Vancouver Canucks (1972 to 1973).

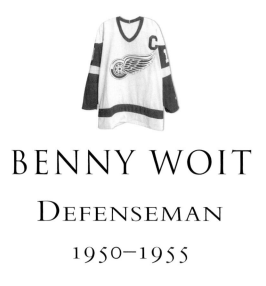

BENNY WOIT

DEFENSEMAN

1950–1955

WHY WAS TOMMY IVAN A GOOD COACH? He had a lot of great players. He knew the game pretty well and he was a great guy, but you couldn't score on Terry Sawchuk.

Sawchuk and I were close. I was his roommate. If he gave up a goal, he would say, "That's the only one I'm giving up. If you guys score two goals, we're going to win." And we would win.

Gordie Howe was a powerful son of a gun. Gordie's shot was a pretty hard one, just a little snap and he could fire it. Gordie was tough. The other players didn't want to bother him. If he got into a fight, it didn't last too long. He was so strong. He liked to fool around in the locker room and pick you up by your neck. He could do that. He was quiet, really, and you couldn't ask for a better guy.

Ted Lindsay was always stirring up trouble on the ice. If you got to close to him on the ice, you ended up bleeding. He got into a lot of fights. Everybody who played against Teddy hated him, and we didn't like practicing against him, either.

Teddy and Gordie played well together and they were good guys, but if they didn't want you playing on their line, you had a helluva time trying to get the puck. Dutch Reibel played with them a while, and I don't know if they wanted him there or not, but I know he didn't see the puck very often. They liked Sid Abel and they didn't want him traded. They didn't want Alex

Benny Woit was known as a strong body-checker during his heyday with the Detroit Red Wings in the early 1950s. He played on three Stanley Cup championship teams.

Delvecchio either, at first, but then they got used to him. Sid was a helluva hockey player. Delvecchio was a helluva player.

Red Kelly was the best defenseman in the league. He used to carry the puck up the ice. They didn't like me to go past the red line, but I would from time to time and then catch heck for it. I was supposed to do the hitting, and I did enough of that. My wife says they carried Rocket Richard off on a stretcher when I hit him once, but I can't remember that anymore. What I remember about Richard is that he was powerful and he could scrap. If he hit you, he could knock you out.

The 1951–1952 season was my first full season with the Red Wings. We had Bob Goldham, Leo Reise, Kelly, Marcel Pronovost, and myself on defense, but I think it was Kelly and Reise who were hurt in the playoffs. All I know for sure is that in Game 1 of the Stanley Cup Finals, I pretty much played the entire third period, maybe coming off for a shift or two. Once when I did come off, Ivan said. "If they score while you are here, you are in trouble. Get back out there."

Jack Adams would sit behind the bench, and you could hear him yelling the whole game. Problem was, Jack couldn't see very well. You would be sitting on the bench, and Jack would be yelling at someone on the ice, thinking it was you.

When that would happen, Abel would turn to me, "Are you getting all of this, Benny?"

We called Adams the "old bulldog." He was always watching you. Even if you didn't see him right away at practice, someone would spot him way up upstairs, watching us. You'd ask, "Where's the old bulldog?" and then someone would spot him. He liked to come into the room after the games and give it to us if we didn't play well. You couldn't repeat most of the things he said.

Trying to talk to Jack about a contract was like going to hell. He could cut you. You knew that. Teddy challenged him. And as soon as he started yapping, he was gone. But despite our problems with Jack Adams, those were great times. The memories are special.

Benny Woit Career Highlights

* Winning three Stanley Cup championships while playing with the Detroit Red Wings.

* Being a member of the 1947 St. Michael's Majors squad that captured the Memorial Cup. The following season, he helped the Port Arthur Bruins win the very same trophy.

* Registering a goal and an assist in the semifinals against Toronto in 1952 when the Red Wings roared to the Stanley Cup in eight consecutive games.

* After his NHL career was over in 1957, playing 10 more years in the AHL, Western League, and Eastern League, among others. At age 35, Woit was an Eastern League All-Star in 1963–1964 when he had 12 goals and 35 assists for the Clinton Comets.

* In 2004, having the Stanley Cup for a day in Thunder Bay, Ontario. Woit was born in Fort William, Ontario. In 1970 Port Arthur and Fort William were amalgamated to create Thunder Bay. Woit's day with the cup was celebrated with a small parade, which went by the Fort Williams Gardens, where he had known many fine moments as a youngster. That area has always been a hotbed of NHL talent. In the 1940s, for example, the Calder Trophy for the NHL's rookie of the year went to natives of Fort William four times: Gaye Stewart in 1943; Gus Bodnar in 1944; Edgar Laprade in 1946; and Pentti Lund, who was born in Finland but raised in Fort William, in 1949.

LARRY ZEIDEL

DEFENSEMAN

1951–1953

WHEN WE WERE ON THE ROAD, we would all pile out of the cabs, go into the old arena, and look at the ice before we went into the dressing room. Our captain, Sid Abel, talked in a Walter Brennan swamp music tone. He liked to get us ready early.

"Boys," he would say quietly, "there's no place to hide out there on the ice."

It was war on the ice back then. That was Sid's philosophy, and it was the philosophy of the organization. When you were on the road, you told yourself that the boos were cheers. If you were getting booed, it meant you were doing something right. Jack Adams. Sid Abel. Ted Lindsay. Everyone back then preached "guts."

League president Clarence Campbell would fine guys for fraternization back then. You could be from the same neighborhood as a player on another team, but if you got caught talking to that guy, it was fraternization. Ted Lindsay and Gus Mortson both came from Kirkland Lake, Ontario. They both played on the Oshawa Generals team that won the Memorial Cup. They went prospecting together as kids. They were friends. But when I was on Chicago playing with Gus and Ted was on Detroit, and we were in an exhibition game, Gus and Ted fought like a couple of pit bulls. I laugh about it now, but that's the way it was back then. We loved the game back then.

56

Nicknamed "the Rock," Larry Zeidel is considered one of the toughest players in Red Wings' history. In the 1950s he was a rough-and-tumble player who could clear the crease and punish opposing forwards.

If you want to win, it's important to have that leadership. Sid wouldn't let up. I was an introvert back then, and even Gordie Howe was quiet like John Wayne's *The Quiet Man*. But Sid would get us going. If we were flat in the first four or five shifts, Sid would yell, "What's going on? The bench is dead."

He would give the bench hell for not talking it up. You were expected to be yelling, "Short shifts. Short shifts. Bear down. Bear down." We wanted fresh legs out there all of the time.

Every team had a couple of chirpers to get on everyone who wasn't doing what they were supposed to do, or to get on the guys from the other team. Vic Stasiuk and our trainer, Lefty Wilson, were the two stars of the chirpers. In fact, Lefty even got muzzled from Clarence Campbell for his chirping.

Every team had hitters. They were like linebackers, and their job was to blindside somebody on the other team. Ted Lindsay was our guy who was always ready to give it somebody, but both teams were like that because it was war on ice. Everyone took it seriously. If you weren't hitting, you weren't doing your job.

But sometimes the opposition guy, doing his linebacking, would blindside someone on our team, and our chirpers would yell, "Give 'em the lumber. Give 'em the lumber."

Leadership was a big part of our team. Once a week, Sid would have a meeting and he would give out what he called the "Academy Award." You were never supposed to let the opposition know that they hurt you. You were supposed to sneak off the ice, even if you had torn ligaments. You weren't supposed to lay on the ice because you were making the opposition look good. But sometimes guys would get blindsided and get knocked out. And Sid would have a meeting and guys would vote on who got the Academy Award. They would argue like a bunch of school kids about who should get it. And everyone would be laughing like hell. There was great spirit on that team.

They instilled in you the winning attitude. I never lay on that ice. If you got a puck in the face, you snuck a peak to make sure your eyeball wasn't in the back of your head, and then you got off the ice.

I was 17 when I went to my first training camp, and it was like Marines going to Parris Island for boot camp. We would spend two weeks at Olympia and we would sleep on cots in the vacant dressing rooms. For the first three or four days, there was a lot of scrimmaging so we could show Jack Adams and the brass that we had the guts to go into the corners and take a hit.

57

Adams always wanted to see what you were made of. In this training camp, I was playing with Jack Stewart and was kind of staring at him because I had him in my scrapbook. I took a hit. I was thinking, *Jeez, I'm in a big league training camp and I have a charley horse, maybe I should put some ice on it.* I decide to ask trainer Lefty Wilson about it.

He looked me right in the eye and said, "Shake it off, kid. You never looked better."

If you played hurt, you got a pat on the back. They taught you to play hurt. Kelly was hurt so many times and he would play even when his body turned every color in the book because of all of the bruising.

The Red Wings didn't tolerate any bad examples on the team They would tell the doctors not to baby the players. Every injury was in your head. If a guy went to the trainers, he was considered a hypochondriac. Adams wanted to get rid of those people.

Usually it would be someone from our team blindsiding someone, like Gordie Howe coming back and ferociously backchecking someone. The guy would be lying there on the ice, knocked out, and when he would come to, our guys would be laughing and yelling, "Did you get the number of that truck?" Or somebody would yell, "You get the Academy Award."

Even when I was 40 years old and playing with the Philadelphia Flyers, I still had that attitude of playing hurt because Sid and everyone else had instilled that in me. All the philosophy I have about winning came from the Red Wings. They taught us not to point fingers. They didn't allow any crybabies.

If someone was complaining, someone would yell, "Hey, Lefty, give him a crying towel." Or someone would call you a seagull because "you are either shitting or you are squawking."

Jack Adams was tough on everybody, even Gordie Howe. Gordie liked to experiment with different moves in training camp. He would have fun with a young defenseman by putting the puck through his legs and going around him. He would do it a second time, and the defenseman would close his legs and stop him. Then Adams would come down and give Gordie hell for trying the same move twice.

Gordie would score a hat trick and the next day in practice he would be like a little kid in a schoolyard, maybe fooling around a little bit. Adams would come down from being high up in the stands to lay into his star.

"What are you doing?" he would yell. "The way you practice is the way you play."

But Gordie led by example. He loved the game so much. What I remember from watching him was how ferocious and determined he was. Gordie would attack, get a shot on the net, there would be a turnover, and the puck would be going the other way. He would be a zone out of the play. But he would be so determined to get back in the play and get a hit in. Once he did that a few times, guys with the puck would be looking over their shoulder to see where he was. He broke a team's rhythm.

I made Jack Adams mad. I had met Wild Bill Hunter, and I decided to play for his team in Saskatoon in 1950 rather than go to Omaha to play for the Red Wings team. Adams was an emotional guy. He had stuff coming out of his nose he was so mad at me as he barreled into the dressing room. He was carrying my skates and he said, "Here, get out of here."

Out there is where I picked up my nickname "the Rock." I made the first team All-Star squad and I played well enough that Adams wanted to turn me pro the following year.

At the beginning of the year, I played with the Red Wings because Leo Reise had injuries. Then, at the end of the year, both Leo and Red Kelly were hurt, so I came up to play in the playoffs.

I logged my time in the playoffs and played my role in our system. One defenseman was supposed to cover in front of the net, and when you went to the bench, they patted you on the back like you scored a goal if you had done your job. With all due respect to Terry Sawchuk, I think one of the reasons we got so many shutouts was our defensive philosophy. Goals win games and defense wins championships. We put emphasis on blocking shots. We would shoot pucks at each other and learn to handle the fake.

The philosophy back then was one puck, and before practice you weren't supposed to have a puck on the ice. But Gordie Howe liked to have one on the ice to work on his moves. There would be 18 guys out there fighting for the one puck. Some guys would try to rag it. You would go after them. And Tony Leswick was trying to lift my stick up and he got me right in the eye. Tommy Ivan came out to start the practice, and I'm looking at the 18 players and see 36 heads. I had double vision and I missed some games, but I did play in the Finals. I was lucky I didn't lose my eye.

When I was on different teams after that, I used to bring out my own puck to practice. I would find someone to pass the puck with. I just wanted to get the feel of the puck, like taking infield practice in baseball. And guys would giggle at me because I had my own puck.

From 17 on, I was a Red Wing. I remember going to that first training camp in 1945. I was there from 8:00 to 5:00 every day, picking up on Jack Adams's attitude. It really was like going to Parris Island to learn that warrior attitude. One time some fights broke out on the ice, and I heard Adams chuckling and saying, "Now the boys are getting in shape."

I definitely feel like a Red Wing. I was on a lot of winning teams in my career, and everything I learned about leadership and winning I got from the Red Wings.

Larry Zeidel's Career Highlights

* Playing for the 1951–1952 Red Wings team that won the Stanley Cup with eight consecutive wins. "I have an article in which Jack Adams says that was his best Stanley Cup team because there was no jealousy on that team," Zeidel said.

* Winning two championships playing with Detroit's Edmonton Flyers' farm team. "Babe Pratt is a Hall of Famer and back then he was a color analyst," Zeidel recalled. "I picked up the paper and he had made the comment that coach Bud Poile had it made with the lineup he got because all he has to do is open the door and say, 'Sic 'em.' In other words, Bud didn't have to do too much coaching."

* Learning how to win from guys like Adams, Abel, Lindsay, Howe, and others: "It was like a family on that team," he said.

* During his career, leading his league in penalty minutes six times.

* Being 40 when he played his last NHL game for the Philadelphia Flyers in 1969.

GLENN HALL

GOALTENDER

1952–1957

WHEN I PLAYED MY FIRST NHL GAME for the Detroit Red Wings against Montreal in 1952, I was using trainer Lefty Wilson's equipment. It was unbelievably bad. I had been called up from the Edmonton Flyers because Terry Sawchuk was hurt. My equipment didn't make it. Lefty's skates weren't sharpened. He was missing the finger in his glove, and the glove bent backwards. It was no good. But I had a really good game and we tied 2–2.

I can't say who scored the first goal against me, but I know Doug Harvey scored the second. I never played a game when I wasn't nervous. I don't remember getting sick before that game, but I do remember stopping the puck.

Even though people think of me as a Chicago Blackhawk, I basically spent nine years in the Detroit organization, which is about as long as I was in Chicago. I think I learned from watching high caliber hockey in Detroit.

Detroit had a roster full of talented players. Defenseman Bob Goldham was sure easy to play behind. He blocked a lot of shots. When Bob retired [after the 1955–1956 season], his wife picked him up after his last game.

"I got out of this game with my teeth," he told her.

I have remembered that forever. He was all scarred up—you wonder how they missed his teeth. He was a great player and teammate.

There is a huge difference in what constituted a good defenseman back then and now. In those days, a defenseman was judged on how good he was defensively. In today's game he is judged on how good he is offensively. Al Arbour was great, too. He copied Bob's style. It took a toll on both of their bodies. I played with Al more than I did with Bobby. I played with Al on the Red Wings, St. Louis Blues, and even in juniors. I knew Al really well. They were both great, but Al was probably the easiest defensemen that you could possibly find to play behind.

Al wore glasses when he played hockey. But it was similar to being a goalie and not wearing a mask—you protected your face a little bit and punished the rest of your body. When those guys went down to block a shot, they were pretty tight to the shooter.

Skating is what made Marcel Pronovost a great hockey player. In those days, defensemen were defensemen. They were trying to bank it off the boards; they weren't trying to make an offensive play out of it. You played defense in your end and offense in the other end. That has changed considerably. Now they talk about transition immediately; I think that gets them into as much trouble as it gets them out of trouble.

I've always said that the most essential ingredient you need as a hockey player is skating. There were good skaters in the old days, and they were basically the top hockey players. For example, it wasn't just Red Kelly's speed that made him a good hockey player, it was his tight turns and how he could handle the puck in his feet. Also, he was a smart hockey player.

Gordie Howe and Ted Lindsay were permitted to do things that other players were not. They worked the crisscross a little bit—that was basically in the days when you were supposed to go up and down. The only people who were permitted to crisscross was the Production Line—they were able to do whatever was necessary. They would be able to create the hole. In those days, players were taught to go up and down their wing. By crisscrossing, you would put different people in the slot. It was from the slot that they would score goals. It finally evolved into the point that everyone was doing it.

Gordie didn't have the big back swing. It was a snap shot rather than a slap shot. You could be pretty sure if he was looking at one corner, he was going to shoot at another one. The good hockey players could do things to you that the average hockey player never even thought about.

I attended a few training camps when Harry Lumley was there. He was a really good goalkeeper. I never put him in the class of Sawchuk, but then I never put anybody in Sawchuk's class. All the good goalkeepers have played

Glenn Hall, nicknamed "Mr. Goalie" launched his Hall of Fame career by posting 12 shutouts and a 2.11 goals-against average to win the Calder Trophy as NHL Rookie of the Year in 1955–1956.

with good teams. He played with a good team. What I really liked about Sawchuk was the low crouch. He worked into that crouch so that he could always see the puck. Players didn't shoot back then with the velocity we see today. Back then Gordie and the Rocket used to cut in and beat the defensemen, and then get a shot on you. As a goalie back then, you worried about deflections, and Sawchuk was great at reading where a deflection was going.

Particularly in years that I was watching, and the first few years that I was in the minors, I was never too concerned about playing with the Red Wings—I just wanted to play hockey. I was quite satisfied with the minors. I know I have been told I should never be satisfied, but I was. It was good hockey in the minors. I just wanted to play hockey, it didn't matter where I was playing.

When you played for Jack Adams, you knew you weren't going to earn big money. The joke around the dressing room, even before I got there, was that as soon as a player got close to making $10,000, he was going to be traded by Adams. That was basically a fact.

When I was playing junior hockey in Windsor, Ted and Gordie would come over the border to watch us. I liked them just because they offered us encouragement. But Adams was mad at Lindsay. He told me not to talk to Teddy once I got to the Red Wings. I told Adams, "If you got into an argument with Teddy, you can choose not to talk to him. But Ted is my friend."

I knew Ted was going to be traded, and I suspected I would be traded. At least I knew they didn't want me. Teddy not only stood up to Adams, he was a very smart guy. He was too smart for the rest of us. Too smart for the owners. He paid the price. Even when he went to Chicago, his heart was with the Red Wings. I always said I could change my loyalty to whoever was signing the check. I don't think Ted could. Ted was still a Red Wing even though he played his guts out in Chicago.

He was as smart off the ice as he was on the ice. I roomed with him and I remember talking to him. He always had the answer—a simple one, even though I was always looking for the more complicated answer. He always told me, make one stop at a time. Now they say, don't give up the rebound. I used to say, "I knew a guy who never gave up a rebound. People would say, is that right? I'd say, yeah he let in the first shot."

Ted was as tough as they come. I'd certainly rather be his friend than his enemy.

"Lindsay could carve a turkey with his stick," former Red Wing and Blackhawk Jerry Melnyk used to say.

Ted and Gordie were together all the time in Detroit. They talked about hockey all the time. Although he has been depicted otherwise, Gordie was just as much for the NHL Players Association as everybody else. I know that Gordie wanted to play hockey just like all of us.

Jack Adams wasn't my kind of people. I didn't like the way he treated people. He liked to be in the position that he was total boss. I know that they made trades to get people out of the league. He didn't acknowledge anything. He lived in his own little world. On the other hand, I loved Coach Jimmy Skinner. I think he knows that I liked him, but I don't think that I told him.

That's the way hockey players are. I probably dug my way out of Detroit. But it didn't help being a friend of Teddy. Eventually I told Jack to go screw himself, and you shouldn't tell your boss that. But it sure makes you feel good.

Glenn Hall's Career Highlights

* Having his 502 consecutive games-played streak, from 1955 to 1963, be chosen by *Sports Illustrated* as the most unbeatable record in all of sports.

* In the 1955–1956 season while playing for Detroit, leading the NHL with 12 shutouts and being named NHL Rookie of the Year.

* Winning the Conn Smythe Trophy in 1968 playing for the St. Louis Blues. The Blues lost in the Finals to the Montreal Canadiens, but Hall played brilliantly.

* Helping Chicago win the Stanley Cup in 1961. He posted a 2.02 playoff goals-against average. He was able to bring the Stanley Cup to his home in Stony Plain, Alberta, in 2005, where he discovered that his name had also been engraved (although it is misspelled) as a member of the 1952 Red Wings team. The oddity of that is that Hall didn't play his first game with the Red Wings until the following season. He was Detroit's minor league goalie in Edmonton in 1952.

* In 2005 the City of Humboldt, Saskatchewan, dedicated a monument to Glenn's career in Glenn Hall Park on Highway 5, otherwise known as Glenn Hall Drive. The tribute includes highlights of Glenn's career from his junior days in Humboldt until his retirement from the NHL.

JIMMY SKINNER

COACH

1954–1958

WHEN PEOPLE ASK ME IF WINNING the Stanley Cup in 1955 was the biggest thrill of my career, they are surprised when I tell them that being named coach of the Red Wings was my greatest thrill. I was out west at my dad's business when the *Winnipeg Free Press* announced that I was going to be appointed the next coach of the Detroit Red Wings.

General Manager Jack Adams hadn't called me. I thought someone was fooling around. I had been coaching the junior team in Hamilton, which was sponsored by the Red Wings. I liked coaching the kids. They would come to you for advice about off-the-ice issues, as well as hockey issues.

I knew Jack respected me because I understood my role in the organization. I knew my job was to develop players, not win championships. My job was to teach fundamentals. We didn't want Tommy Ivan having to teach NHL players how to shoot the puck. I remember telling Jack that Larry Hillman and Dutch Reibel were "wasting their time" playing junior hockey. They were ready for professional hockey. Adams said he couldn't sign them because they weren't 17.

"But there aren't many coaches who want to get rid of their best players," Adams told me, clearly impressed.

The day after the *Winnipeg Free Press* story, Adams called to say that he was naming me head coach. The Norris family also owned the Chicago

Blackhawks, and Jim Norris wanted Tommy Ivan to come there to build up the Blackhawks. Adams said the news had "leaked out prematurely." He said he appreciated that I had handled it well.

A lot of players and coaches were afraid of Jack Adams because he was a disciplined man. He was a perfectionist, even at practice. He didn't like guys fooling around. A lot of guys resented that. Jack and Connie Smythe were the best managers in the sport. They loved their players, but they would never let on. All Jack wanted was disciplined players. He didn't want careless guys on the ice. He kept us on our toes all the time because we were fearful.

When I took the job, people said the only way I could go was down because they had already won six National Hockey League [regular season] titles in a row. And they had two Stanley Cups over a few years. The only way is to go down. There was more pressure on me in that first season than I have ever felt in my life.

"Don't fall in love with your players," Adams would tell me.

To me, respect is the greatest element of coaching. You make players be better players and they respect you for that. They put out for you because they respect you. And you stick up for them. When I would have meetings I would always tell my players, "Respect is the best thing you can have, whether you are working in a factory or playing on a hockey team."

After every game, Jack would tell me to make sure my wife could get a ride home because he wanted to discuss the game. He would say, "Why did you use Red Kelly in this situation?" or "Why didn't you?" You would tell him why you did what you did and he would say "that's logical" or "that makes sense." But if he thought you were wrong, he would tell you. It was good, constructive criticism, and I learned a lot from Jack. I was lucky to have a manager like that.

It bothers me that people don't tell the good stories about Jack Adams.

It was an honor to coach Ted Lindsay. He was one of the best left wingers in hockey history, but he had a little too much mouth. I can tell you that Jack Adams was good to Lindsay. When Lindsay couldn't get rid of a cold in his chest, Jack handed Teddy some tickets to go to Florida for seven to 10 days. And we were in the middle of a playoff fight. But Jack thought about the health of people.

Mud Bruneteau's dad became pretty sick in the middle of the season, and Jack told him, "Go home and stay home until he is out of danger."

Jimmy Skinner has said he wasn't looking to become an NHL head coach when Jack Adams chose him to coach the Detroit Red Wings. He would have been content to continue coaching the junior ranks. He said he liked coaching the kids. He liked teaching the game.

But nobody talks about that. What people want to talk about was the rebellion when Ted Lindsay tried to start a union.

But I can tell you that a lot of people wanted to be traded to the Red Wings. If we traded them, they wanted to get traded back. And when we traded Red Kelly, he had tears in his eyes. It was going to be easier on him to be in parliament, but he hated to leave the Red Wings' organization. I don't know how people can say that Jack was bad for the game.

People behind the scenes put a knife into Jack when he was fired in 1962. Some guys didn't like Jack because he was tough to play for, but he was honest and loyal to his owner.

Guys would come in and ask for a raise, and Jack would pull out the scoring numbers and show them that they didn't play as well as in previous seasons.

"I have to be loyal to my owners," Jack would say. "But I won't cut your salary."

Jack didn't cut salaries and he backed his people 100 percent. To Jack, it was all about respect. He respected players who played hard, and he respected the people he worked for. If Jack got respect from a player, he did everything he could for the player.

When Jack got fired, he had tears in his eyes. Jack was very hurt. He put his whole life into that hockey club. After the games, Jack would call Pop Norris and tell him all about the games. He would talk for an hour with him. When I heard what happened, I went into Jack Adams's office, and I told him, "I'm going to resign, myself."

"Don't you do that," he said. "Just give me a few moments to myself and we will talk."

We went to lunch, and I remember we went to a place right by Olympia, and everyone from the organization was there. We backed out and went somewhere else.

Jack told me to stay because he was concerned about my future.

Some of the players talk about Jack breaking up a winning team in 1955, but there are some lies in that. He had to trade those players to Chicago because the Norris family owned that Chicago team, too, and he had to give them some players. If you ask me, Jack kept the league going. He made trades that would help other teams, even though he was hurting himself. He wanted the league to be strong.

He was a loyal guy to the league. I remember him calling Boston GM Lynn Patrick and telling him he should "take Johnny Bucyk." He had to talk him into the trade.

"We are all partners," he would say. "And the league has to have substance."

A lot of the players we would get back in trades would be lackadaisical. They wouldn't even know how to stay with their wing man. We had to stress discipline to them. We were a disciplined organization. That's why we were successful.

I had some talented players, and they were good guys off the ice. They would worry about me. They knew that Jack Adams expected me to have the team playing well at all times.

Terry Sawchuk was the best kind of goaltender. He studied the angles. But Glenn Hall was a helluva goalie. He didn't come out and play the angles like Sawchuk. He was a flopper—he went down a lot. When I had him in juniors, I stopped the practice once and had players skate while I went down to talk to him.

"When we are talking down at the other end of the ice, don't waste your time," I said. "I want you to flop to your left three times and get back up in position. Then flop to your right and then get back up in your position. Get back up quickly. That's the key."

Glenn looked at me like I was nuts. When I got back down to the other end of the ice, the other players were laughing. They were laughing because they were watching Glenn do what I told him to do. Back then players didn't like what you told them, but they listened. I never made Glenn Hall a great goalie, but I could give him points about his weaknesses and he would listen. He wasn't an angle goalie, and he was weak getting back up. It was the second or third shot that was beating him.

Marcel Pronovost was one of the steadiest defensemen on the club. You could never say that Marcel had a really bad game. He did have one habit. He would give the puck away without looking. We broke him of that. He would stay 15 or 20 minutes after practice to work on that.

Gordie just had natural talent. He could do amazing things. He could shoot both right- and left-handed. He could play right wing, center, or defense. People talk about Rocket Richard, but Rocket was good from the blue line in. Gordie could check.

Teddy and Gordie worked well together. For the star that Gordie was, he was a very good listener. Gordie was already one of the greatest players ever when I was coaching him, but he would still come to me. We lost one night in Boston, and he came up to me and said, "Jimmy, what am I doing wrong?" What could I say to one of the greatest athletes ever? What I said was, "Gordie, you had an ordinary night. Everybody has ordinary nights. But what I will remember about you is that you had a lot more good nights than ordinary nights."

Gordie never brushed off anyone. Fans would hound him. After the games, the lights would be dimming and his wife would be waiting and Gordie would still be signing autographs. He never turned anyone down.

I remember when Gordie fought Lou Fontinato. Eddie Shack started it. He was rambunctious. Gordie warned Shack not to start anything, but Shack got feisty with Red Kelly. But Fontinato was the hero in New York. He was the team's tough guy. Gordie warned him to stay out of it. And Lou probably wishes he stayed out of it. I never saw a guy take a beating like Fontinato took from Gordie.

But the toughest fight I ever saw involved Lindsay and Bill Ezinicki. Neither man gave quarter. The players stepped back and slugged it out in the middle of the ice until they got tired.

The one guy I coached who never got enough credit was Alex Delvecchio. He had more talent than 90 percent of the players who ever played and he always played with a big grin on his face.

Alex had two goals when we beat Montreal in Game 7 of the 1955 Stanley Cup Finals. But all of the guys contributed in that win. People didn't know that Kelly was playing with a hairline fracture of his wrist and Lindsay had a hairline fracture of his shoulder. We weren't going to play them, but they demanded that we play them. They went out and a played a lot when they were hurt. Fans never knew. Sometimes I think they played better when they had injuries.

Jimmy Skinner's Career Highlights

* Being the only Red Wings coach to win the Stanley Cup in his first season behind the bench.

* Boasting a 123–78–46 record in four seasons with the Red Wings.

* Serving as general manager of the Red Wings briefly from 1980 to 1983.

* In four seasons, having his teams finish first in the standings twice.

* According to Legendsofhockey.net, in 1969, Skinner, in his capacity as chief scout, offered two veteran players to the Philadelphia Flyers for prospect Bobby Clarke. The Flyers of course turned him down. Otherwise, the Red Wings' history in the 1970s could have been different.

The

SIXTIES

BRUCE MacGREGOR

RIGHT WING

1960–1971

WHEN I TURNED 18, I STARTED my professional career with the Edmonton Flyers, who were in the professional league in Western Canada. It's much different now. You go into a draft, but back then you were their property and there was no leverage when you came out and signed your first pro contract. The NHL teams used to supplement the farm teams with money, and by doing so they retained the rights of the junior hockey players who played on those teams. I was on the junior Oil King team. I automatically became Red Wings property if I turned pro.

They told you when you came out what you were going to get. If you didn't want to play there, that was your problem because they owned your rights. That's why salaries were all controlled.

The Wings were a veteran team when I arrived; there really weren't any young guys. When you walk into a room like that, it's intimidating. That was the toughest part, getting to know the players. There was a player, Val Fonteyne, who took me under his wing. He was a single guy, and we ended up rooming together.

You find your way around, but it wasn't an easy room to walk into. It was a huge adjustment and a whole different environment that I walked into. I was moving away from home for the first time. I had always had a huge advantage growing up in Edmonton—I had lived there my whole life. The Red Wings were my first venture away, and I was 19.

Bruce MacGregor started his NHL career with Detroit and played 673 games with the club. His best season as a Red Wing came in 1966–1967, when MacGregor led the club with 28 goals while playing right wing on the "HUM Line" with center Norm Ullman and left-winger Paul Henderson. "My style was to play and play hard," MacGregor said.

Jack Adams was very involved with the hockey club. He was hands-on. Everything went through him. That's just the way it was. I had been a center iceman my whole career. Even though I was only 19, I had always played center ice. Jack Adams got it in his head that he was going to make me a right winger. Jack would keep me after practice with a couple of players and a goalie. He would be standing in the far end of the Olympia in street clothes yelling instructions on what I should be doing and how I should do it. That's just the kind of guy that he was. He would do that day after day. If he wanted to make me a right winger, then I was going to be a right winger. I was going to try to be a right winger. That's what you did when you had someone with authority, you didn't tell them you weren't going to do it. If you did, Jack would tell you where your next trip was going to be. You could bet it would be somewhere down in the minors.

I played right wing most of my career. I did play some center, but when I played with Norm Ullman and Paul Henderson, I was a right winger. That was in the mid-1960s. It was a great opportunity to play with Norm Ullman and Paul Henderson; we became a good line and such good friends. I believed that line could've started the changeover with the Red Wings to younger players, but then Norm and Paul were traded to Toronto. That one really hurt. When they made that trade, it may have been the start of all the problems with the Red Wings.

The guys they traded for came in and did some good things. It looked like it could be a good trade, but our line was becoming a dominant line and it was a disappointment when it came apart because great production lines don't happen often. When you think of great lines in hockey that have chemistry, when you find that and it works, it's tough when a trade happens and suddenly it's over. You can't look back, but I would have loved to look ahead and to have been able to play some more years on that line in Detroit.

When Ted Lindsay came out of retirement, I got to have an association with him at a young age; it was a huge boost for me. I had a chance to play with him, and he's the one I always credit with turning me around from being strictly a defensive player, a role I was put in for many years. That wasn't the way that Teddy played hockey. He played at the other team's end, that's where he would start. I played on a line with him and Pit Martin for a while. If we lost the puck in our own end, we would have to skate well enough in the defensive end, but he wanted us to be on the offense. He really turned me around and got me going offensively where I scored some goals. I got back to how it was when I was younger and more of an offensive player than a defensive player. I credit a lot of that to him; he was a great role model for guys like me and Pit Martin, the young guys on that team.

Ted had such a will to win and was a bridge between Gordie and Alex and guys like that because Teddy wouldn't take anything from anybody. When he went into the dressing room, he would give it to Gordie or Alex or whoever if he didn't think they were playing well. The young guys had never heard this before because the veterans had controlled the room before Teddy came back. He could tell Gordie that someone was pushing him around out there, and that was a big part of getting things turned around on that team. He didn't accept losing; he was such a huge competitor. We were all competitors, none of us wanted to lose, but Ted Lindsay was to the highest degree. That has to rub off on you, if you were smart enough to catch on to that and get with it. That was the type of leader he was in the room. On the ice he was getting a little bit older, but that didn't stop the great desire he had to play the game and win.

In the 1964 Stanley Cup Finals, we had an opportunity to win the series at home against the Toronto Maple Leafs. We were up 3 games to 2. The excitement was there in that game, and we went into overtime and lost. I was on the ice late in the third period with Eddie Joyal when he shot the puck and hit the goalpost and the puck went in behind Bower, hit the other post, and went out. Looking back, all I can think is how close he was to becoming a Stanley Cup hero if the puck had went in, it was that close. You reflect back on that kind of stuff and ask, "How close was that to going in the net?" It could have been the winner. Losing in overtime, that was pretty tough to take.

It's so much different in pro hockey than college hockey. When Ned Harkness came in, he was used to dealing with students, whom he could control. In college hockey, Ned was the boss. It was more of a "my way or the highway" relationship between player and coach. Ned had so many strange ways of doing things that he had a tough time fitting in with professional hockey. When Ned couldn't get along with someone, they had to be traded. That's what happened to Peter Stemkowski. He was dealt because in training camp you had to have your hair cut a certain way, and if it wasn't cut the right way, it was a problem. Little things like that became problems with Ned. It became a huge learning curve, and maybe he should have been brought in as an assistant coach because he didn't know the league or the players. The problems just started to multiply as time went on.

At that time, I was a player rep and Ned was driving Frank Mahovlich crazy, to the point that he was saying, "This guy has to go!" Everyone thought Ned was going to go because it was just so obvious to all of us that this wasn't the time or the place for someone like Ned Harkness. But that wasn't the way it was, and Ned started getting rid of players. I had never considered myself to be rebellious, I had tried to do what the coach wanted even if I didn't agree with it because that's the way that things were. I remember lots of conversations with Ned about how he wanted things done. Obviously, somewhere along the way he thought that I was a problem. He traded away so many players that became problems in his mind, but it's the person who hired Ned who should take some of the blame for the dismantling of the franchise.

Being in Detroit as long as I had been, I never wanted to be traded. I always thought I would be a Red Wing. When you're there that long, that's what you are. When it happened, it was a shock to me, although I guess it shouldn't have been. I wasn't playing that well and I had become more a part of the problem than the solution, I guess. But I didn't look at it that way. I always thought I would get out of it and things would get turned around, that

Ned would change his ways and start learning more about the game and the way it should be played in pro hockey. But it just never happened.

For a guy growing up in Edmonton and going through minor league hockey and then the Oil Kings and Flyers, being a Detroit Red Wing was a lifelong dream. Having the opportunity to be in the NHL and play for that organization was a huge honor. Walking into that room and seeing all of their great players like Terry Sawchuk, Marcel Pronovost, Gordie Howe, Alex Delvecchio, and Norm Ullman; and wearing that sweater under Sid Abel and Jack Adams, it's still hard to imagine. There was no bigger thrill than when I had the opportunity to go to Detroit in 1961; when I was brought up and played my first game for the Red Wings at Maple Leaf Gardens. You don't forget those things.

People always talk about Terry Sawchuk, and I ended up rooming with him for quite a bit of my time in Detroit. I got along great with him, and he was always great to me. People are different than they are perceived. I'll never forget when my dad passed away and we were in Toronto playing. Terry was so good to me, he looked after me and made sure that I was okay and could get home to Edmonton. Those are great memories because you develop so many long-lasting friendships, like with Normie Ullman and Paul Henderson. I still enjoy going on golf trips and seeing Gordie, it's just like seeing family. We've spent so much time together, friendships like that don't go away. You might not see everybody all the time, but when you do they're your best friends. That's what I enjoy.

Bruce MacGregor's Career Highlights

* Scoring the first goal against Glenn Hall and Chicago in the Stanley Cup Finals. Detroit won the game 2–1.

* Being called up to the Red Wings in 1960: "A huge day for my family and everyone in my hometown of Edmonton," MacGregor said.

* Playing in the 1964 playoffs against Toronto—"So close and losing in overtime."

* Playing with Ted Lindsay, a "huge influence on me," MacGregor said.

* The influence Sid Abel had on him as a coach and as a father figure.

BILL GADSBY

DEFENSEMAN

1961–1966

WHEN I WAS TRADED FROM the New York Rangers to the Detroit Red Wings for the first time in February 1960, Gordie Howe delivered the news as I slammed him into the boards.

"Hey, lighten up," he said, laughing, "because you are coming here tomorrow in a trade for Red Kelly."

As much as I trusted Gordie, I had also learned not to trust trade rumors. When I was traded to the Rangers from Chicago in 1954, the rumors had me going to Toronto. But as I was pinning Gordie along the boards, he said this wasn't a rumor. It was fact.

I was thrilled with the idea of being a Red Wing. When I was playing in Chicago for player/coach Sid Abel, he would tell me that if he ever returned to the Red Wings he would try to trade for me. My wife Edna and I wanted to go the Red Wings for several reasons. First, they had a good club. Second, we were friends with Gordie and his wife, Colleen. Finally, the Red Wings' minor league team was in Edmonton, which was home to us. We hoped, after I retired from the NHL, I could stay in hockey by coaching or working for the Edmonton Flyers.

After the game, Muzz Patrick did confirm Gordie's story. I had been traded, along with Eddie Shack, for Red Kelly and Billy McNeill. Since Kelly and I were both All-Stars, the trade created a stir. But even after Patrick told me about the trade, I had a funny feeling that it wasn't going to happen. I just didn't think Red would go to New York. But I called Edna and told her that she would have to pack up by herself because I was staying in Detroit. Several of the Rangers' wives came over to help. Gump Worsley's Doreen was there. So was Merle Bathgate and Harry Howell's wife, Marilyn. They worked until 3:30 in the morning. Edna even had to find homes for our kittens.

In the meantime, I knew that Eddie was going to rip New York. He hated it there. I tried to counsel Eddie against saying anything negative about New York. "Maybe this trade won't go through," I said. "You can always say what you want to say later."

But Eddie didn't listen. He lashed out at everyone, including the fans. He said New York was a "zoo."

Imagine the look on Eddie's face when he found out the next morning at breakfast that the trade was voided. "Are you psychic, Bill?" Shack said. "How did you know?"

The trade had been nullified because Kelly wouldn't report. McNeill also wouldn't go because he had lost his wife to polio and was trying to raise his children by himself. He had child care in Detroit and didn't know anyone in New York.

Imagine the shock to Edna when I told her we were staying. She had already written letters saying we were moving. Now she had to write letters saying we were staying. That's the story of the Gadsby trade that didn't happen. Boy, did the fans give it to Eddie in our next Rangers' game at the Garden.

It wasn't until 16 months later, with considerably less fanfare, that I came to Detroit. I was traded for $20,000 and Les Hunt, a prospect who never made it.

Players wanted to be traded to the Red Wings. They had Gordie Howe. They had good defense and goaltending. But it wasn't just about the talent. The Red Wings were just better organized than the other NHL teams. For example, when you would come to the Red Wings, general manager Jack Adams's secretary would have a list of houses that you could rent for the winter. In New York, we had been on our own. Olympia also had the best ice in the league. Everyone said that.

People say Adams was difficult, but he was fair to me. "If you have a good year, Bill, you will get a $2,000 bonus," Adams would say. It wasn't in the contract, but at the party after the season Jack would come around and there

As a Red Wing, Bill Gadsby (left), pictured above with Sid Abel (center) and Gordie Howe (right), achieved several career milestones. He was the first NHL defenseman to record 500 career points, the first NHL player to play 300 games for three different teams, and in 1965–1966, he and teammate Gordie Howe joined former Boston star Dit Clapper as the NHL's only 20-year players. *Photo courtesy of Bettman/Corbis.*

would be envelopes in his pocket. "You had a good year, Bill," he would say as he gave me the money. He gave me exactly what he said he would.

He could be tough. If we weren't playing well, he would come into the dressing room and you could see the Greyhound Bus tickets sticking out of his lapel. He made sure you could see that dog on the ticket.

"Some of you better get in gear or I will have something for you after the game," Adams would say as he patted the tickets.

But I was treated well in Detroit. I probably appreciate playing for that team more now than I did when I played. When I have 65- and 70-year-old people coming up to me and talking about seeing me play in the 1960s, I realize how popular the Red Wings were back then.

When I look back at my years in Detroit, I wonder how in the world we didn't win a title. We reached the Stanley Cup Finals in 1963, 1964, and 1966, and each time I left without a championship. We had a lot of talented players on that team.

Gordie was the best player who ever played because he could do everything. To me, the game boils down to being able to do five things on the ice: scoring goals, setting up goals, playing physical, playing defensively, and killing penalties. You never had to worry about Gordie's man. He would always come back and backcheck. Gordie was exceptional at all areas of that.

I don't think I ever saw him take a full windup for a slap shot. He could get the puck away quickly, especially if it was close to his body. He would bring that stick back about eight or 10 inches. Whack! The puck was in the back of the net. He was so strong in his arms.

Gordie was also a deceptive skater. People didn't think he was a good skater. If there was a man to beat, Gordie beat him. You just didn't think a big guy could get going the way he could get going. He didn't look like he was moving as fast as he was. A lot of great skaters tried to catch him from behind and never made it.

When it came to what happened on the ice, Gordie had a memory like an elephant. If you played it straight up with Gordie, you had no problem. You could take him into the boards and rough him up a bit. I played against him for a lot of years and never had a problem. But if you gave him the stick or slashed him, he didn't forget. He may not get you that night. But he would get you the next game or two months down the road. In the Original Six days, you played 14 games against every team. You had plenty of opportunities.

One night in Montreal, fans were giving him a fine ovation for reaching some milestone and five minutes later they are booing him for something that happened between him and Montreal player J. C. Tremblay. They had both gone into the corner, and only Gordie came out. Tremblay went down like a sack of potatoes. There was no television replay back then, and no one knew what happened. When we got back to the bench, I asked Gordie what had happened.

Gordie said he didn't know what happened. But Gordie was my roommate and after the game, we had supper and I asked him again. "I really don't know," Gordie insisted. "But maybe the thumb of my glove struck him in the eye. That's probably what happened."

That could happen, I told myself, as we walked back to our room in the Mount Royal Hotel. But after I picked up the morning paper, I couldn't resist kidding Gordie the next morning at breakfast. "You must have a really powerful thumb," I said to Gordie as I sat down. Then I showed him the newspaper headline that said Tremblay had a broken jaw.

Not until I did my own book did Gordie reveal that the incident wasn't about anything that Tremblay did on the ice. Apparently, the spring before Gordie had been working as a radio analyst after the Red Wings were knocked out of the playoffs. He had been on a train watching some of the Canadiens playing bridge. Gordie commented that Dick Duff had made a nice play. "What's a dummy like you know about bridge?" Tremblay had said to Howe. That night in Montreal, Gordie had responded to the comment.

People talk about Wayne Gretzky or Bobby Orr being the greatest player, but I can guarantee you those players weren't better at all-around play than Gordie. I played with and against Gordie and my opinion never changed. He's not only the best hockey player I ever saw, but the best athlete I ever saw.

We had many great players on that team. Norm Ullman was one of the better forecheckers I've ever seen. He was even a pest in practice. "Get the heck out of here," I would yell at him in practice. "I'm trying to get the puck out of here." He was a good skater and he turned checking into an art form. He did everything well. He was also a very quiet guy.

We had great goaltending with Sawchuk and Roger Crozier. Sawchuk was a very different guy. I roomed with him after I got to Detroit, and I said, "Good morning, Ukey," and he never said a word. I asked Gordie about it, and he laughed, saying that had happened to him as well. "He doesn't start talking until about two hours after he gets up," Gordie said.

Crozier was a great goaltender. I used to tell him that he must have watched Glenn Hall when he was growing up because Glenn was the only other goaltender I saw who was as acrobatic as Crozier.

I played one season with Ted Lindsay when he came out of retirement, and he had a great year. He was a fiery guy. I didn't care for him when I played against him. He could be a dirty bugger. He had all the tricks. He had to because he wasn't that big of a man. He was tough and he was skilled. He was good in the dressing room and fired up a lot of guys. I enjoyed playing with him.

In hindsight, the loss of the 1964 Stanley Cup Finals series against Toronto bothered me more than any other playoff loss. We were the underdogs in that series, and Sawchuk had injured his shoulder in the first round. He wasn't playing at 100 percent. The town was buzzing about the series, and we had a 3–2 lead going into Game 6 at Olympia.

That game was one I will never forget, and not just because Bobby Baun scored while supposedly playing on a broken leg. Every time I see him I tell him I don't believe he played on a broken leg. Maybe it was a hairline crack of his bone, but it wasn't a broken leg that I would call a broken leg. I jokingly tell him that he got too much ink out of that story. "You skated pretty darn well on a fractured leg," I tell him every time I see him. He just smiles at me.

What nobody remembers about the famous Baun game is that, less than a minute before Baun fired the overtime shot that made him famous, I took a shot that haunts me to this moment. Rushing into the Toronto zone with the puck, I spotted Floyd Smith. As soon as I fed him the puck, he knew I was heading to the high slot for a return feed. We had worked on that give-and-go hundreds of times in practice. Floyd sent me a perfect pass, and I sent what appeared to be a perfect shot over goaltender Johnny Bower's shoulder. It happened so quickly that Bower never made a move. But instead of finding the back of the net, the puck struck the upper shaft of Bower's goal stick. As stunned as I was, I had gotten back into my defensive position when Baun carried the puck over the blue line coming back the other way. I was between Baun and the net. When he took the shot, it was a knuckleball. I had probably blocked a thousand shots harder than Baun's shot, but this shot struck my stick funny and danced over Sawchuk to give Toronto a 4–3 win. I remember turning just in time to see the puck going into the corner of the net.

No one remembers that we lost Game 7 by a 4–0 score. We all know we lost that series in Game 6 in Detroit.

In 1965 I was in my 20th season, and at that time only Dit Clapper and Gordie had played that many seasons, and both of them had won championships. That was one of the stories going into the Finals when we played Montreal. We won the first two games of the series in Montreal and felt like we were in good shape coming back home. But the Canadiens beat us 4–2 in

Game 3, and Ralph Backstrom's third-period goal gave the Canadiens a 2–1 win in Game 4. We lost Game 5, but we still believed we would take the series back to Montreal for Game 7. We expected to win Game 6. Floyd Smith scored for us to send the game into overtime, but Montreal won the game on a very controversial overtime goal by Henri Richard.

Most of the players knew he had gloved the puck into the net with his hand. Crozier had the best view, and that's what he said. Crozier's anger was directed at referee Frank Udvari. Crozier believed that Udvari wasn't in the correct position to make the call. After the game, Richard told newspaper reporters that it had been a "lucky" goal. Although the Red Wings lost, Crozier won the Conn Smythe Trophy as most valuable player. That's how close the series was.

It was a painful loss. When that game was over, I was drained, but I knew that it was time to fulfill a promise. I had always told Edna that she would be the first to know when I was going to retire. She was sitting in the stands, crying, when I got her attention. "Honey," I said, "you've just seen me play my last game."

Bill Gadsby's Career Highlights

* ★ Being elected to the Hockey Hall of Fame in 1970. Gadsby was a seven-time All-Star.

* ★ Being the first defenseman to reach 500 points, on November 4, 1962.

* ★ In the 1958–1959 season, having 46 assists to set a NHL record for most assists in a season by a defenseman. The mark stood until the 1969–1970 season, when Bobby Orr had 87.

* ★ On February 5, 1966, playing his 300th game for the Red Wings, making him the first NHL players to record 300 games with three different teams.

* ★ Fans marched in front of Olympia Stadium in support of Gadsby after he was fired as coach after two games of the 1969–1970 season. The team was 2–0. "What really bothered me was that we had just beaten Chicago and [owner] Bruce Norris had put his arm around me and said, 'Bill, you really got this team going,'" Gadsby recalled. "I told him, 'I think we are going to have a good year.' Two days later, he fired me."

DOUG BARKLEY

DEFENSE

1962–1966

HEAD COACH

1970–1972 ★ 1975–1976

MY EYE INJURY HAPPENED JUST AFTER the Christmas break in a game against Chicago. It occurred on a play that is done a hundred times. The puck came out to the point; I kind of pulled it in and was going to take a slap shot. Just as I took the shot, Doug Mohns came from behind and tried to lift my stick. Of course, I got the shot away, and the stick just came straight up and hit me in the eye. That was the end of it. I don't think there was any intent in it or anything like that. It just happened.

I was able to keep the eye, but the doctors didn't know for sure what was wrong. A couple of specialists were brought in, and it was diagnosed as a detached retina. With a detached retina, if you have 2 or 3 percent torn off it's pretty hard to get back. Well, I had about 80 or 90 percent torn off! So realistically right from the start there wasn't much chance.

But the Red Wings sent me to the Massachusetts Eye Institute in Boston, which was one of the best in the world. I had a couple of operations there. They told me it was very, very doubtful that I would ever get my vision back in that eye. I also went to St. Louis, had another operation, and they said just about the same. I had a little vision after a couple of the operations, but it's just something they couldn't repair. A detached retina is like fly paper. It just pulls together and sticks. They didn't have a way of pulling it back and stretching it out again.

If it happened today, I'm not sure that more could've been done. The eye is such a delicate organ. They've made great strides with the pupil in the middle of the eye with eye injuries—that's new and very effective. But you still have got to have the retina behind it to get any reflections in it. If you can't get the retina set down in place, there's nothing they can do. They've never found anything similar to this gel-like substance in the back of your eye that they can inject to soften it up and get it back to normal.

Truthfully, I didn't know what I was going to do. I had done nothing else in my life except play hockey. I was down in the dumps quite a bit. We had a guy, Baz Bastien, who was a goaltender who lost an eye and was working with Sid Abel. He was a great help. The players were just great. Gordie would come by and say, "Baz, you watch this side and, Doug, you watch the other side, and handle practice for us." They made it easy to be around the rink. Bruce Norris and Sid Abel decided to give me a chance to work in the organization. First, I was an administrative assistant, then a scout, and finally I started my coaching career.

It was certainly the best break of my career when Sid Abel made the trade that brought me to Detroit. If I would have stayed in Chicago, I probably would have never played in the National Hockey League. It was a situation where, defensively, the Blackhawks seemed to be pretty strong. I was also a bit overwhelmed to go to a team like Detroit from a team like Chicago, who was really struggling at the time. Of course, Detroit wasn't.

If you're coming from another NHL club during the Original Six days, you expected that there wouldn't be any problem being accepted in the locker room. I was coming from a minor league team; so going into that Red Wings dressing room, I didn't know how it was going to be. Detroit had Gordie Howe, Alex Delvecchio, Normie Ullman, along with Bill Gadsby and Marcel Pronovost on defense, and Terry Sawchuk in goal. All of them are in the Hockey Hall of Fame.

I had nothing to worry about. They just took me in like I'd been there my entire career. I was just one of the guys. Looking back on it, which I have a lot of times, I don't think many organizations have that family-like atmosphere. We were all family. They did anything they could to make you feel

Doug Barkley, shown here moving past Jacques Laperriere (2) to jam a rebound toward the Montreal Canadiens' net, had his National Hockey League career cut short by a serious eye injury in 1966. He was 29 when he was struck in the eye accidentally by Chicago player Doug Mohns.

at home, not only in the dressing room, but in your everyday life. Detroit has always been a family team. They look after their people.

My relationship with Gordie Howe started from my first day as a Red Wing. When I arrived in Detroit, the Wings were having their golf tournament, and Gordie couldn't play. Gordie asked me, "Are you going golfing?" I said, "No, I don't have any equipment and I'm not that good of a golfer." He said, "Here you go. You can use my clubs and we have the same shoe size. You go and enjoy yourself and have fun." I ended up rooming with Gordie for two years, so I mean, who else better could you learn from? He just took me under his wing and really made me the player that maybe I hadn't been up until then.

Gordie Howe had to be intimidating on the ice because he was a superstar. I think he learned right from the start that he had to protect himself, and he certainly did that. Gordie knew how to play the game. He knew how to play with finesse and he knew how to play it tough. He got a lot of room out there and rightfully so, he deserved it!

For him to play as long as he did and as well as he did his whole career, I don't think there's been any athlete who's had a career like his. He had longevity. If you ask Glenn Hall, Jean Beliveau, any of these guys, they'll tell you he's just a super human being. Even today, anywhere he goes there are crowds. He draws them in. I think the biggest thing about him is he's just down to earth. Let's face it, Gordie's probably met everyone from presidents down to the guy working in the factory; and he always has time for everybody. He'd just as soon talk to you about going fishing or playing golf or something other than hockey. He will stop and sign autographs. We used to kid him all the time, especially on the road, "Gordie, you can only sign 50 so we can get back to the hotel and get something to eat." He would stay forever and wouldn't leave until the last guy had his autograph.

My defensive partner was mostly Marcel Pronovost, and playing alongside him was a great experience. We had Bill Gadsby, too. I didn't get to play too much with Bill, but he was a terrific player. Marcel was one of those defensive defensemen who had a long career; and when you get to play with somebody for two or three years, you get to know each other. You develop a solid chemistry; it worked out perfectly. Marcel was excellent. The whole team was excellent. Three out of the four years I was there, we went to the Stanley Cup Finals. It was just unbelievable for me!

In the 1964 Finals against Toronto, we were up in the series 3 games to 2, and the sixth game was back in our building. We figured that if we win this one, we win the Cup and everything is great. Bobby Baun, one of their mainstays on defense, gets hurt, he goes off the ice, and you're thinking he's out of it. All of a sudden he comes back with his ankle probably frozen and taped. We're in overtime and he takes a shot that I think deflected maybe off of Bill Gadsby or somebody, quite a ways out. Terry Sawchuk didn't see it at all and just like that the series is tied. That was big. Then they beat us in the seventh game in Toronto.

Even though I didn't play in the 1966 Finals because I was injured, I'll always remember it because of the performance of Roger Crozier in the net. Roger was outstanding! We won the first two games in Montreal, but the

Canadiens were a good team and they came back and beat us four in a row. However, Roger's play was the story. He won the Conn Smythe Trophy as the playoff MVP. It was the first time that a player from the losing team had won the award.

Ned Harkness became the Red Wings head coach after having a huge coaching career in college. He had a lot of different ideas and probably some of them were really good, but it was pretty hard for the players to accept them. I think what he had in college was young kids who would do anything he said. If he brought in a play or a set of plays, they would automatically do it. He tried this with the pros and it just didn't work. Ned took away the players' individuality, and I think that was one of the biggest things. The guys who can play, you have to let them play. You've got to give them a little leeway rather than set patterns.

If you look at football, there are so many college coaches who come up and don't get the job done in the NFL. It's a very hard transition, and Ned was one of the first coaches to ever try it in hockey. They may have been dark days, but the Red Wings were just trying to turn it around.

A couple of things stick out in my mind about when I replaced Ned Harkness as coach. One, the team was going to strike; they weren't going to play. That made it a very tough situation to go into. Second, I wasn't ready to be there; I hadn't had enough experience. I loved coaching in the minors because I was able to teach and get the guys prepared to play in the National Hockey League. I enjoyed it. We didn't win a lot of cups or anything in the American or Central League, but we always had good contending teams.

In the NHL, I was coaching guys whom I had played with and guys who were the same age as me. It was tough because it wasn't a teaching situation, it was a management situation and I wasn't prepared for it. I'll admit that I shouldn't have taken it. But how many times do you get a chance to go back to your team and coach it in the National Hockey League? Not many, so I took the opportunity. I was a little more prepared when I went back the second time, but I still think a couple more years in the American Hockey League would have probably been very beneficial to me. With more experience, I could have gone to the organization at the start of the season and said, "Look, I want my own coaches and assistant coaches and I'd like to get this player or that player." That just wasn't available at the time I went in there.

Being a Red Wing, to me, is being part of a family. They look after their people. I want to thank Sid Abel. He traded for me and, right from the start, he let me play a regular shift, on the power play, and on the penalty kill. Sid was behind me 100 percent. I'd like to mention Budd Lynch, who is still there. Bud was on the radio and he became a very good friend of mine.

Lefty Wilson and Danny Olesevich, our training staff, took good care of me; I was injured a lot in my career and, boy, those guys really looked after me, especially after my eye injury. I still have a soft spot for the trainers in any sport.

The fans in Detroit have always been great. I struggled with the fans' support when I was coaching because, let's face it, I wasn't a very good coach. As a player, they treated me outstandingly!

Doug Barkley's Career Highlights

* Being able to room with Gordie Howe for two years on the road. "It was just an unbelievable experience for a young guy to go in there and be with one of the greatest players ever and have him as a mentor," Barkley said.

* Almost winning rookie of the year. He lost out by two-tenths of a point. "I don't know how the voting went in those days, but two-tenths of a point seems a little ridiculous," Barkley said. "I lost out to Kent Douglas who had an excellent year with Toronto."

* The first time he went to the Finals against Toronto. The real bad overtime defeat, thinking we could win it in six, and we lost it in the seventh game.

* Playing with Ted Lindsay. "He came back the one year from Chicago in 1964," Barkley said. "He was a Red Wing to the core and certainly his coming back to the Wings, the year we won first place, was a big highlight for me."

* His last season in 1965–1966. "I'd had a pretty good season," he recalled. "I was up for first half All-Star. Then, I suffered my eye injury and wasn't able to play in the '66 Finals, which Roger Crozier starred in."

PAUL HENDERSON

LEFT WING

1962–1968

BEFORE THE DRAFT WAS INITIATED, NHL teams would sign you as a 15- or 16-year-old kid to play for their junior team. Teams had scouts all over the place, and they would come and try to convince you to sign this C-form. If you signed the C-form, then you were basically that team's property. That was the agreement. All six NHL teams had junior teams in Ontario. Detroit had their team in Hamilton, the New York Rangers had Guelph, Chicago had St. Catherines, Boston had Niagara Falls, Montreal had Peterborough, and the Leafs had the Marlies and St. Mike's.

Three NHL teams were after me in particular: Boston, Toronto, and Detroit. I had a chance to sign with them all; they all wanted me. I wasn't going to go to Detroit. I was going to go to Boston because their guy, Baldy Cotton, was really nice. He came up and talked to my dad, and we just felt good about the Boston organization. The fact that Boston had a bad team influenced me, too. They didn't have any real superstars, so it looked like it might be easier to make the Bruins than other teams. I decided to go to their camp in Niagara Falls, and I told Detroit and Toronto.

The Detroit people phoned me and said, "Well, Paul, our camp starts two days earlier than Boston's. Why don't you just stop in and skate a little while with us and then you can go on. It will give you a better opportunity. We'd like to give you that opportunity." I thought, "Well, geez, that's really nice of them."

I went down to Hamilton, and after the second day they said, "Well, Paul, you've made the team if you want to stay here with us." I phoned home to my dad and I said, "Well, Dad, Hamilton is a lot closer than Niagara Falls. It's another hour and a half getting back and forth. This sort of makes sense to me."

My dad always loved the Detroit Red Wings and Gordie Howe. We talked about it, and I decided to just stay there. I really had had no intention of doing that. Of course, Boston was upset at me, but I hadn't signed a contract.

Back then, my eyes were the size of saucers because these Red Wing players were some of my heroes. I probably would've paid them just to play in the NHL. It wasn't about making money; it was about proving to myself that I could make it. Nobody was looking to make money. I thought if I could play eight to 10 years, it'd be a pretty good career. Then I'd go do something worthwhile. Money was never the driving force.

The first year I was with the Red Wings, I came up at Christmastime. I was a right winger, but they had Gordie, Floyd Smith, Andy Bathgate, and Bruce MacGregor—five right wingers on the team. One night Ron Murphy, a left winger, was playing with Normie Ullman and Bruce MacGregor and got hurt. So Sid Abel just threw me out there. I had never played left wing before in my life. It was just one of those things. I played with Norm Ullman the next eight years. I never had another center iceman.

I hit the jackpot when I was able to play with a Hall of Fame center like Norm Ullman. Anybody could've played with Normie and done well. I would say Dave Keon and Norm Ullman were two of the best fore-checkers that I've ever seen one-on-one, with their ability to cut the ice off. Norm was just an all-around player. He had incredible stamina, he was an excellent playmaker, and he read the play well. He was just a treat to play with. We would rely on each other's strengths. Bruce and I were more the fore-checkers. I had the speed and we would try to get in there; but in our end the secret was to get the puck to Norm. That's what we tried to do. As soon as we got it in our end, we'd get it to Normie and let him make the plays.

If you were in the other end and you got the puck, the first thing you did was try to look for Normie, and he would set up the play. He could shoot the puck; so if he was in position, I would try to go to the outside and Norm would always come into the slot. The guys were always looking for him, and a lot of his shots were one-timers. I would try to turn the defenseman to the outside and flip it back to Norm in the slot.

Once Normie, Bruce, and I started playing together, we established ourselves and became an integral part of the team. The three of us just worked, and it seemed to be the chemistry that allowed us to do it. We were accepted and we were all about winning. There wasn't a guy on the team who didn't want to win. Everybody came to win once the game started, but there was just a different atmosphere in Detroit.

It was definitely a country club in the locker room—a lack of discipline. As a younger guy, I was absolutely flabbergasted. We would get into the playoffs, go down to Toledo, and we wouldn't even practice. They'd take us away from our families, make us live in a hotel, and we wouldn't practice. It just made me think, "What the hell is going on here?" I was a young player and not getting a lot of ice time; so I wanted to go down there to skate and work on things. It made no sense to me.

One year, one of our guys got hammered out of his mind while we were in the playoffs. He wasn't even back at the hotel the day of the game and guys were trying to cover up for him. Sid would have never missed him, but he was getting him some tickets. When Sid called out for the guy, saying he had his tickets, he looked around the room and the player wasn't there. As a rookie, I couldn't say anything, but to me that was bad leadership. If we would've had some leaders on the team, they would've said, "You go out and have a couple of beers, but you better be ready to play the game!" Half the time, guys were more concerned about the horses they were betting on at the track. It still irks me to no end, even today.

Pit Martin and I were the young guys on the team in the era where players would say, "Rook, pick up and carry my bag." We'd go, "Carry your own bag." As a couple of rookies, we just didn't accept that rookie nonsense. We're on the team, we're players, and we didn't take their garbage. In hindsight, we may have just been a couple of cocky rookies, but I was on the team. As far as I was concerned, I wasn't going to be treated like a piece of crap.

We had a great hockey team. Look at the guys we had. Alex Delvecchio and Gordie were poetry together on the ice. MacGregor, Ullman, and I could play with anybody in the league.

In '64 we eliminated Chicago, and that was a pretty good hockey team. I still remember winning that playoff series. It was my first year, and Pit Martin and I thought we'd died and gone to heaven when we beat them in seven. There's no question that once the game started, everybody gave it their best

Paul Henderson played on a line with Pit Martin and Larry Jeffrey in his first season with the Red Wings in 1964–1965. The following season he still enjoyed his first 20-goal season as he helped Detroit reach the Stanley Cup Finals. In 1966–1967, he missed 24 games and still managed to score 21 goals.

shot. To me, it was just the lack of preparation beforehand, but you never questioned a guy on the team. Once they dropped the puck, they came to play.

I was devastated when they traded me. The thing that really got me was that Bruce MacGregor's wife, Audrey, phoned me in the morning and said, "Paul, I just heard on the radio that you, Norm, and Floyd have been traded to the Toronto Maple Leafs." I actually cried when Audrey told me. It was one of the most sickening feelings of my life. I didn't know what rejection felt like. I'd never had a girlfriend reject me, or my parents. I never felt the feeling of rejection until that morning, and it just tore the heart out of me.

I lost some respect for Detroit, specifically for Sid Abel. He didn't even tell us to our face. That was the time that hockey changed for me. I loved Detroit, and Normie and I were playing well.

The first game I played against Detroit as a Maple Leaf was in Toronto. We beat the Red Wings 5–3. Norm was the first star and I was the second star. We each had three points in the game. I especially remember Gordie. I had seen a lot of guys traded, and Gordie would go after them. At the start of the game, I lined up against Gordie. He said, "How are you doing? Is the family doing okay?" I'll never forget that as long as I live. I don't ever remember Gordie giving me a cheap shot after I was traded. I have so much respect for Gordie in that sense.

I think Gordie respected me, but I don't think Gordie was close to anybody, really. He had his own life and he loved to play the game. I never saw anyone who loved to play the game as much as Gordie did. You respected him. He was really just a big kid who loved the game of hockey.

Looking back on it now as I get older, I realize that when I was in Detroit, Gordie was 30-some years of age. He had his circle of friends and his children. I was never invited to the Howe home. I can't ever remember being invited to one of the players' homes, except the MacGregors. That was the thing that sort of confused me. You had the odd team function, but they'd never invite you to dinner as a couple. I thought some of these older players would invite my wife and me over, but that never happened.

I was proud as hell to be a Detroit Red Wing. I wish some of the things could've been better, but I just loved it. If I had my preference, I'd have played my whole career there; so it's not that I didn't enjoy myself. Once I became established, it was fine. You had the Gadsbys, Howes, Delvecchios, and Ullmans. We had an older team; so as a youngster, you'd follow the lead of the older ones.

Paul Henderson's Career Highlights

* Scoring four goals in one game against New York on October 27, 1966. "It was the only time I scored four goals in my life," Henderson said.

* Helping Detroit beat the Chicago Blackhawks in the playoffs in his first season. "We won the first round and were underdogs in that one," Henderson said. "I can remember that like it was yesterday. We won in seven games, and there were some good bonuses involved, but as a young kid it was just really important to be in that kind of an atmosphere."

* Playing with Bruce MacGregor and Normie Ullman on the HUM Line.

* Scoring on a breakaway in the sixth game of the 1966 Stanley Cup Finals against Toronto's Johnny Bower.

* Scoring the series-clinching goal for Canada in the 1972 Summit Series. Most people in Canada over 40 know where they were when Henderson scored.

PETER MAHOVLICH
LEFT WING/CENTER
1965–1969 ★ 1979–1981

WHEN I WAS GROWING UP, before my brother Frank became a member of the Toronto Maple Leafs, I was a Detroit Red Wings fan. It wasn't like today with many games on television. We didn't have all of the images of players like we have today. We played more unorganized than organized games. But we envisioned players like Gordie Howe, Ted Lindsay, and Alex Delvecchio whenever we took the ice.

By the time I was drafted by the Detroit Red Wings in the first amateur draft in 1963, my allegiances had changed because Frank was playing for the Maple Leafs.

But it was a great thrill when my first linemate on the Red Wings was Gordie. In my first few games on the Detroit team, I played left wing on a line with Alex Delvecchio and Gordie. It was fabulous. They gave me good advice as far as what to expect in different buildings.

When you played with Gordie what you noticed is the great respect that other players had for Gordie when he was on the ice. I'm not talking just about his teammates. I'm talking about his opponents. They all knew that stopping Gordie was the big key to being able to beat the Red Wings. But they were still careful to tiptoe around him.

In my first few years it was difficult to earn ice time with Detroit. Back then, you were dressing 16 players and two goalies. I was the 10th forward. I would kill the odd penalty and play the odd shift. I ended up being sent to

Retiring as a four-time Stanley Cup champion from his days in Montreal, former Detroit player Peter Mahovlich has enjoyed a lengthy scouting career. Today he works as a professional scout for the Atlanta Thrashers.

Pittsburgh, which was Detroit's farm team. That was a tremendous experience. I enjoyed playing under Sid Abel. He was a good man.

The first year I was there, I roomed with Bryan Watson. What I remember is that we agreed to split the grocery bill, and I don't think he liked that very much once he saw me eat a couple of times.

I played with a lot of good guys. Nick Libett and I played together in Detroit and on their farm team in Hamilton. He was a good skater and a solid two-way player. He was really a good teammate. He was on the quiet side. I played a bit with Terry Sawchuk. He was quite a character. He challenged you in practices. He didn't like to get scored on anywhere, even in practice. He had tremendous hands.

Another goalie I played with was Hank Bassen. Hank was a practical joker. He was one of those guys who was a little on the sly side. He was always doing something. He would cut your laces or get someone else to do it.

Defenseman Gary Bergman was another great teammate. I also played with Bergy in the Summit Series. He passed away not too long ago. Talk about a guy willing to sacrifice his body to block shots. And they didn't have the equipment they have today.

Late in the 1967–1968 season, the Red Wings traded for my brother Frank. There were some rumors before it happened. It was a huge trade. The Red Wings got Garry Unger, Pete Stemkowski, Frank, and the rights to Carl Brewer for Normie Ullman, Paul Henderson, and Floyd Smith. I think I was down with the Fort Wayne, Indiana, farm team at the time, but I was excited because I thought we might have a little run together in Detroit. It didn't exactly happen like that.

We didn't play a lot together in Detroit, but we had about a season and a half before I was traded to Montreal. I was happy to have the time I had with Frank in Detroit. I didn't have much time with Frank growing up. I was seven or eight when he went to St. Mike's for his first junior. When I was playing peewee, bantam, and midget, he would come on Fridays to see me play the odd game.

We also have an older sister, and we have always gotten along. I hear all about family arguments and I can't think of a time when Frank and I, or my sister, were ever real angry or had a cross word for each other. The only time Frank and I were ever mad at each other came when we played together in Montreal. We were killing a penalty together. It was after a face-off. We both went for the same man and another walked in, and bang, he scored. When we got to the bench, I said, "Geez, Frank, you got the wrong guy." And he thought I had made the mistake. We were both yelling at each other, and Scotty Bowman got into the middle of it. It was the only time I can remember being angry at each other.

Frank definitely clicked with Gordie and Alex. He scored 49 goals in his first full season, and Gordie produced 100 points for the first time in his career.

When I was traded, I was happy to move on because I didn't feel things were going to work out for me in Detroit. But when I was moved, I was thinking, *They just got finished winning the Stanley Cup. Am I going to be able to play there?* But Montreal GM Sam Pollock, ever the psychologist, sensed that apprehension and he said, "We didn't trade for you to play in the minors. We feel that you've got an opportunity to develop and play in the big club and have a good career in the National Hockey League."

I started out with their farm team, but as the year went on they had some injuries and I got a chance to play at the end of the year a lot. I think we missed the playoffs that first year in Montreal with 92 points. I think the first place in the other division was St. Louis with something like 70 points. We were tied with the Rangers and ended up missing the playoffs with 93 points. Then, the following year, we won the Stanley Cup. We ended up beating Chicago in seven games. Frank was traded from Detroit to our team in January, I think, and that could have put us over the top.

I was traded to Montreal in 1969 and I helped get Frank get there in 1971. Al McNeil had felt responsible for bringing me to Montreal and he asked me if I thought Frank would want to play in Montreal. I told him that Frank loved the way the Canadiens played and he had always told me that if he had the chance, he would love to play there. Ron Caron and Sam Pollock were responsible for bringing Frank from Detroit.

In 1979 Pittsburgh traded me back to Detroit for Nick Libett. By then I had had a lot of success, and I think they brought me to help some of the younger players. The first year I played with Mike Foligno. We had Jimmy Korn on defense. Dale McCourt was a young player. In a lot of ways, the way McCourt approached the game reminded me of Alex Delvecchio.

Vaclav Nedomansky was still there. He was one of the first players to come over from an eastern bloc country, and what a terrific skill level. He was introverted and he's still quiet today, but what a nice man.

There had been some problems with the coach before I got there and I think they thought I could help things out. I found out a long time ago, players trying to dictate to the coaching staff isn't what should be done. Management will figure it out. Players play, coaches coach, and scouts scout. Bobby Kromm was my coach at the start, and he did a good job of getting us ready for games. Then Ted Lindsay was general manager, and he felt some pressure to win immediately. He was so determined and he is the type of guy, as a general manager or a coach, who expected players to give the way he gave all when he was a player. And maybe his expectations of some of the players didn't meet the standards of what we needed.

It has always been fun to play in Detroit. You had a lot of Canadians coming across from Windsor to attend games. It certainly had an old-time hockey atmosphere. The old Olympia was a fabulous building, a tremendous place to play. Like in most of the older buildings, the fans were right on top of you. The rink configuration was different than most rinks. The Montreal Forum had really deep corners. Olympia was more egg-shaped. The puck would react differently at times when it came off the boards.

When I look back at my career in Detroit, I feel like there were many missed opportunities for me. Whether it was my fault or theirs, I don't know. I don't point fingers. All I know is that the people of Detroit are terrific hockey fans, and I have great memories about my days there.

Peter Mahovlich's Career Highlights

* After leaving Detroit, winning four Stanley Cup championships while playing in Montreal.

* Playing for Canada against the Soviets in the 1972 Summit Series.

* Having 10 goals and six assists in Montreal's 1971 march to the Stanley Cup championship.

* Posting 30 goals and 42 assists in 88 career playoff games.

* Playing in the 1971 and 1976 NHL All-Star Games.

BRYAN "BUGSY" WATSON
DEFENSEMAN
1965–1967 ★ 1973–1977

I EARNED THE NICKNAME "BUGSY" while playing in Detroit. Before that, I would come to training camps, and when I had to list my nicknames, I would put down "various." I was raised in the Canadiens system, they owned me at age 14, and I turned pro with them at age 19. In those days all we talked about at training camp was first place and the Stanley Cup. When I came to Detroit, the players looked at Montreal and Toronto ahead of them, and their goal was fourth place. I was in shock!

The Montreal dressing room was "rah-rah!" because of the players they had and what they had accomplished with a steady diet of first place, Stanley Cup, first place, Stanley Cup. When I came to Detroit, it was like a country club. No one would say anything. I would sit beside Gordie Howe and Roger Crozier, and between periods I would be the one screaming and yelling. Gordie would sign autographs, and the team would sit and look at me like I was out of my mind. I didn't get these guys, and all I could think was, *What the hell have I run into?* They had great hockey players on the Red Wings at that time like Bill Gadsby, Roger Crozier, and Howe. When we got into the playoffs, I didn't let up. Andy Bathgate and Gordie were in the room and I was on Gordie's ass.

Gordie turned to Andy and said, "He's driving me crazy!" Andy turned to me and said, "You're driving everyone nuts! Will you shut up?"

It is for that reason that they decided to call me "Bugsy"—because I drove them crazy! At the time Jimmy Forney was working for a Windsor radio station and picked up on players calling me "Bugsy." Soon, I was doing an interview with Andy Bathgate and Gordie and we started talking about nicknames, including "Bugsy." Next thing I new, I was traded to Pittsburgh, and Jimmy Forney was the color guy for the Penguins. He started calling me Bugsy during the games and it stuck.

Back then, Bobby Hull was an NHL superstar, a magnificent hockey player on a good Chicago team. One night when I played with the Canadiens, we were in Chicago and playing the youngest line-up that the Montreal Canadiens had ever put on the ice because we had five or six regulars out of the line-up. For whatever reason, I was playing against Bobby Hull. We won the game 2–1, and it was as if we had won the Stanley Cup.

Detroit scouts must have seen that game because they remembered it when I came to the Red Wings and we played Chicago in the playoffs. Chicago had a strong team, and Hull was flying. He scored two goals. Norm, Bruce MacGregor, and Floyd Smith were checking Hull's line in the game. We lost the first game, and afterwards Gordie Howe, Norm Ullman, Bill Gadsby, and I were having beers. I said to them, "I don't know how to say this, but I've played against Hull."

Granted, it was only for one game. But they told me, "Why don't you cover him, then!" Sid Abel had always believed that we needed to get Norm Ullman's line away from Bobby Hull so that his line and Gordie's line could score for us. Either Sid or Bruce Norris must have seen me play against Bobby Hull in that one game in Montreal because I believe I was traded to Detroit for that purpose. The next game, I started against Hull and we won the game. We wound up winning that series.

I did everything I possibly could to get Bobby Hull off his game. My goal when playing him was to stop him from carrying the puck. I would get between him and the puck as much as I could. I was always in his skating lane. He could never wind up and get his shot off. I had great success shutting him down this way. I was also talking to him the whole time as well, I didn't know enough to keep my mouth shut.

I was always a very vocal player on the ice because all I cared about was winning. It wasn't about having a "good game," it was about the team and winning.

It was a big story in the press that someone brand new to the team would play against Bobby Hull. They couldn't believe it when I was able to shut him down. He had no goals and I had two. When you're in the Stanley Cup play-offs, you don't realize how many people are really watching. It wasn't until I went to Montreal and a friend told me, "They're talking about you for MVP of this series!" I couldn't believe it because I hadn't been paying attention to what the papers were saying, but everywhere I went people were talking about it.

Earlier in the year, there was a game where Detroit played Toronto. Afterwards, the plane took us to Windsor and then we drove ourselves home. I was dead tired and driving down the Lodge freeway to my house in Southfield when I saw a police car behind me. I slowed down, thinking that he would pull off, but he didn't and, as soon as I started going again, he pulled me over. I told him who I was and he let me go. After we beat Chicago in the playoffs, we partied all night and as I left I thought, "I have to really be careful driving." I started to drive along, watching the road, and all of a sudden I see police lights behind me. I couldn't believe it! They pulled me over and two policemen came up to the car and opened the door. Only this time, they opened the door and jumped in, saying, "Okay, tell us about the game!" They had sat there all night waiting for me to drive home from the game. That's what I'll always love and remember about Detroit! Detroit always made you feel good about yourself.

In 1966 we played my old team, Montreal, in the Stanley Cup Finals. We were up 2–0 and I heard stories about the Canadiens sitting on the team bus in shock. Our team went outside and, while waiting for our bus, one of our players—I think either Alex or Gadsby—lit up a cigar. The Montreal bus had been sitting in silence until they saw that and Blake let out a scream and said, "Look at them! They're celebrating the Stanley Cup already!"

Oh, my, that started it! I went to Sid Abel to talk to him about it, but I should have kept my mouth shut because that got me in trouble. After that, Toe Blake held a meeting where he talked about putting Jean Beliveau, Leon Rochefort, and Gilles Tremblay against Gordie's line. He told them that if they could shut down that line, Montreal would win the Stanley Cup. We had last change and still lost. We had three of the last four games in our building and the best we could do was to lose in overtime. And to top it off, Roger Crozier got hurt even though he came back and played.

Bryan Watson made "shadowing" an art form when he checked Bobby Hull for the Red Wings in 1965–1966. He played a total of five seasons with the Red Wings in two different tours of duty, but his tenacity and relentlessness made him one of the franchise's most memorable characters.

I told Sid Abel, "I know that you know, but Gordie's line has dried up and we have last change?" He told me not to worry, that they could score against anyone. Too bad it never happened. That was the whole reason we didn't win: that line got shut down.

I've been really lucky because of the great players I've been able to play with in my life. One player that I never got the chance to play with was Ted Lindsay. I never had his ability but thought he was a great hockey player. I did have a similar spirit and stride; the same approach to the game. I loved him! I'll always remember the first time I met him because I was thrilled. I had heard so much about him and we hit it off as if we were old friends instantly.

When I look at the players that I got the chance to play with in Detroit, I think about Gordie Howe. He was so great and easy-going, but a son of a bitch on the ice. I have never seen anyone like him. Whenever Gordie was going for any sort of a record, he was nervous. You had to be careful around him. I drove with him a lot and had to be careful messing around with him. And then there was Gordie on the ice and the things that he was able to do with his stick. I remember getting ready for the playoffs in practice, Gordie wasn't ready for a hit for whatever reason and I knocked him ass over tea kettle into the corner. All I could think was that I was in trouble—I knew what he was like. I had seen him knock a dozen guys out with his stick! I went over to tell him that I was sorry and expected him to scream at me. But he said, "I want to thank you for hitting me because it woke me up. I could have really gotten hurt." I almost kissed him, I was so happy! Here he was thanking me for hitting him.

I wish that we would have won the Stanley Cup in 1966. What was really unfortunate was that we never really built on what we had. Maybe that was the problem we had on the team for quite a few years—we only did so well. We never got better. That was a big disappointment for me in Detroit. That wasn't my job, that was the job of the people putting the team together. They traded Peter for Peter, they never upgraded.

That group that I played with in Detroit was one of the best groups of individuals that I ever played with—championship or not. They were a bunch of guys who really cared for each other and had fun on the ice playing. I just missed the passion coming to Detroit from Montreal because I'm very passionate.

Being a Detroit Red Wing was the greatest experience of my life; both the city of Detroit and the fans at Olympia, as well as the players that I played with. It was a truly wonderful experience. I still get the same feeling whenever I return to the city—the city always makes me feel good.

Bryan Watson's Career Highlights

* Having the chance to play with Gordie Howe and know his family with wife, Colleen, and seeing Marty and Mark grow up.

* Playing with his teammates. "The Red Wing team was the greatest collection of character players I ever played with—we had great camaraderie," Watson said.

* Playing in front of the Olympia fans. "It was my first experience with American hockey fans," Watson recalled. "The whole city was behind us."

* Playing in a playoff series with Bobby Hull. "It put me on the map and is what people still remember about my career," Watson said.

* Scoring his first goal. "Danny Grant scored his 50th goal, and the bench emptied. I scored my first goal in that game, and the bench emptied again for me!" he said.

The SEVENTIES

RED BERENSON

CENTER

1970–1975

ISAW MY FIRST PRO GAME IN OLYMPIA when I came to the University of Michigan as a player. My coach, Al Renfrew, helped me get tickets to see the Red Wings play Montreal. One of my best friends, Billy Hicke, was playing for Montreal at the time, so I went out with the team after the game. I couldn't believe what these guys drank! Wow! I was pretty naïve at that time. All these people were asking for autographs from the team, and I tried to tell this lady that I wasn't a player, but she wouldn't believe me. I looked across the table and there was a guy who looked like me with a short brush cut, Jean-Guy Talbot. So I wrote "Jean Talbot" as my autograph to this woman.

When Montreal came to town the next couple of years I would always go to see Hicke. And soon after I played my last game for Michigan in the NCAA tournament, I signed with Montreal. I played the last four games with the Canadiens that year. Sure enough, where was our last game of the year? Detroit. I scored my first NHL goal in that last game at the Olympia against Hank Bassen. It was a big deal in those days for a college player to go to the NHL, so my whole college team had come in to watch me play. I said hello to them after the game, but I had to leave with the Canadiens. We went to the same place after the game, and the same lady comes up for an autograph. I tried to explain to her that I wasn't Jean-Guy Talbot and I ended up in this big argument with this lady over who I was. I ended up signing Talbot's name for her again, anyway. Detroit was a neat place, and visiting teams loved to

Red Berenson was among Detroit's best players in the early 1970s, scoring 28 goals and adding 41 assists in 1971–1972. But he's probably more known to Detroit-area fans as the long-time coach of the University of Michigan hockey team. Berenson played at Michigan before turning pro with Montreal.

play at the Olympia because there was a great history there. It's sad that the final years there were not that good.

It was a tough trade when I came to the Red Wings because I was solidly entrenched in St. Louis. I was the team captain at the time and their leading scorer. There were definitely some political implications with the Players Association. I was president of the Players Association at the time, and

Timmy Ecclestone was the player rep, so it was ironic that we were both traded to Detroit. I'm not so sure if Wayne Connelly wasn't the player rep in Detroit at the time, and he was sent to St. Louis in that trade.

Detroit had Gordie Howe and Alex Delvecchio and it was an honor for me to play with them. Yet the franchise and the team seemed to be in turmoil with the recent change in coaches and general manager. It seemed like we had more players living in the motel in Dearborn than we had living in the city. It was a really unstable situation. I felt bad for the new coach, Doug Barkley, who was trying to hold everything together while the players were having a tough time. We weren't nearly the team that we should have been, and it was not one of those proud times to be a Red Wing.

I think the leadership of the organization was going through a difficult period. Sid Abel had a power struggle with Ned Harkness. It was a tough time for the organization in terms of stability and leadership. Yet Detroit was still a great place to play because they treated us like pros. It was a good organization with some good prospects, but I'm not sure how good their drafting was. In a lot of cases, they may have expected too much from their draft picks. These guys shouldn't carry the team when they're 18- or 19-year-old kids. Even players like Marcel Dionne and Guy Lafleur in Montreal took a long time to develop.

You need to have a good base of players on the team and then let the young guys develop; you can't rush them into leadership roles immediately. The same holds true today. There is the odd player, like Sidney Crosby, that you can put on a pedestal and they can lead your team, but that's usually with a losing team. You can even look at Steve Yzerman's early years in Detroit where it was probably unfair for him, as well. You have to be patient and have a decent team, but if you had a decent team, you wouldn't be getting that high of a draft pick. It's a catch-22.

College hockey didn't have a lot of credibility when Ned Harkness tried to coach the Red Wings. It might have been different if he had been a pro player or pro coach, but he was coming from college hockey with a lot of new terminology like "breakouts" and different systems. He wasn't used to players who were undisciplined or different from college players. He had a hard time with all of that. He was gung ho and probably had some good ideas, but I think if Scotty Bowman had done the same things Ned Harkness did, there would never have been a question asked because Scotty had the credibility. Ned didn't.

It wasn't difficult for me to adjust to Ned because I played college hockey at Michigan. It was really difficult for the rest of the team. Ned Harkness was the general manager when I came to the Red Wings, and people in the front office, in some cases, were saying that he had done a great job in getting the scouts more organized to do a better job. But the team itself still seemed to be lacking leadership. I can't tell you that it came from Ned, but that usually comes from the top. We also had so many new players; I can't tell you how many players played for the Red Wings in the few years that I was there. It was probably twice as many as most teams.

The coaches I played for with the Red Wings were Doug Barkley, Johnny Wilson, Alex Delvecchio, and Ted Garvin. With Ted Garvin it was probably unfair to put him in that situation, and he was only there for 11 games. After Johnny Wilson and Garvin, it was Alex Delvecchio. I don't know if Alex agreed to retire one day and coach the next, but he went right from playing to being the coach. There were at least those four coaches in my time in Detroit. Maybe if we had less coaching changes we would have had more stability, because one season we had close to 90 points and didn't make the playoffs. We had some great players, but there was just something missing; I can't even tell you what it was. There would always be some crisis, some problem, or some issue that ended up affecting the team one way or another.

I liked Detroit and there were a lot of positives to playing there. The first thing I did after the trade was buy a house. I tried to get some stability. My one regret is that I didn't play as well as I feel I should have. I should have done more. I gave a lot of respect to Delvecchio, Howe, and the guys who had been there, like Bergman, rather then becoming more of a leader like I could have been in Detroit. Alex had been a captain for years and years, so how could you say something when you had a player like that who was your captain? But we definitely were not living up to our potential as a team. When I look back, I think that with the team we had we should have done a lot better.

Olympia was a great building historically and nostalgically, and I liked playing there. Our fans were great and there were a lot of good things going on, but we just didn't get over the hump for some reason. It was disappointing. Soon after, Alex Delvecchio took over as general manager, they made some trades, and I went back to St. Louis. The Red Wings crowds continued to slowly go down because of more issues and a new era of players. I remember them getting Terry Harper after making that deal with L.A.,

113

where Dionne ended up going to the Kings. That was a big hassle. It was just one thing after another, and it never seemed to take off in the direction it should have. Whether it was the combination of the draft picks, trades, leadership, or coaching, the problems were on and off the ice.

I don't know what happened with Marcel Dionne leaving the Wings. I think he liked Detroit, but he was very young, and they made him captain. That wasn't fair to him. There was enough pressure on him just to show that he was a great young player without having to be a captain. Personally, I think that was putting a lot on his plate. And then Mickey Redmond's back went and he couldn't play. And all of the sudden, who are your best players? It starts with the ownership and the leadership up top and it filters down to what's happening on the ice. That was a low point in Detroit's history, when you think of their great years in the 1950s and part of the 1960s. When I was in St. Louis, we played Detroit and they had Mahovlich, Delvecchio, and Howe on a line. They were as good as anyone in the league.

The Red Wings players got great support from the fans and the people in Detroit. Every player who came to Detroit, for the most part, really liked playing for the Red Wings and liked being in Detroit and living there. That was a real positive even when the team wasn't doing as well. We did have our good moments. I remember the night that Mickey Redmond scored his 50th goal, but then we didn't make the playoffs and that was the down side. And when Marcel came up, they had a good draft pick. I had good friendships with the players like Nick Libett, whom I still stay in touch with, and Bryan Watson, Arnie Brown, and also Gary Bergman, who passed away. It would be hard to believe, when you look at our record, but there was chemistry and friendships with the players even when we went on to other teams.

Even though our owner, Bruce Norris, lived in Chicago, he was a sports fan. Mr. Norris would come with his entourage to some of the home games and come down to the locker room afterward, if we had a good game. I remember at the end of the year I suggested to Doug Barkley and Harkness that they take the team to Florida, like St. Louis did, to help the team build friendships and a good relationship with the owner. They did take the whole team down because Norris owned a resort in Florida, and everyone had a great time. I thought that would be a real positive step for the organization.

Bruce Norris would do unusual things, like, he gave me a Newfoundland dog. He knew I was interested in dogs and he had a friend who was a breeder of Newfoundlands. Harkness also had a Newfoundland dog. So he gave me a Newfoundland. It wasn't like he didn't show an interest in any of the players; he just seemed to have a hard time relating to everyone. People may slam Bruce Norris for a lot of reasons, but there were some good moments, too.

You had a different feeling playing for an Original Six team like Detroit and Montreal than you did playing for New York. You just didn't have that feeling in New York. Even though we played at the "historic" Madison Square Garden, it really was a pit. It wasn't like the Forum or the Olympia. Montreal and Detroit had winning histories. Now, living in the Detroit area and coaching at the University of Michigan, Detroit is the team that I follow. They have a terrific history, so it's nice to see them back to what they were in the 1950s.

I feel fortunate and proud to have played for the Detroit Red Wings. They were one of the teams that I grew up with in the Original Six era. Gordie Howe was from Saskatchewan, so as far as I was concerned, he was from my hometown. It was a thrill for me to play for the Red Wings and to play with Gordie Howe.

Red Berenson's Career Highlights

* Scoring my first NHL goal in Olympia with Montreal.

* Rooming with Gordie Howe.

* Playing with Gordie Howe and Alex Delvecchio and getting to know Ted Lindsay—all players I looked up to.

* Representing the Red Wings at public functions.

* Being an assistant captain on the Red Wings.

* Scoring six goals in one game versus Philadelphia on November 7, 1968, while with St. Louis.

JIM RUTHERFORD
GOALTENDER
1970–1971 ★ 1973–1981 ★ 1982–1983

W HEN THE RED WINGS LET ME GO to the Pittsburgh Penguins in the waiver draft in 1971, it was because general manager Ned Harkness believed I was too small. When Harkness traded Ron Stackhouse to Pittsburgh for Jack Lynch and me in 1974, my comment to the Red Wings was, "You know, I haven't gained an ounce or grown an inch."

But joking aside, I love playing in Detroit. We didn't have great teams when I was there, but hockey was big in the city. As soon as you walked into Olympia Stadium and smelled the beer and popcorn, the game was on. It was a great old building. It seemed like the fans were sitting on top of you. The corners were very shallow. There was hardly any room behind the net. It was difficult for a goalie because it felt as if you were closed in. If you were in an exciting game at Olympia, there was nothing like it. It was a fashion show for the women. They would all come decked out in their nice dresses and fur coats. Men came to the games in a shirt, tie, and sports coat. Many of the men would be wearing fedoras. Sunday night games were big in Detroit.

If there were a Lions game at Tiger Stadium, people would attend that game, go to Carl's Chop House for dinner, and then to the Olympia. Then, after the game, everyone would go to the Lindell Athletic Club for drinks.

When I came to my first Red Wings training camp in 1969, I was probably more in awe than I should have been. Gordie Howe was still on the team.

Jim Rutherford's 96 career wins rank him seventh on Detroit's all-time for wins by a goalie. He had 10 career shutouts, even though he played primarily during an era when the Red Wings didn't have competitive teams.

Gary Bergman was there. Bill Gadsby was the coach. Roger Crozier was there. Crozier was such a great goaltender. He battled through illness to play at the NHL level. I was excited to be in the same dressing room with these guys. I felt like I should be asking these guys for autographs, not playing on the team with them.

The biggest mistake the Red Wings made in the 1970s was letting Marcel Dionne go. To allow a franchise player like Dionne to get into a contract dispute and leave the team for the Los Angeles Kings is almost unforgivable. The team lost their building block and they probably didn't recover until they drafted Steve Yzerman. When Dionne signed with Los Angeles, Terry Harper and Dan Maloney came back [as compensation]. They were good players, but they didn't make up for Dionne. He was probably one of the 10 best players of all-time. You paid to see Dionne. He was so highly skilled that he brought people out of their seats. I remember once he scored when we were playing two men short. In the 1974–1975 season, he set an NHL record of 10 shorthanded goals in a season. [The record is now 13, set by Mario Lemieux in 1988–1989.]

If all the sports were successful in Detroit, I think hockey would be number one. That's why it was sad that we didn't have any success in the 1970s. At one point, we had three legitimate 50-goal scorers on the team in Marcel Dionne, Danny Grant, and Mickey Redmond, and we couldn't make the playoffs. That sort of summed up the chaos of that period. I think we had 10 or 11 different coaches in my time in Detroit.

Mickey shot the puck at the level they are shooting at today. He always had the new sticks and high tech sticks of those days, but they weren't quite at where they are today. It would be interesting to see how hard he could shoot with these new sticks.

He could really wrist the puck, too. He did a lot of work on his shots. He would be in the corner, working on those shots from the sharp angle, shooting for the narrow spots.

Danny Grant scored because of his accuracy and quick release. He could shoot the puck in full stride, and he caught goalies off guard with his release.

Alex Delvecchio was probably my favorite teammate of all-time. He's actually probably my all-time favorite person in hockey, and my favorite coach. He was a man's man, but he was so easygoing and always willing to help you. He was also a good coach; he had a real understanding of his players. He was a good communicator. He just didn't have enough quality players to be successful as a coach.

Gordie Howe's last year in Detroit was my first. He was a true gentleman, really good with the younger players. I didn't get to see him in his best years. That was the season they asked him to play defense, which I thought was unfair. But you could always see that he gave it everything he had. Every day, he came to play.

But even if the crowds were smaller back then, there was a lot of interest in the Red Wings. When Toronto came to town, it was probably 60–40 in terms of rooting for the Red Wings or Maple Leafs. So many people came across the river from Windsor to watch the games that it had a real Canadian atmosphere at Olympia.

When I came to Detroit, the team moved Roger Crozier to make room for me. My favorite goalie growing up was Glenn Hall, and I tried to pick up some of his traits. But when I came to Detroit, some people said I was like Crozier because we were about the same size. But there was really no one like Crozier. He was an acrobat. He was up. He was down. He was diving around constantly. He was the most exciting goalie I ever saw.

Because I played under so many different coaches with different styles, I saw a lot of funny things happen. Times were really changing when Ned Harkness came in from Cornell to coach the team in 1970. He wanted to do things back then like we are doing today, particularly with regard to conditioning. But it wasn't accepted. He took over a team that had recorded 95 points the year before, and we still had the big line of Gordie Howe, Alex Delvecchio, and Frank Mahovlich. We had old-school guys who came to training camp to get in shape, and Harkness believed you needed to stay in shape year-round. His approach was different. He made Gordie a defenseman and played him there for a big part of that year. He thought his puck-moving would help, but that was really unfair to Gordie.

With all of this going on, there was a big player rebellion in Buffalo. I was called out of my room for a players-only meeting. Essentially, no one wanted to play for Ned. The point of the meeting was to figure out if we could get a new coach.

That meeting evolved into a meeting at Olympia, and Alan Eagleson came in to help represent the players. Eagleson was my agent. When the meeting was over, Ned was not our coach anymore. Doug Barkley was our coach, and Ned was the general manager.

That night we were walking out the back door of Olympia. It was Eagleson, Bruce Norris, and I, and Norris put his arm around me. "Jimmy," he said, "you are going to be a Red Wing for life."

A few months later I was sent to Pittsburgh because I was too small.

When I came back, the coaching carousel was still going. I played for nine different coaches during that period. A lot of things that we were doing with Ned, they are trying to do now, but it wasn't accepted. Then Larry Wilson came in from the Philadelphia organization and wanted us drinking beer after the game in the locker room. He ordered no soft drinks anymore; he threw all of them in the garbage. His coaching philosophy was: you have to drink together, play together, stick together, have fun together, and fight together. One day he told us were weren't going to have practice. Instead, he said, we were going to have boxing matches. He matched up fighters with non-fighters, like Dennis Polonich fighting Bill Lochead. You were supposed to spar. But it didn't work out. He wanted his two goalies to fight. Eddie Giacomin said, "I'm not doing that." He was by no means afraid of me, but he just didn't think it had anything to do with playing hockey.

It was just a strange time to be a Red Wing because we had so many different coaches and everyone had a different idea of how we could be successful.

People seem to remember my goalie mask with the Red Wings logo over the eye hole. Here's the story about the mask: when I was with the Penguins, I wore a blue mask to match the Penguins color. After I was traded back to the Red Wings, my first game was in Toronto, where I met up with goalie-mask designer Greg Harrison.

"Don't paint it red—just paint it white," I told Harrison.

I was still a bit upset about the trade because the Red Wings organization had gotten rid of me before.

Greg said he would have it by game time, and when he showed up with the mask, it was white but it had the logos painted around the eye holes with the holes serving as the wheel. I didn't want that, but it was too late to repaint the mask, so I wore it.

Everyone loved it. People talked about it. We tied the Leafs 2–2, and I decided to leave the mask the way it was. After that, all the goalies painted their masks.

Jim Rutherford's Career Highlights

★ Wearing the Red Wings sweater. "Maybe it means less now because there are 30 teams, but it was a big deal to wear a jersey from one of the Original Six teams," Rutherford said.

★ From December 21, 1975 to January 10, 1976, posting a shutout streak of 217:38 to break Terry Sawchuk's team record. It still makes the NHL's Top 15 list of longest shutout steaks. Rutherford etched another mark in Detroit history in the 1975–1976 season. Included in his streak were a 4–0 win against Washington on December 31, a 1–0 blanking of Toronto on January 3, and a 5–0 shutout of Minnesota on January 8. He joined Terry Sawchuk, Clarence "Dolly" Dolson, and Glenn Hall as the only Red Wings netminders to post shutouts in three consecutive starts.

★ Helping Detroit down Atlanta 3–2 to clinch the best-of-three 1978 first-round playoff series. Bill Lochead scored a late third-period goal. Lochead squeezed by Atlanta defenseman Dick Redmond, brother of Mickey Redmond, to streak down the ice and score the game-winner at Olympia. "We weren't supposed to win a game in that series," Rutherford. "And people still talk about that game. What people forget is that, right before that, I had made a save and was down and Guy Chouinard hit the crossbar. From there we got the puck up to Lochead."

★ Joining Sawchuk as the only Red Wing ever to play with the team on three separate occasions.

★ In the second round of the 1978 playoffs, helping defeat the eventual Stanley Cup champion Montreal Canadiens in the opening game of their playoff series in 1978. The Canadiens were 59–10–11 that season.

DANNY GRANT
LEFT WING
1974–1978

I HAD BEEN PLAYING IN MINNESOTA FOR SIX YEARS, and the organization had some internal problems. There was kind of a power struggle between the owners, represented by Walter Bush at the time, and Wren Blair, who was general manager. Some of the players got caught up in the middle of it—guys like me, J. P. Parise, Jude Drouin, and a number of other guys.

Management just felt that everybody had been together for so long and maybe a change was due. I was looking forward to a change, too. I loved Minnesota and loved living there. My children were born there and it was great, but it was time to move on. There was also a big movement within the North Stars to acquire as many American players as they could get, Henry Boucha in my case. Henry was an American boy from Minnesota.

He was flamboyant and he was young. A trade was made, and I became a Red Wing.

Going to Detroit was certainly going to be a challenge, but Mickey Redmond was there. Mickey and I were, and still are, the best of friends; we played our juniors together. They also had a young future superstar coming in Marcel Dionne, as well as solid veterans like Nick Libbet, Bryan Watson, and a few other guys.

Playing for an Original Six team was also appealing. I liked the idea of playing in the old Olympia. Along with Chicago Stadium, it was my favorite rink to play in because the people were so close to the ice. It was such a lively building, and Detroit always had such great fans, win, lose, or draw. The tradition and the history with Gordie Howe, Terry Sawchuk, Bill Gadsby, and Alex Delvecchio were really interesting for me.

When I went to Detroit, I was a veteran player and Alex Delvecchio was the coach. I thought Alex was a great coach for handling veteran guys. I don't think coaching the younger guys was his strongest suit. He was such a great player that he took so much for granted. He felt that if you played at that level, you should be able to do certain things; but younger players needed a lot of teaching. Remember, Alex came from being a player to a coach in only a couple of years.

From my point of view, Alex was fantastic not only as a coach but as a friend. He let me play my game and he allowed me to do things that really helped me personally. It couldn't have worked out better.

There's no question Marcel Dionne was the real deal. He could do so many things with the puck. He was a very deceptive skater, strong on his skates, and he saw the ice tremendously well. From the first time I played with him I thought that if you were lucky enough to come along at the same time and played with him for 10 years, you could put up Hall of Fame numbers. Look at 50-goal scoring wingers and the centers they played with. You don't play with third- and fourth-line centers and score 50 goals. Dionne was a true superstar.

We ended up with Phil Roberto on the right side of the line with Dionne and me. There were a number of guys there during the course of the year, too many to really count. Phil came along out of St. Louis and was a big, strong, tough kid. But Phil had a serious injury to his hand, and by the time he got to Detroit, he was certainly not the player he originally was at St. Louis. Marcel and I were not physical players, yet when Phil came along, he allowed us to do things we couldn't do before he arrived. He was the type of guy who always had his nose in there; he was always a tough kid even with his hand injured.

Nobody understood how losing Dionne could've happened. You have a kid at that time who's 21 years old and had another 15 or 16 years of great hockey in him. Even though they traded for Terry Harper and Dan Maloney, who were both definite assets, they were certainly not in the same category as Marcel Dionne. It would've been great to have Terry and Danny along and still have Marcel there. Then we would have had tremendous improvement; but the way it was, we gave up way too much, especially when you're trying

Although Danny Grant was never considered a fast skater, he was considered a strong skater and a mentally tough performer. He worked hard, and he used his creativity and accurate wrist shot to become a 50-goal scorer for the Red Wings.

124

to get a franchise back on its feet. You look today, and everybody in the league, all 30 teams, are all looking for a franchise player. Every team is looking for something to build around, and the Red Wings had it right in the palm of their hand and let it go. Any hope you had for things to improve disappeared with the loss of Dionne. The message was really, really not good.

Everybody was just grasping at straws. We had glaring weaknesses on the team. I was there for four years, and in my fourth year we still had some of the same weaknesses that we had the first year I was there. The franchise got to a point where everyone was desperate to find something to cling to. We were a team that had some talent and had some glaring weaknesses. We were an exciting team, but we couldn't win. We had so many coaches and so many different philosophies that we never got to the point where we could have one direction.

Scoring 50 goals was something. I started out playing that year with Bill Hogaboam at center and Mickey Redmond on the right side. Our line got off to a pretty good start. Then Hogaboam broke his ankle and Mickey's back went out on him. Nick Libett was playing on the left side with Marcel, and here I am a left winger with nobody to play with. So they put Nick on another line with Red Berenson and I took Nick's place with Marcel. From the moment we played together on the first shift, it was magic. In total, I think I played 50 to 55 games with Marcel, and it was as if we were just made for each other.

When I got around the 35- to 40-goal range, we were out of the playoffs and the fans were desperately looking for something to cheer about. The old Olympia was filled every night. In my four years there, I knew more people around the glass. In the warm-up you could talk to them and they just kept coming and cheering you on. I don't want to sound corny, but I wanted to give something back. I had a chance to be the first left winger in the history of the Red Wings to score 50 goals. It was just one of those years where I could put my name in the history books from a personal point of view and really give some meaning to a disappointing year for our team and our fans.

In those days, you weren't rewarded the way you are today. Let's say for the sake of argument, if you scored 35 or 40 goals, you got a $5,000 raise. If you got 50 goals, you got a $6,000 raise. You raise your expectation level as a 50-goal scorer, but the reward was minimal. A lot of times you got to a certain point and thought, "What benefit is this to get to the 50-goal plateau outside of it being a personal accomplishment?"

I remember sitting down with Mickey Redmond, and Mickey had scored 50 a couple seasons before that.

"Danny, you've got to go for it," Mick said. "You might never get another chance. Look at me, my back's gone. I'll probably be out of hockey in another year. The one thing I have got is a 50-goal year behind me, and it's something very few people do. You've got to go for it."

I said, "Yeah, you're right Mick. I'm going for it."

Then I went to Marcel and said, "Marcel, I want to get 50 this year." We just went from there. When I was in the 40s, I was getting so close that I kept thinking about a guy like Frank Mahovlich, who ended the season with 49 but he never got that 50. It was our last game of the year at home; we had two games left after that. We were playing Washington, and I had 48 goals. I scored the 49th and 50th that night.

When I scored the 50th goal, it was just the fact that I did it. I never kidded myself into even dreaming of being compared to a Bobby Hull or any of those guys who had 50 goals previous to me. I knew I was a good goal scorer and I could've easily gone through my career averaging 33, 34, 35 goals, which was probably quite good. But to put the icing on the cake, to really solidify yourself as a goal-scorer, scoring 50 is something they can never take away from you.

In 1975 Marcel was gone and Mickey was in bad shape with his back. Doug Barkley became coach, and he had ideas. Things started out as everybody anticipated—not good. Mickey and I were put in limbo because the Wings wanted to develop a team game. They didn't want to depend on one or two guys to do all the scoring, which I found quite strange. So in the first few games of the season, we weren't going to see a whole lot of ice time because they wanted to see what other players could do. You figure that out.

As a result, I was thrown into a game against Atlanta after sitting on the bench for two periods. That's when I got hurt and the injury eventually ended my career. I should have never played again. I should have never put on another pair of skates. I kick myself even today. I remember asking the doctor about playing again and he said, "Absolutely not. If we can ever just get you walking normal, then you will have accomplished quite a thing."

It was just a case of bad ice and getting hit the right way. It wasn't a dirty thing. The ice was just terrible in Atlanta. They had something else in there the day before and it was soft and there were spots that went right through to the concrete. The puck went into the corner. I got a skate caught and at the same time got hit and everything just went from there. I don't remember anything.

The injury was called an anterior thigh rupture. I tore off the muscles that are attached to just below your knee. The muscles receded into my thigh where there was a big tennis ball at the top of my thigh. There weren't any muscles attached to my knee or to the rest of my leg. At that time the doctor said he had only seen two previous injuries like this and they were from tennis players who had the muscles almost torn off their elbow. This was the first time he had ever seen this, and this was at the Mayo Clinic.

All in one year's time we lost Marcel, we lost Redmond, and we lost me; with nobody to take our place. If you look at a case like that and you take 150 goals out of a lineup today, look at what you'd be left with.

I was out the rest of that year, but came back the next year and tried to play. It's a miracle that I didn't do some real damage that would stay with me the rest of my life. The next season I was dealt to L.A., and for the first few weeks everything went really good and then my leg just gave out. With my leg being in a cast for over a year, and the type of injury I had, the strength just left it.

In 1979, when I retired, I couldn't even walk on an uneven surface. It took me at least two years after I retired before I could even go fishing or do anything. I was going to the gym and did everything I could to build the muscle up around the injury to get it to where I am today—it doesn't bother me a bit.

While I was still with Minnesota, my wife, Linda, and I got a collie dog. During the summer we'd return to Minnesota and, one year just before we went back to Detroit for training camp, the dog was hit by a car and killed. We get back to Detroit and, during a game, Linda was sitting with Bruce Norris, the owner of the Wings. She was telling him how bad I felt because we lost this dog. Soon after that, I get a call from Bruce Norris, who said, "There's a package waiting for you at the airport."

We drove out to the airport and there in a kennel was a three-month-old Newfoundland dog. Mr. Norris gave me a dog. We called her Sugar. We had her for years. You either thought the world of Mr. Norris or you didn't. As far as I was concerned, he was a true gentleman.

Even though my career ended there in an unfortunate way, going to Detroit was still one of the greatest things that ever happened to me. There's something special about playing as a professional athlete in the city of Detroit. I didn't just hang around with players on the team. We had friends in Milford; we had a lot of good friends. It was just a fantastic area to raise a family.

Detroit is such a great sports town. I think it's the greatest sports town in the world. I know other people have said that a lot, but it's fantastic. I have no regrets whatsoever. I had some great relationships with guys on the team and with people in the community.

Danny Grant's Career Highlights

* Being named captain of the Red Wings.

* Scoring 50 goals.

* The standing ovation he received the night he scored the 50 goals.

* Playing in the Olympia with all of its history.

* "Being able to play in front of some of the greatest hockey fans in the world," Grant said.

DENNIS POLONICH
RIGHT WING
1974–1981 ★ 1982–1983

I F YOU'RE AN ATHLETE AND YOU'RE SMALLER in stature, you have to fight that battle for the rest of your life. People are always going to test you and say that you're too small and you can't do this or that. That is huge motivation. I always turned it into a positive. People like an underdog. They like a little guy who tries hard. My work ethic was never a problem; that was a big skill that I had. Detroit's a blue-collar town, fans like the tough and rough kids. It didn't take long before they came on my side and started chanting, "Polo! Polo!"

I had a very good start to my career until I got hurt. There was a time that I didn't like to talk about the Wilf Paiement incident, but time has passed. Wounds slowly heal. I talk about it now because I'm 52 years old and people ask me because they're fans and they want to know. I have nothing to be ashamed of. I did what I thought was right.

Why he did it is beyond me. You would have to ask him, but he probably doesn't have an answer either.

Obviously, he just snapped. He maintains 'til this day that he was provoked, that when I went to ice the puck, I high-sticked him. Because I was knocked unconscious, I don't know if I did or didn't. Even if I did, it doesn't give him the right to two-hand a player across the nose with a baseball swing.

At 5'6", 165 pounds during his playing day, Dennis Polonich is considered one of the toughest players ever to wear a Detroit sweater. He became an instant fan favorite because of his tenacity and bravado. On March 24, 1976, in a 7–3 victory against Washington, Polonich set a club record by sitting out eight penalties—five minors, a major, and a misconduct.

The Wilf Paiement incident happened on October 25, 1978, at the Olympia. I was out for a month and a half after that. I have some unbelievable pictures where my eyes were swollen shut. I looked like death. I remember Ted Lindsay coming to the hospital, and I was squeezing his hand so hard that he almost had to let go. I didn't have kids at the time, so my wife spent the night in the hospital putting ice on my eyes. I still couldn't see in the morning. Without a doubt, it was traumatic. I suffered some permanent disfigurement and breathing impairment.

I think it was an isolated incident with Wilf Paiement. At the time, he played with the Colorado Rockies and was a frustrated hockey player because they were losing. You have to have humor in the game and try to turn every negative into a positive. Now my buddies say, "What did Dennis Polonich say when Wilf Paiement hit him in the face with a hockey stick?" And they answer, "Thanks a million."

Was it worth the almost one million dollars? I don't know. Did it hurt my career? Certainly, it hurt my career. Look at my stats: I had 11 goals, 18 goals, 16 goals, and after that my play dropped. I was never the same type of player in Detroit. Was I black-balled because I sued another player? I don't know. I can live with it.

There has never been any remorse from Wilf Paiement. Had anyone with the Colorado Rockies, the owner, the general manager, or Wilf called me while I was in the hospital or afterward and said, "Dennis, I am totally sorry for this and that..." maybe there wouldn't have been a lawsuit. I don't know. I do know that what Todd Bertuzzi did after what he did to Steve Moore was the right thing to do. He tried contacting Moore and he couldn't, or his calls weren't returned, so he apologized publicly and was very sincere and very emotional about it. Good for Todd Bertuzzi, he made a mistake and he admitted it. Wilf Paiement made a mistake and he hasn't admitted to it. But Wilf Paiement has to live with it, I don't.

There were a lot of guys who wanted to kill me because of the way I played. I was a pretty good disturber! I use to really get under the skin of Fred Shero, Dave Schultz, and the Broadstreet Bullies. This one time, I remember Schultz coming off the bus at the Olympia for the Flyers' morning skate, and he started accosting me in the driveway.

I pointed to my watch,, and said, "Relax, the game doesn't start until 7:00. Go home, have your pregame nap and six-pack of bananas, and I'll see you at 7:00."

Another time when Schultz was with Pittsburgh, he was yelling at me from the bench, "I'm going to kill you, Polonich! I'm going to kill you! I'm going to take your head off!" The face-off was right in front of the bench in the off-sides circle. I was playing right wing and was close to the bench. I just turned around and said, "Schultzey, how can you kill me? Your coach doesn't play you. You don't get on the ice!" Johnny Wilson was our coach and he had to turn away because he busted out laughing. The veins were just popping out of Schultz's neck—he wanted to come after me so bad!

Marcel Dionne wasn't my teammate for very long before he went to L.A., but my second year as a pro, he and I were in Kalamazoo for training camp. I was having a really good camp and was looking forward to playing in an exhibition game against St. Louis in East Lansing. When the lineup was posted, my name wasn't on it. I was pretty disappointed. I stayed behind, showered slowly, and did some extra weights. I walked across the parking lot to the hotel, got to my room, and I saw the phone's red light flashing. It was a message from Jimmy Skinner. I called him and he asked me if I wanted to play in the game because Marcel wasn't going. He had the flu. Of course, I said I wanted to play!

Lefty Wilson had already taken the equipment to East Lansing. So when I went back to the rink, I had to find somebody to let me into the room to pack my own gear. When I got to the game, I found out that they had only taken 20 sweaters. I had to wear No. 5, Marcel Dionne's sweater. Back then there were no names on the back of the sweaters. I got dressed and went onto the ice. Marcel had just had a season where he had 100-plus points and won the Lady Byng Trophy. Everyone was yelling from the stands, "Marcel! Marcel!" I pretended I was Marcel. I'm the same size and a right-handed shot.

St. Louis had a tough team with the Plager brothers, Frank Bathe, Battleship Bob Kelly, and John Wensink. In the second period there was a five-on-five fight on the ice. One of our guys was getting it pretty good. I wanted to leave the bench. I was trying to go, but Billy Dea had a hold of me by the jersey. I tore away; grabbed this one guy, Howie Heggedal, who had been a top scorer in the Central League the year before. He was 6′ or 6′2″. I dropped him with a couple of quick rights and the crowd went nuts, chanting, "Marcel! Marcel! Marcel!" They thought Dionne had turned into this little tough guy. I was Marcel Dionne for that one day.

The Olympia in Detroit, along with a few other rinks like Boston Garden and Chicago Stadium, were suitable to my style. They were small with oval corners. I remember playing against Bobby Orr when he was with Chicago. I ran him in one corner but he was so competitive that he took a piece of me in the other corner. Then the puck turned up the ice and we started jawing at each other. He said, "Oh, you're up from the minors trying to make a name for yourself!" I said, "Yeah, I may be from the minors, but I'm not impressed by your press clippings." We ended up fighting.

While we were in the penalty box, people from the Olympia started streaming down from the stands to stick their programs underneath the glass.

131

Orr's picture was on the program, and they wanted to get it signed. He had a pen and he was signing these programs. At the same time I was trash-talking him. Little did he know I was thinking, "Bobby, could you please sign one for me, too?" I was in such awe of him. If he only knew how badly I wanted his autograph. Just last year, 30 years later, I golfed with Bobby Orr and he signed that same program for me.

My biggest memory at Joe Louis Arena was playing Hartford and facing off against Gordie Howe and Mark and Marty. That is a Hall of Fame memory—Gordie and his two sons—that will never happen again. Bill Hogaboam was on right wing and Jean Hamel was at left wing, and I took the face-off against Gordie. We played the game and the crowd was going nuts. At the buzzer, I asked Gordie for his stick and he handed it to me. A friend of mine who lives in Detroit sent me a tape of the game, and at the end of the game you can see Gordie handing me his stick. Just this past year, I caught Gordie at the airport and he signed the stick for me.

That was Gordie's last game in Detroit, and at the end he came back out onto the ice and skated around for an encore. He took one of his gloves by the string and he twirled it 'round and 'round and then threw it up in the crowd. He then skated around to the other side and did the same thing there.

Another great memory for me was when the Detroit Red Wings were celebrating their 75th anniversary. The Ilitch family flew back 18 ex-captains. We were there for three days, and the accommodations were first-class. They had a big event for us at Hockeytown Café and put us on the back of convertibles with replica sweaters that had a "C" on them and drove us out onto the ice. It was after the national anthem when the players were lined up on the blue line and Steve Yzerman came over to the car and said, "Congratulations, Polo, you deserve it!" Steve Yzerman is very classy. He respects the guys who played there before him and helped make Hockeytown what it is today.

Just like hundreds of kids across Canada, I didn't know what it was like to be a Red Wing and I didn't care. I just wanted an opportunity.

Luckily for me, it was with the Detroit Red Wings. Once I joined the organization, things started to become apparent to me. This was an Original Six team! Now at 52 and retired for a number of years, I look back and it was a great thrill and an accomplishment that I'm quite proud of. I played for an Original Six team for 12 years; I was able to stay 12 years with the same organization through some tough times. I was never traded. I became captain of an Original Six team. It gives me goose bumps and great pride in the fact that I played for the Detroit Red Wings.

I'll never forget the people and places in Detroit. My oldest daughter was born in Detroit. Detroit is a part of me.

Dennis Polonich's Career Highlights

* Getting drafted by the Red Wings and playing seven seasons at 5'6", 165 pounds.

* Playing in the Olympia for my first NHL game.

* Being named Red Wings' captain in 1976.

* Being interviewed on *Hockey Night in Canada* (after watching it growing up).

* "Facing off against the greats of the NHL, players I idolized—Bobby Orr, Wayne Gretzky, and Gordie Howe," Polonich said.

REED LARSON

DEFENSEMAN

1976–1986

FROM TIME TO TIME AT GOLF TOURNAMENTS, banquets, and other events, former players will come up to me and tell me my shot broke their ankle or bones in their foot or their hand. Someone told me once that I broke his shin pad and gave him stitches.

After being asked by many people why I had such a hard shot, I finally thought about it enough to realize it resulted from a combination of factors. It was stick design, repetition, practice, technique, timing, and strength in certain muscles. I would hit the ice about six to eight inches before the puck. It leaves divots in the ice and thus the stick flexes like a bow. The muscles that are important are more in your back and top of your shoulders—the outside muscles. The slap shot involves the whole upper torso.

I water-skied my whole life, barefoot on slalom courses. I wrestled and I did gymnastics. I did high bar, parallel bars, rings, and floor exercise. I did that until I was 14. I think all of that helped. I didn't do weights. I played on football teams. I played at 6', 198 pounds, and I think that everything I did contributed to my balance and well-rounded muscles.

The funny thing was that it was the refs and linesmen who talked to me most about the shot. They would come up to me in warm-up and say, "Whatever you do, don't hit me."

I was pretty good about keeping the shot down. I do have a video of a game in Quebec when one of my shots went off a blade and went up and hit goaltender Clint Malarchuk in the mask. It broke his orbital bone. His eye just turned red. He was a tough player, and when he skated off the ice he said, "Nice shot."

He was being sarcastic. He was really mad. He didn't realize then that it had just ticked a defenseman's blade and took off and caught him flush on the cheekbone.

I've hurt people in the crowd when deflections would go into the stands, and it would scare me. I hate talking about it, but I've broken some bones. I even took the blades off the bottom of skates. Dennis Hextall was standing in front of the net, and I wiped his blade right off. The puck went into the net. He got a goal, but he had to limp to the bench.

One of the funniest stories is when I broke Plexiglass two years in a row in Philadelphia. During a game, I just missed the top corner with a shot and hit the side brace. The glass didn't just crack. There was a little chip and then, almost like a chain reaction, the entire pane disintegrated in five seconds. It cut a fan in the front row.

The next year I was in Philadelphia—and this is a true story—I broke the glass again and it hit the same guy. The same pane. What're the odds? I got a letter and it said, "I know you don't like us fans, but you have to stop doing this because I can't take it anymore."

135

It was pretty funny.

The only time they ever timed my shot was just after Joe Louis Arena was opened. New Plexiglas was just put in, and some highway patrolmen came down with handheld radar guns. We weren't skating up to the puck like they do in competitions. This was done over the course of a half hour. We got to come all the way down the ice and shoot the puck on the fly.

Obviously, the accuracy back then wasn't what it is today. But I remember that John Ogrodnick had some shots between 115 and 120 miles per hour, and I had some over 130.

I know today there are some guys with the new stick technology who can really shoot. But when players were first starting to compete at the All-Star Games for the hardest shot, I had played with or against most of them, and I thought that I could shoot with them—like Al Iafrate, who was clocked at over 100 mph.

I have fond memories about my days in Detroit, especially the year we beat Atlanta in the playoffs. The Flames had a good team with players like Guy Chouinard, Willi Plett, Eric Vail, Tom Lysiak, Bobby MacMillan, and others. The Flames had a big team then. That game in the Olympia when Bill Lochead scored the big goal was special. That was fun. We should have built on that, but I think we made too many changes right away. If you look at the best teams, they only change one, two, or three players per season.

The team made Eddie Giacomin retire. One of my career highlights came in my first year when we beat Montreal 1–0 in Olympia. The whole place was shaking with people shouting, "Eddie, Eddie, Eddie." Playing in Olympia was awesome.

Coach Bobby Kromm let me go, and I give him credit for that. I took pride in being an all-around defenseman. I'm not the biggest, not the strongest, not the toughest, but I tried to be balanced. I just tried to help out. If there was fighting that had to be done, I tried to do it. Some players can hit, and some can play defense, and some could shoot, but I tried to do a little bit of everything. I was not a heavyweight, but I took on Clark Gillies, Willi Plett, Dave Schultz, Bob Nystrom. Most of the fights came in the early years of my career, maybe 1978. Then Bob Probert and Joey Kocur came along and they would look at other teams' rosters like a menu. What are we going to have for dinner tonight? They were really good at what they did.

My other highlight was being the Red Wings' representative at the NHL All-Star Game at Joe Louis Arena in 1980 when Gordie Howe received the long ovation. Five minutes is long for any ovation, but I bet that one lasted 10 minutes. Gordie is so humble. I can remember he was shuffling his feet and saying, "We got to get this game going."

He was 52 then, and I know how my body feels at 49. He was joking about how he couldn't keep up with us. But he played well in that game. He was smooth and graceful, maybe like Jean Beliveau played. He never made a mistake or bobbled the puck either. He always made the right play at the right time.

Whenever I see him, he treats me like a son. He is a prince of our sport. He set a standard for how you should behave as an athlete and how you should treat fans and your teammates.

I have fond memories of my days in Detroit.

Reed Larson will probably be remembered as owning the hardest shot in Red Wings' history. A tough two-way defenseman, Larson holds the Detroit record of 67 power-play goals by a defenseman. He also wasn't shy about dropping his gloves, often fighting some the league's top heavyweights.

Reed Larson's Career Highlights

* Being the first American-born player and the sixth defenseman to score 200 career goals. At one point, Larson was the highest-scoring American-born player.

* Holding the Red Wings record of 27 goals by a defenseman in a season, set in 1980–1981.

* Getting named Detroit's captain from January 10, 1981, to September 1982.

* At age 20, playing in the NHL All-Star Game with the likes of Darryl Sittler, Lanny McDonald, Brad Park, Marcel Dionne, Gilbert Perreault, and others. "These were guys I used to watch on TV, and now I'm getting dressed with them," Larson said. "It's a weird feeling, but they were very nice to me. I sat in the corner and watched everybody."

* Becoming the third defenseman in NHL history, after Bobby Orr and Denis Potvin, to score 20 or more goals in five consecutive seasons when he achieved the feat in the 1983–1984 season.

VACLAV NEDOMANSKY
CENTER
1977–1982

WHEN THE DETROIT RED WINGS traded for me on November 18, 1977, I was very happy because the reason I defected from Czechoslovakia was to play in the National Hockey League.

First I had to play in the World Hockey Association because I was under suspension for defecting from my country. I had offers from NHL teams when I was young, but it was not possible to leave. Finally, I left when I was on vacation in Switzerland, but it is a long story and too complicated to explain how I defected.

There was no news about the National Hockey League when I was in Czechoslovakia, but I had traveled with the Czech National Team since 1963 and I had some information from the Canadian press.

My memories of Detroit are very good. I loved playing in Olympia. I was playing for the Birmingham Bulls in the WHA when Ted Lindsay came down to watch us and ended up making the deal.

When I came to the Red Wings, I found out that the NHL was cleaner than the WHA. I lived 19 years in Detroit and my memories are very good. My teammates were good friends. It was a good memory when we beat Atlanta in the playoffs. Bill Lochead scored the winning goal. It was fantastic. Then we beat Montreal in the first game, and had them down 2–1 in the second game. We were improving each year. I had a number of coaches, including Ted Lindsay for 20 games. Bobby Kromm. We also had Wayne

Czech legend Vaclav Nedomansky was one of the pioneers of the European migration to the NHL. He played 344 games with the Red Wings, scoring 108 goals with 139 assists. He led the team in scoring in 1978–1979, posting 38 goals and 35 assists for 73 points.

Maxner. Bad memories of that. Painful. But even when the team wasn't good, it had great support from the fans.

I felt strongly about my move to defect. I never questioned it. I thought it was good for my family and me. But I don't think about whether it would have been better if I were younger when I left. When I was young, I attended the University of Cominsk in Bratislava (now in Slovakia). I got a degree in physical education and biology. I have a master's degree. My life would not be as complete as it is now if I had left earlier.

I coached overseas in Austria and Germany. I knew Rogie Vachon from Detroit, and when he became the manager in Los Angeles, he asked me to scout for him. Now I am happy and enjoying my life very much doing that.

One of my most dominant hockey memories came from the 1978–1979 season when the Red Wings were scheduled to play the Soviet Wings at Olympia. The Russians indicated that they wouldn't play the game if I was allowed to be in the lineup. It was all about my defection.

Our team had a meeting, and the players decided that if I didn't play then there would be no game. The players said the Russians shouldn't even come to Detroit. Within 24 hours, the Russians faxed back, "Okay, no problem, let's play."

The game was played on January 4, 1979. [A former Soviet National Team standout] was doing the radio commentary going back to Russia, and he wasn't allowed to use my name. Because I had defected, he had said I had been killed in an accident. So when he was broadcasting the game, he just called me "Number twenty."

We won that game 6–5, and I had a goal and an assist. I remember Dennis Hull was my linemate. I was so proud that our team stuck together and gave me the opportunity to play in that game.

Vaclav Nedomansky's Career Highlights

* When Nedomansky was signed by the Red Wings, Gordie Howe, who had played against Nedomansky in the WHA, predicted he would be a 30-goal scorer for the Red Wings, even though he was 33 years old when he came to the team. Howe compared him to Phil Esposito. Nedomansky was a 30-goal scorer twice for the Red Wings—netting 38 in the 1978–1979 season and 35 in the 1979–1980 season.

* On October 28, 1978, at Olympia, scoring his first career NHL hat trick, sparking the Red Wings to a 7–2 win against Chicago Blackhawks. In that same season, he became the first Red Wing to record back-to-back hat tricks.

* In the 1977–1978 season, being crucial to the Red Wings ending a seven-season playoff drought. In the postseason, he had three goals and five assists in the Red Wings' seven playoff games.

* Before coming to the NHL, dominating international hockey. In 1972 he helped Czechoslovakia win the bronze medal at the Sapporo Olympics. This was four years after the Soviets invaded the Czech Republic with tanks to quell a political uprising. The Russian vs. Czech Olympic game was a war on ice at the 1972 games. Former Red Wings player Mark Howe has called it the "most brutal game" he had ever witnessed. He recalled Nedomansky, who was second in the tournament in scoring, was huge in that game. "The Russians were ahead in the third period and the Czechs were on the power play, with a face-off in the Russian end. They won the draw and the puck went to Nedomansky, but he just turned and wired a shot into the Russian bench." Also, in 1972, Nedomansky helped Czechoslovakia win the gold medal at the World Championships, ending the Soviet Union's streak of nine consecutive World Championships. He had 15 points in those 10 games.

* Winning four Czechoslovakian scoring titles and almost scoring a goal per game during his career. Counting his Czech league play, international tournaments, WHA days, and NHL career, Nedomansky scored 789 goals.

PAUL WOODS

LEFT WING

1977–1984

THE FIRST TEAM I EVER PLAYED ON, with my older brother John, was a squirt team called the "Detroit Red Wings." We had the dark red jerseys. So my first memory of hockey is wearing the Red Wings sweater. The Red Wings have been with my family for a long time, and to come full circle and wind up playing for them was funny. It was where I ended up and where I started. It means everything to me.

I was drafted by the Montreal Canadiens and played two years with their American Hockey League team in Nova Scotia. In my third year, I played with the Canadiens during the exhibition season and then was sent to the minors. It was a bitter disappointment because, after two years in the minors, you think you're ready and then you're back in the minors again. There were other players whom I played against in the AHL who were up in the NHL, and you get frustrated seeing them go up when you're not. Back then, you were locked into the team's system, and there was no way to get out. I was back in Nova Scotia and not very pleased, wondering if it was ever going to happen for me.

It was also the first year of the waiver draft, and I got a call from someone who asked me if Detroit took me in the waiver draft, would I go? I said definitely. I went to practice and to lunch with the team like normal, and while driving in the car I heard on the radio that I was selected first overall in the waiver draft by Detroit. That was the happiest moment of my life. All the time I had spent trying to get to the NHL, it was finally going to come true. I was all excited but then got into a panic mode, wondering if I could really do it. It was all very quick.

The next morning I was on a flight to Detroit. Billy Dea picked me up at the airport and told me they were holding up practice for me, which really made me nervous. I got there, got fitted for equipment, and when I hit the ice I realized I had one moment—and it was right now. I was probably a little bit tired from traveling from Nova Scotia, but when I got to Detroit I just flipped into overdrive because I knew it was finally my chance to make it in the NHL. I had to go really hard. I played in the game the next night against Toronto at home. It was the first game of the year and we tied them 3–3. I never looked back after that moment.

When I younger, I was a different type of player. I wasn't known for my speed or as a great skater, but I developed into one. In Montreal, they knocked me down and told me I had to start playing back in my own zone. I had never done that kind of stuff in juniors, like blocking shots. I wouldn't dream of it—risking getting myself hurt. But you change when you start to understand the other side of the game and you start to like it. That happened more and more when I got to Detroit, but the process started in the minors. When you're in professional hockey, you need to learn that defensive side of the game. That's the difference between junior hockey players and college players and pro hockey players—we understand both sides and the things you just don't get as a young guy. I enjoyed that part of the game and started to thrive off my accomplishments in that area of play.

Playing against Montreal was always a great feeling since I was drafted by them; those games were always thrilling for me. Guy Lafleur was their top guy, and getting that assignment to be against him, it was exciting. Same with playing against Wayne Gretzky—I had the opportunity to do that as well for a couple of years. I went up against a lot of good players—Bryan Trottier, Gil Perreault, Darryl Sittler. Back then, the best defensive line always played against the best offensive line. I was out there a lot in those situations. With the really skilled players, the great ones, it's the determination and intelligence that makes them stand out. They are so smart, they work so hard, they're willing to fight through the defensive coverage to create scoring chances and win the game. It was always a battle.

Gretzky and Guy Lafleur were the two toughest match-ups. They could do so many different things and were so dynamic. Wayne Gretzky wasn't

Speedy Paul Woods was a fan favorite long before he climbed into the broadcast booth as the team's radio analyst. Claimed by Detroit from Montreal in the 1977 waiver draft, Woods became an instant fan favorite because of his speed and aggressiveness. He finished his career with 72 goals and 124 assists in 501 regular-season games.

really a great skater, but he was unbelievably quick and intelligent. Before he hurt his back, in his first couple of years, he would sneak up on a defenseman, lift his stick, steal the puck, and go back on a break-away. He was also a pinpoint passer. With Lafleur, he was explosive—lightning fast and skillful. And he had the passing of Montreal's defense at the time with Larry Robinson, Serge Savard, and Guy Lapointe—it was very much like Detroit today. They could move the puck to the forwards. You just did the best you could. There was no real method beyond that for trying to stop those two.

The first couple of years were definitely the best years for me in Detroit. We were in the playoffs my first year with the Red Wings. We were just starting to turn the corner because they had the foundation of a pretty good group there. We had some older veteran players who were good, strong guys in Dan Maloney, Dennis Hextall, Nick Libett, and Terry Harper. We had a good blend of youth and age. We played together. I was very happy to be in that situation.

Three guys I really respected were Hextall, Maloney, and Reed Larson. It was such a great advantage for a young player to come into a system with a Hextall and a Maloney—two guys who were so serious and knew how to do it the right way. Sometimes organizations think that young players are already there, that they've had enough tutoring, and they get rid of the older guys. That's a mistake, moving too quickly. You need the veteran players to show the guys how to become good pros, how to do the right thing, when to talk and when not to talk. There are so many things to learn from a good pro; if you get that schooling at a young age, you can gain so much.

My only time in the playoffs was in 1978, and it's something I'll never forget. We played Atlanta in the first round. It was a best-of-three series. We beat the Flames on the road and we returned to Olympia with a chance for a sweep. It took a great goal to close out the series. When Bill Lochead came down that left side, he was a right-hand shot, and cut in on Dan Bouchard. I thought he was going to go behind the net and center it, but he tucked it back in. We were linemates, so when we got past the goal line behind the net and scored, I was so excited that I just dove at him. We crashed against the boards. It knocked the wind out of him. Back then the players could come off the bench on a big goal and we had this big pile-up in the corner. It was only a playoff game, but it meant so much to our fans. It was an unbelievable feeling, our crowd was so loud. That was a great moment and it reflected that team.

We played Montreal next, and after three close games we were down 2–1. In Game 4 we got beat 8–0. With five minutes left to go, there was an icing call against Montreal. We were racing down to touch the puck first. The crowd gave us a standing ovation. We're down 8–0, and these Red Wings fans were giving us a standing ovation because they knew we were a team that wasn't as talented as Montreal but we worked hard. And they liked that team.

That's when I learned about Detroit fans—that if you worked hard and were determined, if you played your heart out, that's all they wanted. Do the best you can and they'll accept it; they can't accept the other way. When you aren't doing what you're capable of doing, they'll turn on you. I don't know of another city where something like that could happen, when a team is getting beaten that badly at home in a playoff game and the fans are still respectful. That always stuck out in my mind.

The Olympia was a beautiful place with a lot of noise. It's hard to describe how good Olympia was. The ice was good and the fans were right on top of you. When we switched to Joe Louis Arena, the new building, it was a sad day for us because the building didn't have the same chemistry, the same feeling. However, Joe Louis has developed its own history over the years. It now seems like the same kind of place, with the same sort of feeling that Olympia had back then. Yet, when we moved, we couldn't understand as players why it made sense to leave a great place like Olympia to go to a new place.

When you see magic happen in front of you, it just stays with you. The last game at Olympia was a really big game. All the old Red Wings were back to watch it, and we were down 4–0 after two periods. We got a goal in the third period, and momentum started to build, and then it just took over. We came back and finally tied it up with a couple minutes left against Quebec. It meant so much to not lose that last game because there were some many great players before us and a lot of them were there that night. It was so important to so many people. They had a party after that last game. All the old guys were there. It was a neat night.

Steve Yzerman was a very nice person who really handled himself well when he joined the Red Wings. You could tell he was a good player, but he was very young and still had junior eligibility left when I was a Red Wing. He was highly skilled and determined. Steve never over-stepped his boundaries as a good young player coming in. He always had respect for the game and the people playing it. I always appreciate and admire the players who have such great respect for the game.

Over the years, Yzerman has really developed, he has an ability to adapt, he's always improving, and he keeps getting better.

With Mario Lemieux retiring, everyone tries to think of who was the greatest player of all-time. In his era you would have to compare Yzerman to Lemieux and Gretzky. If you ask who was the best defensive player of the three? It was Steve Yzerman. Who was the best penalty killer? It was Steve Yzerman. Who was the best face-off man? It was Steve Yzerman. Yzerman's

147

numbers may have been behind Gretzky's numbers, but they're not far behind the rest of the pack. He is one of the rare guys; he's your best offensive player and your best defensive player. How many guys like that in NHL history did we actually have?

Making the NHL is a family sacrifice and reward. It takes a whole group to get you there. My family was a hockey family, so when you make the NHL it means a lot to you because you've gone through all those things; but you also see what it does to your family and how it affects them. The first time you see your parents after you've made it is the most unbelievable event to describe—just the look in their eyes. You think no one knows what you go through, but they do because they've been through it with you.

You look back and realize all of the sacrifices your family made over the years in minor hockey, in juniors, and all the ups and downs. Without my brother John and my parents, there was no way that I would have made it to the NHL. The rings I received from the Ilitches for the three Stanley Cups, I gave those to my family: one to my dad, one to my mom, and one to my brother. I knew how much it meant to them.

Paul Woods's Career Highlights

* Playing his first game at Olympia. "It was my first NHL game versus Toronto—I had finally gotten there," Woods said. "I lost the face-off clean in my first shift and they almost scored." He scored 19 goals in his first Detroit season.

* Scoring first NHL goal at Minnesota against Gary Smith.

* Having five points in seven games in the Red Wings' 1978 playoff run.

* Currently serving as the analyst on Red Wings radio broadcasts.

* Playing for Canada at the 1979 World Championships.

The
EIGHTIES

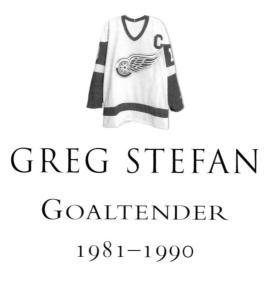

GREG STEFAN

GOALTENDER

1981–1990

WHEN I PLAYED MY FIRST GAME with the Detroit Red Wings there were only about 5,000 people in the stands.

Bruce Norris owned the team when I came aboard. The franchise was in a bad funk. Wayne Maxner was the coach. Jim Skinner was the interim general manager. Maybe it was fortunate for me that the franchise was struggling because the team didn't have many goalies.

When Mike Ilitch bought the team, the crowds began to improve. He wasn't afraid to sign guys. He brought in new management, coaches, and scouts. You could see the team changing. There was more enthusiasm. He even gave away a car at every game, and I think that helped. You could see he was going to do something about the Red Wings' situation.

We were right at the bottom when I started, and I watched us climb near the top through the years with Jacques Demers and Bryan Murray as the coaches.

Demers was the key when we reached the Conference Finals in 1987 and 1988. He was the most visible guy on our team because of his personality and how he dealt with the press. He was the story. And he got the best out of us. Demers was one of the greatest motivators that I ever played for. He had good relationships with his veterans. He liked the character players. At that time, we had guys like Dave Barr, Mike O'Connell, and Jim Nill. Jacques wasn't as good with the x's and o's. And he had a harder time with the younger guys, like Joe Murphy and Adam Graves. But I have a lot of respect for Jacques. He supported his veterans. Guys went to bat for Jacques.

We were a close-knit team. This was just before the old-time hockey players gave way to the new wave. We were a muck-and-grind team—we played better defense than most teams, and we scored timely goals. We were also a very tough team.

The one-two combination of Bob Probert and Joe Kocur was one of the reasons why we were so good. They were feared. We went into tough buildings like Philadelphia and Chicago, and all the other guys on our team got tougher. That was our identity. We won a lot of games because of our physical toughness. We were a difficult team to play against.

Joe Kocur was probably one of the most feared one-punch guys. I remember when he fought Winnipeg Jets defenseman Jim Kyte right in front of me. Kyte was a big tough kid who wore a hearing aid. When Kocur hit him, the hearing aid popped out of his ear. When Kyte landed on the ice, I was scared that he was seriously hurt. Kyte had a hard time getting off the ice.

Greg Stefan's 115 wins rank fifth on Detroit's all-time goaltender victory list. He played on the Detroit teams of the 1980s that paved the way for Detroit's success in the 1990s. He had 11 playoff wins from 1987 to 1989.

Probert and Kocur were feared around the league. Bob was pretty amazing. When he came into the league, he wasn't the greatest fighter. At first, it was trial and error. He lost his first few fights. But he was fearless and he got better and better. The scary aspect of Bob is that the longer the fight lasted, the tougher Bob became. As the fight progressed, he got stronger. He was two different fighters. Sometimes he just wasn't in the mood. And then there were other times when he was teed off. That's when he was scary. When Bob was into the fight, you knew you were in for a long battle.

We had a lot of interesting players. Shawn Burr played with a chip on his shoulder, and Gerard Gallant was a good player. I roomed with Petr Klima. He was a talented kid. He could skate. He brought a lot of excitement to the Red Wings organization. He could shoot the puck, toe drag it, and do amazing moves. He was the new breed of European players who were coming over. I think the organization and the players, myself included, share some blame for not giving him more guidance. The Wings brought him over here, and then he was just on his own. It's hard to say how good Petr could have been with some guidance.

We didn't have any superstars except Steve Yzerman. Steve came into a situation where there were a lot of veteran guys at the end of their careers. There was a lot of selfishness on the Red Wings then. He was brought in when we were a losing team. He wasn't brought up properly. He was about goal scoring and getting points. Then he changed as a player. And when he started changing his ways is when the Red Wings started becoming a great team. That's why I have so much respect for Steve.

Was he the greatest leader? Not in the early stages of captaincy because he was brought up in a selfish environment. Then he became one of the best captains in the history of the game. It was no longer enough to get goals and assists, he wanted championships. That's why he is as respected as he is.

In 1987 we beat Toronto in seven games to reach the Western Conference Finals to play against the Edmonton Oilers with Wayne Gretzky and Mark Messier. The Oilers were one of the greatest teams ever. Everyone said we would lose four straight to the Oilers. But we went into Edmonton and won 3–1. It was the only win I had in Edmonton.

Did we think we could beat Edmonton? I don't know if we really believed we could win, but we weren't afraid. We just didn't know what we could do. When we beat them in the first game, I think we woke them up.

Really, I had two careers in Detroit—one that started with no pressure, no expectations. I could wing it and have some fun. I didn't have good leadership. When we started to improve as a team, I had to change my game. I was used to facing 45 or 50 shots, but there was no pressure. But when Demers came in, we played a more defensive style. We faced fewer shots and I had to learn to play a different game. There were times when I wouldn't get a shot for four or five minutes, and I had to learn to concentrate more than I had in the past.

Maybe near the end of my career there was more pressure because we reached the Conference Finals twice. The goalies who came after me faced more pressure. I was treated pretty well by the fans.

I love it here. Michigan has been my home since 1982. I now work for the Carolina Hurricanes as a professional scout and goaltending coach, but my second favorite team is still the Red Wings.

Greg Stefan's Career Highlights

* Winning NHL Player of the Week honors twice, including once when he beat the New York Islanders twice in one week. This was the great Islanders teams that include Mike Bossy, Bryan Trottier, and Denis Potvin, among others. He shut them out once in Detroit and beat then 2–1 on Long Island.

* Beating the Edmonton Oilers 3–1 at Northlands Coliseum in Game 1 of the 1987 Conference finals. "Everyone said we had no chance," recalled Stefan.

* Being picked for Team Canada once. "But I broke my thumb in the final game of the season and couldn't play," Stefan said. "I got into a scrap with Al Secord in a playoff. It was a highlight that turned into a disappointment."

* Winning a playoff series against Chicago while keeping his goals-against average under 1.00.

* Playing his entire career with the Red Wings.

JIM DEVELLANO

GENERAL MANAGER

1982–1990 ★ 1994–1997

SENIOR VICE PRESIDENT

1997–Present

WHEN I WAS HIRED BY MIKE ILITCH, I already knew what Detroit Red Wings' tradition meant. The Original Six meant much to me because I had grown up in Toronto during that era. I knew about the history of the Detroit Red Wings. I knew about Jack Adams. I knew that Gordie Howe might have been the greatest player to ever play the game. I watched Ted Lindsay beat up on the Toronto Maple Leafs. I saw Red Kelly play defense for 12 years for great Detroit teams and then come over and play center late in life and win another four Stanley Cups for the Maple Leafs. I was aware of Sid Abel and his accomplishments as a player, as a coach, and as a manager.

When I was growing up listening to Foster Hewitt broadcast games, I aspired to be a general manager. That's a little unusual because most youngsters aspire to be players. But that's what I wanted—to run a National Hockey League team. So it was a dream come true when I became general manager of the Red Wings in 1982.

After I had established myself with the New York Islanders, my profile was starting to grow because all of our draft choices were starting to play and we started to win Stanley Cups. I was the second guy there to Bill Torrey. My name began to be mentioned for general manager openings.

After the Islanders won their third Stanley Cup, the Norris family decided to sell the Red Wings after 50 years of ownership. Mike and Marian Ilitch of Little Caesars bought the team. At the time of the sale, the franchise was in a bad state. The challenge we had when I was named the general manager on July 12, 1982, was daunting.

After the press conference, I turned to Marian because I knew she would be the financial person, and asked, "How many season tickets do we have?"

Marian said, "When we bought the club, Bruce Norris said we had 5,000. But why don't we go down to the box office and find out."

We went down to talk to Bob Kerlin, who was the head of the box office, and he said, "Marian, I hate to tell you this, but it's only 2,100 season tickets."

Right away Marian gathered her family in what I called the "war room." They all got on the phone and they called all the people they did business with through Little Caesars and everyone else to sell these tickets. So in 1982 we started the season with 4,000 season tickets. That year we averaged 7,800 fans per game in Detroit. We inherited a team that had missed the playoffs five consecutive seasons and missed the playoffs 16 of the previous 18. This was in a league where 16 out of 21 teams made the playoffs! Even with all the expansion teams put in, the Red Wings were really a poor team.

155

I wanted to build the team through the draft, just the way we did with the Islanders. But I found that I couldn't entirely do it that way. I had to find some older, broken-down players. There wasn't great free agency in those days. In order to get the media interested, I would go out and sign a Reggie Leach, a Colin Campbell, and Rick MacLeish. Anyone who had a name or who had done anything, we would try to sign them for a year or two. We had to wring a little hockey out of them as we waited for our draft picks to mature. The big break: our first pick in our first draft was Steve Yzerman. Obviously, here we are 24 years later, and we are still watching him play.

Out of that same draft we landed Bob Probert, Joe Kocur, and Petr Klima. It was a good draft to get us started. However, the only one who could jump in and contribute immediately was Yzerman. He was small. And I always remember his first training camp in 1983 in Port Huron, Michigan. I was sitting in the stands with Nick Polano. Danny Belisle was running practice. We were getting our first look at 18-year-old Yzerman. I had spent a lot of time with Yzerman that summer.

"Steve," I said, "I want to be very careful now on how we handle you. I want to make sure that you're ready. You need to be prepared, because we may send you back to Peterborough."

Yzerman had two years of juniors left, and I wanted Steve to know what we were thinking. He came to camp knowing there was a chance of him going back down to Peterborough if the game was too physically demanding for him. That was my concern. He wasn't very big. It's training day number two for Devellano and Polano, and out comes Yzerman. Now the good news is, within five minutes and three shifts, Yzerman was our best player on the Red Wings. Remember he is 18 years old and weighs 155 pounds. Now the bad news also was that he was our best player. If a 155-pound, 18-year-old could be our best player, you can just imagine what our other players were like.

Steve Yzerman was a great foundation, but what made the Detroit Red Wings into a dynasty, or at least a terrific team for the last 12 or 15 years, were the Europeans. The Russians, the Swedes, the Czechs all helped us. I'm going back to Sergei Fedorov, Vladimir Konstantinov, Slava Kozlov, Nick Lidstrom. It's a long list.

And of course, Scotty Bowman did a great job in getting Igor Larionov and Slava Fetisov. They fit in masterfully well. And here we are now, as we go into the new millennium, and we're living off the backs of a bunch of Swedes. It's phenomenal. The Europeans really made this franchise. It opened up a whole new market for our franchise.

At one point, Mike Ilitch wanted to hire Mike Keenan to coach the team, and I said I didn't think he was the right guy for the team. "Well, then who is?" he asked.

I said it was either Scotty Bowman or Al Arbour. He asked me if I could get one of those guys, and I said I could. We ended up with Scotty Bowman.

I remember I was on the radio with Art Regner, and he asked me: "Is it true that there is a lot of infighting with you and Scotty?"

"We've won divisional titles," I said. "We've won conference championships, and we won a Stanley Cup last year. There is a little bit of that going on, but let it continue."

I said that live on the radio. Scotty and I had our differences, but we are the best of friends now that we don't have to work together. We are in a competitive business, and I called the other places that Scotty worked, and I understand how he worked. Scotty has to be the Guy. There was some

Sharp and charismatic, Devellano was the architect of the Red Wings' success during Mike Ilitch's ownership of the team. He drafted players like Steve Yzerman, Sergei Fedorov, Bob Probert, Joe Kocur, and others, and hired Ken Holland as his protégé. He subscribed to the idea that the Red Wings needed to win and needed to be entertaining. That philosophy has made the Red Wings' one of the league's most successful franchises.

friction, but I enjoyed it. I thought it was good for the team. The players had troubles with Scotty, but they could also see that I had troubles with Scotty. And Kenny had troubles with him. The players didn't take it so personal. It worked for us.

I never minded a little controversy because I understood we were in the entertainment business. We had very poor coverage in the newspapers back in the early years. We signed players and made trades to create interest any way we could. I like to keep moving. I like the ability to announce moves so fans could see we were trying to improve. Even bringing in Jacques Demers was for that reason. He was brought in to make us better on the ice, no doubt about that. But I also knew there was a show business element to him. He could stir up attention and get the media to love him and to talk to him. He did that like nobody could. How colorful he was. That was all part of it! Because our team wasn't good enough to sell itself on its own. Our league had expanded, and teams weren't getting as many good players out of the draft. That's how we got through the 1980s.

In those days it was important to be a very tough team. The Philadelphia Flyers succeeded with that approach, and we had to sell tickets in Detroit. We had to get tougher. The drafting of Probert and Kocur were by design. We took the toughest guy in Ontario in Probert and the toughest guy in the West in Kocur. We were going to have a tough team to sell. Their off-ice antics were bad, but in a screwed-up way, it was what helped make them popular. They had a mystique, and people in Detroit loved them. It was with the arrival of those players and the greatness of Yzerman and then some good signings like Harold Snepsts and others that helped get us through. I traded a pretty good little player in Kelly Kisio to get Glen Hanlon, and that solidified our goaltending.

Meanwhile, for a two- or three-year period, Jacques was so good with the press. He could fire up the city. That was at that point—in 1986, '87, '88—when we started to approach sellouts. We got to the Final Four in back-to-back seasons. And that kind of got hockey off and running in Detroit. Then, of course, the Europeans started to come. The first one was Fedorov, then Slava Kozlov and Lidstrom and Konstantinov. Their skill level was so good, it really helped our club. I was told when we drafted Lidstrom that he was a young, skilled player who wasn't strong enough. We were told if we leave him in Sweden and let him play, the skill level is very high, the skating is good, and he will get stronger. Guess what? We left him alone, and the results are evident. There has been stability in how we have handled prospects here.

My lowest, lowest moments were during the 1985–1986 season after making the playoffs in my second and third seasons and creating a little bit of a revival for the franchise. In year four we finished at the bottom of the 21-team league with an embarrassing 40 points. There was a lot of really bad criticism of me personally. I had gotten into really bad public battle with Brad Park, who we made coach halfway through that year. It just wasn't a good time. Now the perception in Detroit was that Jimmy D's regime isn't working, that what happened in the Island was just luck. That I couldn't get the job done.

I remember that year the *Hockey News* put a cartoon in of me behind a great big eight-ball, my glasses hanging around down by my nose and me behind an eight-ball. It wasn't very pleasant. You might say my regime probably was hanging on by a thread. Fortunately, we would turn it around. We would bring in Jacques Demers and we would make a lot of moves, and we doubled our point total. Everything was fine. It turned around in a big hurry when we made some changes.

You can say Mike and Marian Ilitch are like the O'Malleys with the Dodgers and the Griffiths with the Washington Senators. They are approaching a quarter of a century of ownership. The stability has helped this franchise.

The other thing we know about Mike and Marian is that they were great hockey fans and great supporters of the game way before they bought the Red Wings. They owned season tickets at the Olympia, put ads in Bruce Norris's game magazine, and, I think, one year they had a box. As they were building up their pizza business, they were sponsoring youth hockey teams. They still do. It says that they have a great passion for the sport. They were both raised by European ethnic parents in Detroit. They are Detroiters. The city means a lot to them. They moved Little Caesars downtown. Comerica Park is in downtown Detroit. When you get a family that has that type of passion for a city, for the sport of hockey, both at the amateur level and at the major league level, you've got pretty committed owners.

Money has never been an issue for Mike Ilitch. He made it very clear to us: if we needed something or wanted to sign a player, and we were acting responsibly, money was not going to be an issue. You would see it every year at trade deadline. We had some duds in there. But for the most part it was very helpful. To describe Mike and Marian, I would say they are very driven and superbly committed both to the city and the franchise. Mike is trying to run the Tigers the same way. It is just a little more difficult. It's been good and stable.

Back in 1982, Minnesota's general manager, Lou Nanne, strongly recommended me to Mike Ilitch. It was a terrific thing that he did for me.

One time I asked Mike Ilitch whom he had interviewed for the general manager's job, and he told me his list included David Pole, Red Berenson, Ron Mason, and Pat Quinn. I told him that was an impressive group, and Mike laughed and said, "But none of them have won the Stanley Cup." I am very proud of Kenny Holland. The second year I was with the Red Wings,

I had signed a small little goaltender to be my goaltender in Adirondack. His name was Kenny Holland. He played two or three years in Adirondack and actually played a couple of games for us in Detroit.

I knew he wasn't going to make the big leagues, so I released him. We had an opening for a Western Canada scout and two days later I got call from Adirondack coach Bill Dineen, urging me to hire Kenny.

The first person I approached was Darcy Regier. He had been one of my draft picks on the Islanders and had been coaching in Indianapolis. He was a western Canada guy, and I offered him the job. He respectfully turned me down because he was going to be an assistant coach with Al Arbour.

Dineen calls me and says, "Jimmy, I got your man. I want you to hire Ken Holland."

"He's never scouted before," I reminded Bill. "He's a nice young man. He's been a player. Besides, he has three kids. I don't know if he wants to get in his car and go to a game every night for 14 straight days."

"I know, Kenny," Bill said. "I'll stake my job on it. I've had a lot of hockey conversations with him. He's a smart hockey guy. Jimmy, I want you to hire him."

I agreed to call him. Remember, I had called him three days before to tell him I was releasing him. Now I'm calling him telling him that Bill Dineen is really pushing me hard to hire him as the western Canada scout for the Detroit Red Wings.

He said he was interested, and I reminded him that he had to go to Moose Jaw, Saskatchewan, and Prince George and everywhere else. I reminded him he would be away from his family.

"I know that," Kenny said, "But I have a good wife. And I will have the summers with my family."

That was true, but the other eight months you are on the go. I said, "Okay, let me speak to your wife." I talked to her, and she was all for it, and we hired Ken Holland. It was a great hire. In 1989 when Neil Smith left me to be the general manager of the Rangers, I promoted Kenny to head scout.

In 1994 Brian Murray and Doug MacLean left us. I then brought Kenny in to be the assistant general manager of the Detroit Red Wings, and then, of course, the big three-headed monster was formed: Scotty Bowman, Jimmy D, and Kenny Holland. And we kept things interesting for about six years. There were rumors…wasn't it exciting? Say what you want, but it all worked out, didn't it? I never minded a little controversy.

One laugh that Kenny and I share involves the 1984 and 1986 drafts. In 1984 the Penguins finished dead last and got Mario Lemieux. The Detroit Red Wings finished dead last in 1986 and got Joe Murphy. Kenny and I often say, "What would the Detroit Red Wings have been like if we had been last in 1984 and got Mario Lemieux to go with Steve Yzerman?"

Talk about how timing affects your situation. You can say we made a lousy pick in 1986, but Jimmy Carson and Neil Brady were the second and third picks. It just wasn't a great draft year.

When I took over the team, I said we would win the Stanley Cup in eight years. It actually took 15 years. But we got there.

Jimmy Devellano's Career Highlights

* ★ Choreographing the transformation of the Detroit Red Wings from a floundering franchise to a franchise that is one of the league's most valuable. Today the Red Wings sell out their arena for every game.

* ★ After missing the playoffs 16 times in 18 years, the Red Wings made the playoffs in Devellano's second and third seasons.

* ★ Having his ring collection include six Stanley Cup rings (New York Islanders 1980, 1981, 1982; Detroit 1997, 1998, and 2002); three Calder Cup championship rings in the American Hockey League with Adirondack (1986, 1989, and 1992); two Adams Cup championship rings in the Central Hockey League (Fort Worth 1978 and Indianapolis 1982); and one Riley Cup championship ring in the East Coast Hockey League (Toledo 1994).

* ★ Having been with the Red Wings for 24 years and now also now helping shepherd the Detroit Tigers.

* ★ Being named Minor League Executive of the Year by the *Hockey News*. He returned to New York in 1981 as the Islanders' assistant general manager.

EDDIE MIO
GOALTENDER
1983–1986

THE FIRST HINT THAT I WAS GOING TO BE TRADED by the New York Rangers to the Detroit Red Wings in 1983 came from Wayne Gretzky.

I had just spent two days in Toronto with Gretzky and his then-agent Mike Barnett. We had met some members of the Oakland A's baseball team, and the trainer and the pitching coach had invited us down to the stadium. We went down to the dressing room and met everyone. The next morning, I was having breakfast. Wayne and Mike were going to take off and we were going to meet in Niagara Falls. As I was coming back to my room, Wayne and Mike were going out.

"By the way," Wayne said, "Craig Patrick's trying to get ahold of you."

"What?" I said, surprised.

"Yeah, he called the house," Gretz said.

Wow, that's strange, I thought

Patrick was the Rangers' general manager. My only thought was that it was about my contract. I was negotiating my own contract during the season, and before the playoffs we weren't getting anywhere. I just said, "Craig, listen. Let me get through the playoffs and then we'll talk again."

I probably had the two best years of my career with the New York Rangers. I thought I may have found something with the Rangers. We had a good squad. We had just taken the New York Islanders to six games in our division finals. The Islanders had gone on to win the Stanley Cup.

When I called Patrick, I made a joke. "Craig, what's the matter? Did I get traded?"

"Well, as a matter of fact, you did," he said.

I went quiet. I had been just throwing that out there as a joke.

The Rangers sent Ron Duguay, Eddie Johnstone, and me to the Red Wings for Willie Huber, Mark Osborne, and Mike Blaisdell.

When Patrick said I had been traded to Detroit, my thought was that it wasn't the worst place I could be traded. I grew up across the river in Windsor and idolized Gordie Howe and goaltenders Terry Sawchuk and Roger Crozier. I was envious of Crozier because he was a left-hander and he looked so cool making a save. I was just shocked to be traded to Detroit. I had to recover from the shock.

When I returned to New York, Duguay was still there. We went out to dinner, and I said to him, "You know what? Ron, you had your problems with [Rangers coach] Herb Brooks. This is a new beginning. We will get a chance to play every game. They are counting on us."

The Red Wings had only made the playoffs twice in 17 years when I was traded to them in 1983.

When I got home to Windsor, my friends were excited. I hadn't been home really since 1971 when I left for college in Colorado. Now I was basically coming home. The only scary part was we had a saying in hockey: "Your career is near the end if you get traded close to home."

Ironically, in three years, my career was over.

It took that whole summer to sink in that I was now coming to an organization that was changing for the better. There was going to be pressure.

Even players who didn't grow up in the Original Six era understand that it's special to play for an Original Six team. I felt a little bit of that even when I was with the New York Rangers. Goalie John Davidson bred that tradition into me. But I understood Red Wings tradition because I had grown up in Windsor. Father Cullen was the coach at Assumption High School in Windsor and he knew all the people in the States, so we got to play some games at Olympia. Sometimes we would get tickets to Red Wings games, and I can remember back then we use to sit up in the rafters and just say, "Could you ever imagine playing on the Olympia?"

Certainly I remembered what it was like for me to watch Budd Lynch and Bruce Martyn when they used to do play-by-play of Red Wings games on Channel 50, or maybe it was Channel 20.

164

Although Eddie Mio played just three seasons in Detroit, his colorful style made him a memorable player. He's also known as one of Wayne Gretzky's close friends. He was the best man at Gretzky's wedding. The two played together in the World Hockey Association.

Now I was going to be involved in that atmosphere. Once I got my contract done with the Red Wings, I was excited. Mike Ilitch had just taken over as the team's owner, and the whole organization was trying to change. We knew we had a good owner. Mike came down to the dressing rooms more then than he does now. He was there after the games sometimes, but not a lot. We could all call him by his first name. I think we saw Marian more than we did him.

We made the playoffs in my first season of 1983. We lost in the 1984 playoffs to St. Louis. After the season, Mike had thrown the year-end party at his home off of Lahser. At the end of the night, there was an envelope waiting for everybody. It wasn't for the players. If the player had a wife, it was a check for $1,000 in his wife's name. If the player had a girlfriend, it was in her name. In my case, I didn't have a girlfriend or a wife, so he made it to my mother's name. It was special. That's when you knew Ilitch was committed. He was happy we had made the playoffs for the first time since he had the team.

That party seemed like it was a sign that the organization had turned the corner. Stevie Yzerman had a beautiful year. John Ogrodnick scored 42 goals that year. Duguay played very well on that line. We had reached the playoffs and now we wanted more. In 1984–1985, we did it again. It was the first time the Red Wings had made it in back-to-back seasons in a long time. You could see that the organization was moving forward. Stevie got hurt the next season, and the team was in disarray. We took a step backward. When something like that happens, you reevaluate. I was pretty much done.

For a year, I was a little bitter. But I was still a Red Wing at heart. Once a Red Wing, always a Red Wing. The whole summer took a toll on me to a point that I didn't even try to land a job. I remember sitting with Mickey Redmond, and he wasn't a broadcaster at the time. Mickey gave me a nice pep talk. Sure enough the Red Wings alumni called and helped me find a job in the automotive business. The Red Wings alumni association is very special to me because they were out there for me. You have to remember back then we didn't make a lot of cash.

I think it took maybe six months after I retired to really understand what it meant to be a Red Wing in Detroit. I think I really knew what it really was to be a Red Wing when I was in the alumni association with guys like Alex Delvecchio, Ted Lindsay, Johnny Wilson, Shaky Peters, and the late Gary Bergman. They bled red.

You've got to remember, I had three years here and two of them were pretty volatile with the Red Wings. Yet after the Red Wings won the Stanley Cup in 1997 and 1998, the team invited the alumni to be in the parade. There's no better feeling than to be part of an organization when you were playing and still being a part of it after you stop playing.

I like to believe that my Detroit teams helped get the organization turned around by making the playoffs those two seasons. I can walk the streets and anyone who watched me play in my era still knows me. That's what being a Red Wing is about. It's a great hockey town, and fans will still acknowledge and say kind words about you after you are retired. Your notoriety goes on forever. New York's athletes were recognizable in my days there; Edmonton is good; but I don't think I have ever been to a town that compares to Detroit. That's why I'm still living here in Detroit.

If you have ever worn the Red Wings' colors, you are in our alumni association. It's hard to describe the feeling you have when you wear that color. If anyone took off a Red Wings sweater and dropped it on the floor, everybody would be on him. That's what it means to wear the jersey with the spokes on it, to be a part of city that loves its players. I don't think it gets any better.

I played a sport I love in a city that is always behind its players. You will be recognized not just for what kind of player you were, but for just getting to the team when a lot of guys couldn't get there. That means a lot to me.

When you retire, you realize that being a Red Wing alumnus may be even better than being a Red Wing. When you are retired you really start to reflect about how special it was.

Eddie Mio's Career Highlights

* Playing his first game at Joe Louis in front of his parents. "I can't remember if we won it or not, but to be able to have my mom and dad at the building that they have watched on TV," Mio said, "that was definitely a highlight—to be able to look up and see my mom and dad every night when I played. I left home in 1971 as a 17-year-old and really never came back other than a few weeks for the summer."

* Helping the Red Wings make the playoffs for the first time in 6 seasons.

* A former Colorado College goaltender, being named one of the top 50 players of the Western Collegiate Hockey Association's first 50 years in 2002.

* Playing with Wayne Gretzky on the Edmonton Oilers in Olympia Stadium in the 1979–1980 season. "We lost the game 4–3," Mio recalled. "But I think I had 48 saves or something like that, and I remember coming into the locker room because I had let a little sneaky one in, in the third and apologizing to Gretz [Wayne Gretzky] and Mess [Mark Messier], and they all told me to shut up." He was the best man at Gretzky's wedding to Janet Jones.

* Practicing at Olympia Stadium. "At one point when we got to practice there during the morning skate, I kind of looked up at where I used to sit on New Year's Eve and whenever I could get a game in. That was a very special moment for me."

* Playing with Steve Yzerman and Wayne Gretzky and watching them both grow up.

SHAWN BURR

CENTER

1984–1995

I DEFINITELY GREW UP A LEAFS FAN. I'd usually watch the Wings game on Sunday afternoon to fall asleep. Since I was a Toronto fan, it didn't really matter when the Wings drafted me.

My parents were both very active in my hockey career; my dad was the manager all the way through. So initially I thought if I made the team they could come to all my games. If I had to play out in L.A. or someplace far away, it would have been a lot tougher for my parents to see me play.

I didn't think I was going to be picked by Detroit after Montreal took Petr Svoboda with the fifth pick. The day before the draft, Jimmy Devellano had interviewed me and told me if nothing special or unexpected happened, they were going to pick me. I thought the Wings might pick Shayne Corson or Doug Bodger. They were both good players and were available. However, the Red Wings said they had their list and they took me with the seventh pick.

That first training camp with the Wings was a little weird. I was probably bad and didn't have a very good camp, but they kept me around just to give me a taste. There were a lot of older players: Ivan Boldirev, Dwight Foster, and Danny Gare. The next year, again, there were a lot of older players, a lot of guys who were kind of holding onto their careers by a thread. We did have a few younger players: Steve Yzerman, Lane Lambert, and Claude Loiselle. I wasn't really accepted by anyone, the older guys or the younger guys.

I actually stayed for the first month of the season, and then Jimmy Devellano came to me. He said, "Shawn, we're not going to have a good year. This team is not going to be good. Why don't you go back to juniors, have a great year, and then start." I went back to juniors and I had a good year with 60 goals and 76 assists. The Wings ended up with only 40 points.

It was my next training camp that was definitely the resurgence year of the Red Wings. They broomed out a lot of those older players and they signed a lot of college free agents in Adam Oates, Ray Staszak, and Tim Friday. Detroit also got Basil McRae. Plus they added Steve Chiasson and me, and they brought in Jacques Demers as coach.

I had played 11 games in the NHL and I think I had five different coaches. Personally, this will sound weird, but out of all my coaches, Doug McLean, who sat in for Bryan Murray a bit, was my favorite. He was emotional, smart, and he played me, too.

As far as playing time, Jacques Demers played me all the time and I owe him that. He was a great coach at getting the best out of the role players. From a technical standpoint, he wasn't the greatest. He went out and hired some guys he thought would help him. I won't mention any names—Colin Campbell—but he was the one who undermined Jacques. He had secret meetings behind his back and tried to get him ousted as a coach. Jacques brought him in as an assistant. I didn't like that at all.

Was Colin Campbell right in a lot of the things he was saying? He probably was, but was it the right thing to do? I'm a pretty loyal guy, and if somebody brings me in, I stand beside him. It just wasn't right. I walked out of the meeting. I wasn't going to listen to that. The meeting was pretty much "this is what we're going to do, these are the things we've got to do, and Jacques isn't going to know anyways."

Jacques was a motivator; he kind of knew when to push the buttons. Whether you won a face-off or blocked a shot, you'd come off, and Jacques would acknowledge it. He seemed to know who to put on the ice at different times, even though he wasn't the greatest x's and o's guy.

When we were playing Edmonton in the playoffs, Jacques came in before the first game and said, "Guys, the game tonight, the biggest game we play as a team. The boys, they cannot play this game. You see, we need the mens to show up. The boys, you cannot play against this Edmonton Oilers team. The boys, you stay at home, we need the mens to play. Go get 'em boys!"

We just died laughing, the way he butchered the language. Little did we know back then that he couldn't read. He used to carry five or six newspapers all the time, so I don't know, maybe they were just weighing him down in the wind.

It was depressing not fitting in with the guys in the dressing room. I went home and I would just lie there thinking, "Gosh, do I have to change? Do I have to sit there and not say a word?" I was always a pretty vocal person and liked to try to be real rah-rah. The dressing room was always quiet. I was always used to having fun playing. I honestly thought after the first year, "Oh, wow, the NHL is a lot different than anything else I ever played in!"

Until I realized that it wasn't me who had the issues—I played in the World Championships in 1989 and everybody was the same as me. That World Championship over in Switzerland was probably the most fun I've ever had playing hockey.

Stevie Yzerman—I don't know if he still feels this way or not—probably never liked me when we played. I'm totally the opposite of him. He's very focused on hockey. We didn't understand each other until the Wings hired a team psychologist. Stevie started talking one time about how he handles pressure. For him, it was to be very quiet. I'm one of the few people whose heart rate goes down when they talk. I talk to relax. At that point, I was thinking, "Hey, maybe Stevie doesn't talk to me not because he's better than me, he's just quiet and he keeps everything inside." I think Stevie started thinking, "Hey, Burr isn't a big-mouth, he's just nervous before a game so he talks."

My relationship with Sergei Fedorov started in the summer the year he came to Detroit. Jim Lites called me up and said, "Hey, Shawn, I have this Russian kid, and he's living at my house, and he hasn't done anything." I said, "Well, I'm going on my boat. I'll take him out."

Sergei shows up and he's got a Speedo on. Here's me, not a body of a Greek God, and here's this kid, with a body of a Greek God, and he's in a Speedo. I said, "Sergei, not a chance." He couldn't speak English, so I gave him a big pair of watermelon boxers that went down to about his knees.

Every once in a while we'd go out on the boat. All he could say was, "Milk, steak." He'd drink milk and eat steak, that's all he ever did. I could never figure it out. I'm eating all of this lean meat and he'd have steak with sour cream on it and a baked potato loaded with butter. He was chiseled out of steel and I was chiseled out of a marshmallow. I was thinking, "Maybe we're eating wrong in this country."

Shawn Burr, the Red Wings' first-round pick in 1984, had his best Detroit season in 1989–1990, when he had 24 goals and 32 assists for 56 points. The gritty forward was always popular with fans.

Like Stevie, Sergei keeps all of his emotion inside. As a Russian, you never show your emotion. But he's very emotional. I think it bothered a lot of guys because they didn't think that he cared, but he does. He just doesn't show it.

We did have a lot of fun together and did a lot of stupid things. I remember we went to San Francisco one time. Here's two hockey players—and we walked for about an hour holding hands down the street. You know, we wanted to fit in. We got no reaction at all. We were laughing ourselves, but we used to go around saying, "We're going to San Francisco."

Sergei is one of the greatest Red Wings to ever put on the uniform. It was a sad day when he left Detroit, but maybe it was time for him. Everybody always thinks during their career that maybe the grass is greener on the other side of the street. I think he realizes now that it's not. The Wings would not have won any of their Cups if it weren't for Sergei.

Probably the worst time of my hockey career, believe it or not, was the NHL Stanley Cup Finals. I played on a line with Dino Ciccarelli and Keith Primeau. In the semifinals against Chicago, we had a great series, and I played a ton. Once the Blackhawks were eliminated, it was on to the Finals to play New Jersey.

Before the series even started, Scotty Bowman pulled me into his office and said, "I don't know if I am going to be able to play you against these guys, Shawn. They're a lot faster and I don't know if you're going to be quick enough to play." I just looked at him, wondering, *What are you talking about?*

Then the second game against New Jersey had the infamous handing the stick to Scott Niedermayer. I was driving home after the game, and Scotty was on the radio and said, "I'll tell you why we lost. Shawn Burr hands Scott Niedermayer the stick right in the slot for the winning goal." I was thinking, *Holy crap, what was he watching?* I've actually played that play over in my head a thousand times and that's not how it happened at all!

I was in to forecheck their defenseman behind the net, and Scott Niedermayer was hooking me—this was at their end. So with Niedermayer hooking me, I grabbed at his stick to try to get it out of there. I kind of pulled it loose out of his hand. I was going to hit their defenseman, but Niedermayer's stick was caught up in my mid-section, and the puck went around the boards to Ciccarelli. It was around their right side, so Dino got it on his backhand and he turned with the puck to face me in the slot. Well, I had a stick in my chest, so I couldn't shoot the puck with two sticks in my hand. I just pushed the stick free and tried to open up for a one-time pass from Dino. He passed it across the slot and, when I threw the stick out, Niedermayer regrabbed it. He intercepted the puck. Now, we were in front of their net, and Niedermayer took the puck and kind of weaved down the ice. He took a shot off the boards, and Paul Coffey went down on one knee to block it. He walked around him, the puck went off the boards, and Mike Vernon kind of tripped and fell down. Niedermayer tapped it into the net. There was no indication that I was going to be the one at fault for the goal by giving Niedermayer his stick! But that was me, "handing him the stick in the slot."

It bothered me maybe for a year or two, but I have never felt any repercussions because of it. I don't really worry too much about things I can't control or didn't do, and I didn't do that. I think it was a stupid comment by Scotty Bowman. Everyone has their insecurities; if it made him feel better about himself, then so be it, I guess.

Scotty Bowman pays attention to detail. That's the one thing I learned from him. He made a good team great by detail. He was the weirdest guy you'd ever meet. He said a lot of things that were wrong, but he paid attention to detail. When you have a team with a bunch of superstars, Scotty was always bigger than the guys were, and I think that's important for a coach. Did I like him as a coach? I respected him as a coach. I didn't really know him outside of hockey. Maybe he was different. When I was traded, Scotty Bowman was the only one who called me. He basically said, "Hey, I enjoyed having you as a player."

As a Red Wings player, whenever I skated out onto the ice, I was always the first player out after the goaltender. I always hit both posts and the face-off dot. Then I usually looked up. My wife sat right behind the net, and my mom and dad sat kind of behind the visitors' bench. That's what I'll always remember.

Being a Red Wing is the proudest thing, other than being a dad, that I have. I put a lot of hard work and a lot of years in. All the guys who have played here still have a lot of pride. I was the vice president of the Red Wings alumni association and now I'm the president. Ted Lindsay was at a meeting the other day and he said, "If you're going to run around this town beating your chest, saying 'I'm a Red Wing,' then you're obligated to do the charity work." That's fine with me because I'm going to run around beating my chest, saying I was a Red Wing. I was proud and still am proud to be a Red Wing!

Shawn Burr's Career Highlights

* Skating onto Joe Louis and seeing his wife and parents at every game. "My parents never missed a game, ever," Burr said.

* Scoring the overtime goal against Chicago in Game 3 of the 1987 playoffs.

* Helping Detroit come back from a 3–1 deficit in games to beat Toronto in 1987.

* Mentoring Sergei Fedorov.

* Playing his first game in Maple Leaf Gardens.

HARRY NEALE

COACH

1985–1986

WHEN I WAS GROWING UP IN SARNIA, ONTARIO, thinking I was going to be a National Hockey League player, Gordie Howe was one of my favorite players. I have fond memories of listening to Detroit Red Wings games on the radio in the 1940s. Sid Abel. Terry Sawchuk. Marcel Pronovost. They were all my heroes in those days.

Even when I was in the Toronto Maple Leafs organization, I looked forward to playing against the Red Wings.

Every year my dad would take me to Detroit, to Briggs Stadium, to see the Tigers play and then over to Olympia to see the Red Wings play. I saw my first game in the mid-1940s, when the Red Wings played the Blackhawks. Mud Bruneteau played for the Red Wings and Bill Mosienko was on the Blackhawks.

I was so excited in 1985 when I received the chance to coach a franchise that I was very familiar with. I was certainly looking forward to the challenge. They hadn't been a good team in the two or three years before I came there. But I felt as if I had enough experience to bring them out of the woods.

This was probably the third year that Mike Ilitch owned the team. He was willing to spend. The Wings had signed a bunch of college players, like Ray Staszak, Adam Oates, and Chris Cichocki. They were good players, particularly Oates, but none were ready to be contributors in the National Hockey League. Oates went on to have a distinguished career, but at that time he just

174

Although Neale didn't coach long in Detroit, he is remembered by Detroit as the long-time analyst of *Hockey Night* in Canada. He also coached Gordie Howe in Hartford. Neale once said of Howe, "If you equate greatness with longevity and superior play, there is no match for Gordie Howe. I think he's the greatest and, under those circumstances, I don't think there is even a challenger." *Photo courtesy of Getty Images.*

wasn't ready for the length of the season or the size of the players. The Wings had signed Warren Young from Pittsburgh, but he couldn't duplicate what he had done playing on a line with Mario Lemieux. We had also picked up Ron Duguay from New York. But we just weren't a good team. I lasted 37 games and then I was harder to find than Jimmy Hoffa.

When you are in the middle of that kind of season, you don't actually think about whether you are going to be fired. You just are trying as hard as you can to win the next game. I wasn't shocked to be fired, but I was surprised. How I heard the news of my firing is actually a funny story. Right after Christmas, we lost 8–3 in New York and chartered back home. We landed in Windsor, and I drove back to Detroit through the Windsor Tunnel with my assistant coaches, Colie Campbell and Danny Belisle. It had to be around 1:00 A.M. or later, and we were trying to find the out-of-town scores on the radio. Just before we entered the tunnel, the sportscaster said, "The rumor is that there is going to be a shakeup with the Red Wings. Coach Harry Neale and general manager Jimmy Devellano could both take the hit."

Then we promptly entered the tunnel and lost our signal. When we came out, the sports show was over. We didn't know if was rumor, fact, or speculation.

This was a day or two after Christmas, and my wife's parents were at our house. My children were young. And Christmas was a big time in our house. I was sure that when I arrived home the lights would be on and everyone was going to be waiting up because they had heard the report. But there were no lights when I came home. Everyone was asleep, and I went to bed.

The next morning a couple of reporters called me about the situation, and I decided I had better phone Devellano. He had a scouting background, so he usually didn't get up until 12:00, but I found him.

"What's going on?" I asked.

"I was going to tell you when you got down to the rink for practice," Devellano told me.

I figured there would be four television cameras and three radio stations there, so I told Devellano to check the last line of my contract, which stated that if I was fired I would still be paid whether I found another job or not. I had another year left on my contract.

It really was a bitter pill to swallow. I look back now and think that I didn't have as much time as I would have liked to turn it around. I tried everything I could, but I couldn't get them to play better. We really just weren't good enough. They brought in Brad Park to replace me, and he didn't do much better than I did. Then they stole Jacques Demers from St. Louis and added a few guys, and Jacques did a nice job to get the Red Wings back to respectability.

When I was with Vancouver, I had done some work for *Hockey Night in Canada* after the Canucks got knocked out of the playoffs. I used to tell executive producer Don Wallace, "When I get fired as coach, I expect a job on *Hockey Night*."

"Just call me when it happens," he told me.

Before I could call him after I was fired by Detroit, he called and told me to be in Montreal on Saturday night. That was the year that TSN came aboard to do a 20-game television package. The network had no commentators. That was my lucky break. I did that and then John Davidson quit as *Hockey Night*'s principal color guy and went to New York. The timing was perfect for me. Don Wallace saw something in me that I didn't see in myself. The rest is history. Since then, I've been able to go to the Finals every year. I could never say that when I had a real job.

My season as a Red Wings coach was a good opportunity that didn't work out. When I go to Detroit now, I always look at the board and see that, at one time, I was coach of the Detroit Red Wings. There were a lot of good coaches on that board. I wasn't one of them, but it was nice to be there.

Harry Neale's Career Highlights

* Coaching Gordie Howe at New England in the WHA. He was there when Howe scored the 1,000th goal of his pro career. "I would not seriously try to convince anyone that Bobby Orr or Wayne Gretzky wasn't as good as Gordie Howe because that argument could go on forever," Neale said. "All I know is that I had Gordie when he was 49 and 50 years old and he was a phenomenal athlete."

* Coaching New England to the Avco Finals in 1978.

* Being general manager of the Vancouver Canucks from 1982 to 1985.

* Coaching Team USA at the 1976 Canada Cup. The U.S. squad included Lou Nanne, Craig Patrick, and Mike Milbury, among others.

* Coaching the Canucks before coming to Detroit.

JACQUES DEMERS
COACH
1986–1990

THE BEST COMPLIMENT THAT ANYONE ever gave me was when Mike Ilitch said that I taught the Red Wings organization how to win.

I always say that the best coaching job I ever did was in Detroit, even though I won the Stanley Cup in Montreal. When I came to the Montreal Canadiens, it wasn't a bad hockey club. In Detroit, I took over a team that had 40 points, and we went from being the Dead Wings to the Red Wings. I was asked to take a team that was a laughingstock and improved the team by 50 percent. But that wasn't good enough for me.

But I can tell you that it wasn't Jacques Demers. I had solid backing from Mr. and Mrs. Ilitch, Jimmy Devellano, team president Jim Lites, and assistant GM Nick Polano. Jimmy D was a very smart hockey man. He put things together. We worked well together. But it was the players who earned the success on the ice. They believed in me, and I believed in them.

I turned to guys like Stevie Y, Gerard Gallant, Shawn Burr, and said, "Boys, you are the new leaders. They just went with it, and we took. We went from 40 points to 79 points and we went to the Western Conference Finals. People said it was a fluke and we went to 93 points. Those two seasons were as good as any I've had in the league. It was the first time in NHL history that a coach had won back-to-back coach of the year awards with the same team.

I've coached some Hall of Famers, but I always say that the greatest player I ever coached is Steve Yzerman.

The only problem Steve ever had was that Mario Lemieux and Wayne Gretzky were in the league at the same time. If they would have come three years after him, or 10 years before, he would have been known as an even greater player. He had 60 or more goals two years in a row and three more years when he had 50 goals.

Healthy, injured, or sick, Steve competed hard every night. He was very consistent in his desire to win. He has changed in that he's much more talkative. He was very shy back then.

When I named Yzerman captain, it was controversial only because he was just 21 years old. He was the youngest captain in the team's history. Neither owner Mike Ilitch or general manager Jimmy Devellano fought me. At a tender age, Steve didn't hesitate. He just took off with it. And he had his best years. He was just an awesome player. An awesome captain. He led on the ice and also led in the locker room.

We had to start somewhere. I was a new coach trying to establish a new attitude in the organization. "I'll take full responsibility," I said to Mr. Ilitch.

I never hesitated on that decision. I knew from day one that Yzerman would be my captain. I'm very proud of him. Some people said he could never win the big game, and now he has led the franchise to three Stanley Cup championships. He carried that team by himself for years, and all he needed was to be surrounded by good players. You can't win a Stanley Cup by yourself.

In those years, we were not the most talented team. But we had players who did what they had to do. Harold Snepsts, Lee Norwood, Glen Hanlon, Tim Higgins, Mike O'Connell, Jimmy Nill, and Joe Kocur. They loved each other as human beings and they worked for one another.

With Bob Probert, Kocur, Gallant, and Snepsts, we were probably the toughest team in the NHL. No one fooled around with our captain. Everyone looked after him, but Gallant played on his line and really looked after him. Gerard was a hard-nosed winger, limited in talent but blessed with a tremendous amount of heart. He got there when he needed to. Gerard and Steve were made for each other.

Probie and Kocur really helped our team to play the exciting brand of hockey because very few people would try to manhandle our team even on the road. Probie ended up playing in an All-Star Game one year. He is one of the five best heavyweights in NHL history.

Jacques Demers, shown here celebrating with his Detroit players, is one of the most popular figures in Red Wings' history. The effervescent coach won 137 games in his tenure in Detroit and guided his team to the Conference Finals twice.

Another interesting character was Petr Klima. He was a bit of a flake, but I liked him and he played some good hockey at times. He scored some big goals. Even with the problems I had with some of those guys, I loved those teams. Some of those players simply had deep-rooted problems. To me they were all good people, some with medical problems. I didn't take it personally.

My time in Detroit provided me with great memories. I only had two sad moments in my days there. My first was when Bob Probert was arrested at the Windsor-Detroit border in 1989. There was great sadness in seeing Probert, my friendly giant, with all of those problems. I had a lot of anxiety over that team. Now we know why I put up with Probert and some of the guys because my dad was a deeply rooted alcoholic. I was trying to help him out because my dad was difficult to deal with. Probert could have been a consistent 300 penalty man and a 30 to 35 goal scorer, 65 to 70 points a year. For a big guy, he could skate and he had good hands. He was fearless. He could have been another Clark Gillies.

The other sad day was the day I got fired, because I loved Detroit. But the Ilitches handled my firing with so much class and respect that I couldn't even be mad at them. Firing is just part of this business. Mr. Ilitch was like a second father to me. I came in with no money, I was broke. He took care of me. When he let me go, it was more like a separation, and it gave me the opportunity to win a Stanley Cup, too. Who knows how long it would have taken for us to win a Stanley Cup. I just love that man.

How can I forget the fans in Detroit? How many ovations did we get there? Hundreds on the ice. It's hard to explain what it was like to be coach of the Detroit Red Wings. I had watched on television before when fans would throw an octopus on the ice as part of the Red Wings playoff tradition, and then I'm in Detroit waving an octopus.

When I received the opportunity to coach the Red Wings, I remember thinking that Gordie Howe wore a Red Wings' sweater, and Terry Sawchuk, Alex Delvecchio, and Bill Gadsby. There is a long list of great players. The Red Wings represent the Original Six and class. Those red sweaters are so classy. And the ownership there is so classy. I was honored to be given that opportunity and I'm still honored today.

Jacques Demers's Career highlights

* Winning a Stanley Cup with the Montreal Canadiens. "I thank Mike Ilitch for helping me get there," Demers said.

* Coming back from a 2–0 deficit in a best-of-seven series to beat Toronto in the playoffs. "I remember Toronto coach John Brophy gave us the choke sign," Demers said. "We didn't need much more than that to get us going…we just killed them in Toronto and then came back home for the last two games and shut them out."

* Seeing Steve Yzerman scoring his 60th goal. "I was so proud of my captain," Demers said

* Becoming a general manager of the Tampa Bay Lightning.

* Working with writer Mario Leclerc to produce his autobiography in French. It was highly successful in Quebec.

DAVE LEWIS
DEFENSEMAN
1986–1988

ASSISTANT/ASSOCIATE COACH
1988–2002

HEAD COACH
2002–2004

WHEN I WAS WITH THE LOS ANGELES KINGS, Jimmy Devellano was hired as Detroit's GM, and I know that he tried to trade for me, but the Kings didn't want to trade me. However, I'm jumping ahead of myself.

My association with the Red Wings can be traced back to the 1973 NHL Draft. I was drafted in the third round by the New York Islanders, and the man who selected me was Jimmy Devellano. I'm not sure if he was the Islanders' head amateur scout at that time, but it was Jimmy D who picked me. After spending a number of years playing for the Islanders, Kings, and Devils, I was almost at the end of my career when Jimmy Devellano called, asking if I would be interested in coming to Detroit as an unrestricted free agent. The whopping negotiation price of the transfer was about $25,000 extra, which isn't much in today's terms, but it enticed me to sell the house, move my family, and come to Detroit.

Dave Lewis entered the coaching ranks immediately after retiring as a player on November 6, 1987. He was the associate coach on Detroit's three Stanley Cup championship teams. Lewis coached Detroit to a 96–41–21–6 record in two seasons, but he was replaced after the team didn't have postseason success. He is now the head coach of the Boston Bruins.

Prior to the year I got there, the Wings had 40 points and missed the playoffs. Detroit was in a state of turmoil. So they brought in some veteran players, including me, hired a new coach in Jacques Demers, and were beginning to accumulate good, young players in Steve Yzerman, Petr Klima, and other guys who came into the mix, like Bob Probert.

We were a team of workers—I can't remember all of the players, but on defense it was me, Gilbert Delorme, Lee Norwood, Darren Veitch, Harold Snepsts, and Doug Halward—a bunch of guys who were not what you would call highly skilled.

Our team fit Jacques Demers pretty well. Jacques wasn't big on tactics, but he understood that emotions played a big part in the game and that's what he tried to touch on with all the players. We had a lot of guys with a lot of hockey sense. They could relate to the younger guys and knew what was important to win. That was one of the things that Jimmy D saw in us and Jacques picked up on it. We became a playoff team.

The most remarkable thing about the playoff run in 1986–1987 was that this rag-tag bunch of guys, who were rejects from other teams, were all of a sudden playing the high and mighty Edmonton Oilers in the semifinals. We were as close as any Red Wings team had gotten in years to that Stanley Cup Trophy. We were really proud of that. Jimmy D did a great job in picking the right type of people to get the team turned around. In one year we went from being a 40-point hockey club to losing to the Edmonton Oilers in the semifinals. It was quite an accomplishment.

Playing my 1,000th game at Joe Louis Arena against Philadelphia was a really special night. Mrs. Ilitch, Jimmy D, and my family were on the ice for a presentation where I received a beautiful Rolex watch. It's something I still cherish today. Once the game started, I was relieved because, during my 999th game, I kept thinking, *My god, can I get through this game and make it to 1,000?* It was kind of strange because, as I got closer to my 1,000th game, I worried about ever getting to that point.

One of the things I did for my 1,000th game was change my number. Before I came to Detroit, I always wore No. 25. That number belonged to John Ogrodnick, so I wore No. 52 with the Red Wings. Ogrodnick was traded to Quebec, so I thought it'd be sort of neat to play my 1,000th game in the same number that I started with in Long Island. I got permission from the league and, after the second period, I changed jerseys and finished the game wearing No. 25. The scorers had to make the change and it had to be recorded on the official score-sheets.

After the game, Glenn Resch, who was the goaltender for Philadelphia but also my longtime teammate in New Jersey and Long Island, gave me an autographed stick with all of the Flyers' names on it. I still have that stick framed along with that picture of Mrs. Ilitch, Jimmy D, my family, and myself on the ice.

My career came to an end the next year. The game wasn't about winning or losing anymore, it was more about survival, and that really scared me. I recognized it and it didn't last long because Jimmy Devellano and Jacques Demers talked to me about retiring, and I knew it was time. I guess it took them a little longer to recognize it—at least that's what I'm hoping anyway. I did retire.

Detroit asked me if I wanted to stay on and become an assistant coach.

I thought it was quite an honor to say yes to that. I didn't do a whole lot that first year; just sort of got acclimated to what it was like to be on the other side of the bench, upstairs in the press box, and communicating with the players at practice. That transition I was ready for because my body had worn out.

Jacques Demers was the type of coach who was fiery and emotional. Bryan Murray was very analytical, very organized in his direction. They were on opposite sides of the spectrum. Both of them were extremely successful coaches but exact opposites on what is expected of the players and how they dealt with the players. There was a learning curve there for me and it helped me along the way to get settled in with Scotty Bowman.

It took me time to get to know Scotty Bowman. You hear things about him: you hear about reputations, you talk to people who have worked with him or players who have played for him, and everybody has their different story to tell. I guess the one thing that was really important was that his winning record was what we were looking for in Detroit. That was the most important thing for me because I had never won a Stanley Cup and he had, so he must know the way to get it done.

I spent a lot more time talking with Barry Smith than with Scotty. But once we were in close quarters—you see each other every day, you travel together, you go to dinners together, and you watch hockey games together on the road—I got to know him much, much better. It took time, and the adjustment was a slow process, but as it turned out it was obviously a very successful coaching group with Scotty being the lead man.

Preparing for a playoff series, whether it's the first round, second round, or third round, the process is always the same. Our pro scout at the time, Danny Belisle, would watch the team we were playing and prepare a scouting report. We were going to be playing Phoenix, and Danny's report was a breakdown of their lines and a breakdown of their systems. All that information was supported with video. Barry and I spent three or four days where we had meetings with players, we had group meetings with penalty-killers and power-play. We had match-up meetings. We talked to the defense about what we were going to do and we talked to the forwards.

All of this preparation was supported by video, and the info from Danny Belisle's traveling was thrown out after the first shift with Phoenix. Scotty said, "All that stuff, we're scratching it all. We're going to do this now." That was the first time that ever happened to me and it never really happened again; but for whatever reason, Scotty wanted to change the whole outlook of what we were trying to get done. I don't know if he had been thinking about it or if he had just decided after one shift when the game started that he didn't like what the shift looked like.

Most everybody looks at the March 26 game in 1997 against Colorado as the turning point for our team. It was a turning point because we found a way to beat Patrick Roy. I think he was in our head. We just couldn't beat Roy. Colorado had owned us; they had beaten us the year before and eliminated us. Going into the game, we were thinking that Roy wasn't going to play. Colorado had nothing to gain by playing him.

We looked at the game this way: if we beat Patrick Roy then we beat him, but if we don't, all of a sudden we're right back into the same mindset. If we beat Colorado and Patrick Roy isn't in the net, well that's not quite the same as beating Colorado with Patrick Roy in the net. For me as a coach, the turning point wasn't so much the fight, but that we beat Patrick Roy by coming back and winning in overtime.

There were a lot of labels before the Red Wings won the Stanley Cup: "You could never win with so many Russians" or "You didn't have the right captain as your leader" or "Steve Yzerman will never win." Those ideas, internally I think, affected our group—and when I say "our group," I mean the coaches, players, and management—because we really believed we could win the Stanley Cup. We hadn't done it and we didn't talk openly much about it, but it was a bit of a driving force of "We'll show you guys. We'll show the rest of the world what we can do as a group."

As it turned out, it was an incredible run and an incredible experience to win that Cup in '97. We were fighting all different types of adversity; whether it was unflattering labels, injuries, pressure, or expectations—the guys found a way to get it done. My God, was it a relief when we won that Stanley Cup! Emotionally, the relief was like a blown-up balloon when you let it go, the air was just going out of it as fast as it could. You could sense it. We accomplished something that the team hadn't done for 42 years!

The fabric of the Red Wings crest seems to be woven into the community, and I'm talking generations here. I'll never forget the parade in '97. There were grandfathers with their kids, who were with their kids, who were with their kids! I saw three or four generations of families sitting on the street, lined up with tears in their eyes. It was an amazing vision to see. We were sitting on Ford Mustang convertibles waving and were taking pictures of our fans taking pictures of us. That's how bizarre it was.

You're emotionally as high as you can get as a professional athlete or as a coach and you're supposed to enjoy and celebrate this great, great victory. We did get to celebrate it, but only for five or six days and then the tragedy happened with the limo accident with Sergei Mnatsakanov, Vladimir Konstantinov, and Slava Fetisov, who actually recovered. It was as low as you could get after as high as you could get. The emotions and the mood swing that night, the next morning, the day after that, and for the entire summer is difficult to describe. Emotions were rampant in the hospital that night. All of the players and their families were there to find out what had happened.

The next year, I sensed that the resolve of the organization and the team was that we knew we weren't going to lose. Mark Howe told me the same thing. He was a scout at the time and he knew we were going to win the Cup again. There was that prevailing feeling amongst the guys. It didn't matter what happened in the regular season, but let the playoffs start and we'll show you. We'll show you what we can do for these two guys.

The players normally don't observe what goes on, on the big screens, but when they would show Vladdy sitting in a super-suite on the screens, our guys would look up and, if they were tired, if they were hurt, or if they made a major mistake, that would refresh them and get them refocused on the task at hand. Vladdy was still part of the team.

Beating Washington in the Finals in 1998 was great, but what really stands out was Steve Yzerman presenting Vladdy with the Stanley Cup after Slava

Fetisov and Igor Larionov rolled him onto the ice in a wheelchair. It's one moment in sports that I'll never forget.

Another incident that motivated us in the playoffs occurred in 2002. It was Dominik Hasek's stick measurement. Somewhere along the way, Colorado's coach, Bob Hartley, received a Dominik Hasek stick. We were getting ready for Game 6, facing elimination, and someone from the Colorado side tipped off our training staff about a possibility of a stick measurement. Because they had one of Dom's sticks, Colorado was convinced that Hasek used an illegal goaltender's stick. We were told to make sure Hasek had a legal stick because, at a crucial point in the game, Hartley was probably going to ask for a stick measurement. As things would be, Dominik received a brand new shipment of sticks that particular morning for that evening's game. Colorado did call for a stick measurement right after they had just gone on the power play. The stick was legal, we ended up winning the game, and the rest is history.

All of us heard about the possible stick measurement. We just didn't know for sure if it was going to happen. When it did happen, our guys were indignant. If you have to do that to win, well, let's just say, if anybody was not in tune with what was going on, this helped motivate the team for the rest of the game and obviously the rest of the series. It worked for us.

What it means to be a Red Wing is more than what meets the eye. You become a part of what's important to so many people in this state, to represent the team and what they believe in. It was a great honor to put the sweater on and play for them, and to coach and be involved with the franchise for as long as I have been. The people who make the team work are also the fans and it's an incredible place to be involved in hockey.

Dave Lewis's Career Highlights

* ★ Winning the '97 Stanley Cup.

* ★ Winning the '98 Stanley Cup.

* ★ Winning the '02 Stanley Cup.

* ★ Playing in his 1,000th game as a Red Wing.

* ★ Being named head coach of the Detroit Red Wings.

JIM NILL

RIGHT WING

1987–1990

JACQUES DEMERS'S KNACK AS A COACH was that he could make the little guy feel like superman. He was a great motivator.

We had a bunch of hard-working muckers and grinders on those teams in the 1980s. For guys like Tim Higgins and myself, Demers would make us feel very important to the team. He would put us in situations in which we didn't think we would be. He would throw us out on the power play. He knew how to build us up. We would go through the wall for him. He was a player's coach.

The way he coached, we started to believe in ourselves. The franchise had some tough times and then suddenly we had some playoff success. The year we played Edmonton in the Campbell Conference Finals, I thought we could have beat them. In the first two games in Detroit, we were all over them. We were a hard team to play against.

That was the time that Stevie Yzerman was starting to take over. He had been named captain and he was becoming a 50-goal scorer. Gerard Gallant was chipping in. The veterans we had on the team were veterans who already had known success. They brought that to the team. Many players contributed. Doug Halward. Dave Barr. Mike O'Connell was a very smart defenseman. He wasn't a physical guy but he always had the puck. He would go into the corner and find a way to get the puck. He was a steady guy. Mel

190

As a player, Jim Nill was a third-line contributor. But as an NHL executive, Nill is a premium performer. Now serving as the Detroit Red Wings assistant general manager, Nill is highly regarded for his ability to scout and assist in the management of the team. He is a valuable right-hand man to general manager Ken Holland.

Bridgman had come from Philadelphia where he had a lot of success. These guys would say, "This is the way we do it and let's go do it."

We had a bunch of guys who had been assistant captains or captains. It was a good relationship between Steve and the veterans. He needed some help, but other players didn't overstep their bounds. They let Steve grow into the role. He was respectful enough of veterans that when Harold Snepsts talked, he would back him. He didn't have the attitude like, "This is my team and let me do all the talking." I think he's still the same way in the dressing room today. If Brendan Shanahan stands up and wants to talk, Steve is fine with that. Steve is a quiet leader. Most of what he did was on the ice. But when he did speak, you knew it was something that should be listened to.

We had some funny moments with Jacques. He liked to have a big impact. Once, when we were struggling in a game, just not playing well, Jacques started talking to us. We were paying attention, but maybe not paying attention the way we should. There was a big table in the middle of the room for the tape, and Jacques grabbed a goalie stick and slammed it down on that table. But it didn't break. The guys in the room went from wondering what was going to happen to chuckling under their breath. Then, goalie Glen Hanlon broke the ice by grabbing another stick and giving it to Jacques. "Maybe this one will break," Hanlon said.

There was another time when Jacques was mad at us. He was fuming and he grabbed a stool. Our trainer's room had glass in front of it and he wanted to make a point. So he threw a stool against the glass. But it didn't break. He just kind of turned around and walked out. Like I said, he was a motivator.

We had some characters on the team, like Petr Klima. He could win a game for you, or he could lose a game for you.

We had quite a crew back then. We weren't the choir boys. There was always something going on. We played hard on and off the ice. You never knew what was going to happen around our team. We had a colorful team. Doug Halward was a team joker. If you fell asleep on a plane, your tie would get cut. You would get shaving cream in your hair. We went to Quebec where they had wooden floors, and someone hammered a rookie's shoes into the floor.

Harold Snepsts was a popular player. Back then, he had no helmet. He was very visible and he played hard. He was a big guy. He was tough. When we played in Chicago, he would battle Al Secord in front of the net. He was a tough guy to play against. Back then, there weren't too many guys bigger than Harold.

I had been on teams where I had to fill that role. And I remember going into Chicago. Chicago Stadium was a tough place to play. I remember thinking, *I had better get ready.* All of a sudden, I look and there's Bob Probert pushing around one guy and Kocur is with another guy. And I'm thinking, *Is this ever nice. I don't have to worry about it anymore.* In the past, I might have had to be a protector, but not with Probert and Kocur on the team. But if someone got in trouble, Probie and Kocur both knew that Doug Halward or Jim Nill would be in there to help them. We were a tough, tough team.

We used it to our advantage. There would be a face-off by the bench, and the two wingers would be lined up, and Probie would be telling the guy on the other team, "Hey, I'm going to get you the next shift." I don't care who you were, if you heard Probie say that, you couldn't be sure what was going to go on.

Probie was a really good player. He turned himself into a good player. He started to make room for himself, and he turned himself into a complete player. He could score goals. He was a valuable player.

Guys would fight Probie, but no one wanted to fight Joey Kocur because, if he hit you, you were done. I remember on Long Island, Kocur fought Brad Dalgarno, and it was unbelievable how he hurt him. [Dalgarno suffered a fractured orbital bone and then retired the following season, although he did come back.] The other scary fight he had was against Jim Kyte. There was probably five minutes left when they carried Kyte off, and I remember the rink went quiet. It was scary. I remember players on both teams just went back on the ice and said, "Let's get this game over with."

There was another time in Chicago. Probie walked Behn Wilson around the ice. It was like Probie was saying to the Chicago, "This is your tough guy that I'm doing this to." He wore out Wilson, and that's what Probie could do. If a fight went on an hour, he would still be going.

We had other tough guys. Dave Barr was tough. Gerard Gallant was tough for his size. Lee Norwood was tough. Not everyone was a heavyweight, but we were like a pack of wolves coming at you. And Gerard was chirping all the time. I remember playing against him, and he would be chirping. I would look and he would have Bob Probert standing next to him. I would say, "Get Bob Probert away from you and then chirp." I still kid him about that.

Probert didn't go looking for a fight until things started to happen, and then he would say "Okay, you guys want to do this." Then, lookout!

I remember a fight with Gary Nylund when Probie was losing. Nylund was a big guy in Chicago and was starting to beat Probie. They were going at it. The funny thing was that if Probie was fighting and his opponent hit his helmet and knocked it a little crooked, it would bother him. It was like he wasn't comfortable. And it would get him more involved in the fight. Probie would hold the guy back and straighten up his helmet. That's what happened against Nylund. He straightened up his helmet and then gave him an undercut that brought Nylund to his knees.

Guys would think they had to go hard early against Probie and he might still be sleeping, but Probie could go forever. The guy would just be worn out, and Probie would just be getting warmed up.

We were a difficult team to play against, and I think Jacques got all that he could out of us. Stevie was just starting to come into his own. Gallant was good. He was very deceptive. He could really shoot a puck and he knew where to find the holes. I think one thing that you could say about us is that we played hard.

It was an honor to play for an Original Six team and it's still an honor to be associated with the team. The Ilitch family treats everyone first-class. I know that Jimmy Devellano, Kenny Holland, and myself take pride that we are not big ego guys. We know that this organization is about team success. We feel like we built a team the right way.

Jim Nill's Career Highlights

* Playing for the 1980 Canadian Olympic Team. Although he's a proud Canadian, he is happy that the Americans won the gold medal. "I might not have the job I have today if the Americans hadn't won," Nill said. "There wasn't much interest in hockey in the States before they won the gold medal."

* Scoring a goal and getting three assists in his first game for the Red Wings. It was against the New York Rangers in Madison Square Garden.

* Playing for Vancouver in the 1982 Stanley Cup Finals.

* Playing for the Red Wings in back-to-back conference finals.

* Serving as the Red Wings assistant general manager today.

TIM CHEVELDAE

GOALTENDER

1988–1994

MY FIRST YEAR IN ADIRONDACK, I received a call from the Red Wings trainer around 1:00 in the afternoon. Greg Stefan had hurt his back, and the team needed me to come in and back up Glen Hanlon for that evening's game. He said the flight left at 2:00 from Albany, and anyone that knows the geographical region of upstate New York knows that it's at least 45 minutes to an hour drive from Glen Falls to Albany. With everything I had to do, grabbing my bag, my clothes, and getting my ticket—I missed that 2:00 flight. I phoned the trainer, told him the situation, and he said that there was a 6:15 flight from Albany to Detroit. The flight is about an hour and 15 minutes, and from Metro Airport to Joe Louis is about a 35-minute drive. The game started at 7:30, so the plan was to have some police officers meet me at the gate and rush me to Joe Louis Arena in a police car. The police chief heard this and thought of a quicker way for me to get there. The police airport was right beside Metro Airport, and they could put me on a police helicopter, so that's what they did. They flew me in and we landed on top of Cobo Hall. The Red Wings assistant trainer met me on top of the roof. We ran down to Joe Louis Arena and I got dressed in between the second and third period. That was my first introduction to the NHL.

I missed the first two periods of the game and Detroit had no back-up goalie until I arrived. I heard that if Glen Hanlon would have gotten hurt, the guy who was next in line was the team psychologist who used to play goalie but hadn't played in 20 years. That would have been an interesting situation if Glen had gone down. I think the Red Wings may have forced him to play even if he had a broken leg.

The second time I was brought up, the Red Wings were on their western Canada road trip that they always started out the year with, playing Calgary, Edmonton, and Vancouver. They played their first game in Calgary, lost 10–7, and, again, Greg Stefan hurt his back. That happened on a Thursday and they played Saturday in Vancouver. I flew from Albany to Chicago to Vancouver on Friday. I arrived at the Vancouver airport, got off the plane, and picked up all my baggage, except my goalie equipment didn't show up. I talked to the people at the airline and they said it would be delivered to the rink the next day and everything would be fine. I went to the rink the next day and it wasn't there. I was supposed to play that night against the Canucks! It got closer and closer to game time, and Jacques Demers, being very emotional, is freaking out and about to fire the trainer for this. It's about 20 minutes before the warm-up and I was getting dressed in Greg Stefan's equipment because I have no other equipment. The situation arose that Glen Hanlon had to play. My equipment showed up 10 minutes into the warm-up, but Glen played the whole game. That was my second introduction to the NHL.

195

It was a whirlwind my first two trips up to the Red Wings. I remember flying in the helicopter, thinking, "Oh, my God!" I had 8 million different emotions running through my mind. And then walking into the dressing room and seeing Steve Yzerman, Mike O'Connell, and all these people there—that was my first time in a NHL dressing room and there was no warm-up, you just get off a helicopter and sat on a bench—cold, stiff, and excited. I just prayed, "Okay, Glennie, please don't get hurt! Please don't get hurt, whatever you do!" It was a pretty amazing experience.

Going into the locker room for the first time, you just walk in, look around, but you don't want to stare. You feel like a really little kid who just walks into a room with a whole bunch of new people and stares down at the floor, looking at his feet. You wouldn't say a word; you're like a church mouse. The guys were great, though, and there were a few jokes and laughter between the periods. My heart was racing. You would think that you would enjoy this moment, but there's so much happening. Everything seemed to go by so fast and so quick that you couldn't really capture the moment 'til maybe two weeks down the road, when you thought about the situation you were in.

I'm not really sure how the expectation for the Red Wings goalie position started, but somehow it started to snowball and got bigger and bigger becoming the en vogue thing to talk about in the media. It was like the magnifying glass had been turned up to five or six times the effect on the goaltending in Detroit. In the media, you're going to talk about what fans want to talk about; and it became the popular thing to call a radio show and bitch about the goaltender. The media picked up on it and ran with it. Now it has pretty deep roots, and I don't know if it's ever going to change in Detroit for the goaltenders. You're underneath the spotlight and people have grown up with it over the last 10 to 20 years. It's instilled that people are going to wait for something bad to happen and then say, "Oh, here we go again with Detroit goaltending!"

Momentum is a big thing. People talk about momentum in sports, but momentum in the media is also big. If you're an athlete and you play poorly, I don't think you mind the criticism. The tough part for anyone, if you're an athlete or just a human being, you just want to start with a clean glass every game. And it seemed to become that if you gave up a questionable goal, you were never given the benefit of the doubt; it was automatically a bad goal. That was tough. I've heard the term before "Being Cheveldaed" and I think of the movie *King Pin* where the guy got "Munsoned." I don't know if that's a good or bad thing to be associated with.

When I look at it, though, it was something I could have handled better. It affected my play and was certainly a tough situation, but I didn't deal with it well. I let it effect me too much. I've learned now that you only have a certain amount of energy, of focus, and you have to focus that energy on things you can control—like becoming a better goalie, or mentally stronger, or more physically fit. If you focus that energy on something you have no control over, then your game is going to slip. That is what happened to me. If I had done things differently, things might have been different.

The way it negatively affected me was playing at home the last few years, I had better records on the road. If you're .500 on the road, that's pretty impressive. At home, when you start to let in questionable goals, or even if you let in two of the greatest goals in the world in the first 10 minutes, the crowd would be on you. It affected me because I got tight. I would think, "Oh, no! Here we go again." I had to answer all the media questions after every game, no matter how I played. Once I lost my focus, I made a bad situation into a worse situation. I didn't really say much at the time, but every

Tim Cheveldae won 128 games in Detroit to rank fifth on the team's all-time goaltender wins list. He averaged 34 wins per season between 1990 and 1993. He won 38 games for the Red Wings in 1991–1992 and was named to play in the National Hockey League All-Star Game.

once in awhile I needed to say, "Hey, I didn't play that bad today. That game two weeks ago, yeah, I was horrible and I'll take whatever blame I deserve. But today, I've been treated unfairly and, if you look at those goals on the tape, they were all good goals." I needed to do that every once in a while to get it off my chest. You don't want to do that all the time, but there were situations where I was blamed for something and I didn't deserve it. Those are the situations where I should have stuck up for myself.

During the time when the fans were really on me in Detroit, Monica Seles got stabbed by that deranged fan. Of course the media came to me, wanting my reaction. When I got home, I was telling my wife about it and, while chuckling, asked her, "Why is the media talking to me about this?" And she asked, "Are you concerned about a fan attacking you?" I sort of found it amusing that they weren't talking to Steve Yzerman or anyone else in the dressing room, they were only talking to me about this situation. I thought, "Are you trying to tell me something? Should I be concerned about that?"

Losing to Toronto in 7 games in the 1993 playoffs was a huge disappointment because we had a really good hockey club and I didn't play as well as I would have liked. We got a lot of criticism for that series and the following year we brought in Scotty Bowman. We wanted the new season to be a fresh start to regain our confidence and the fans' confidence. I got hurt and missed the first six weeks of the year. When I came back from my injury, I was playing pretty well.

We were playing the New York Rangers and were up 3–1 in the third period, and Kevin Lowe took a slap shot from the blue line. I was partially screened on it and it went in. To the general public's eye, it looked like a bad goal because it was from far out. The crowd right then got all over me. It got so bad that five minutes later, Scotty Bowman pulled me and put Chris Osgood in. There was the mock cheer and everyone in the crowd was happy to see Ozzie in. I had played well up until that point and with that one mishap, whether it was my fault or not, I knew then that the fans, or certain people, were waiting for something bad to happen. I realized that they were probably going to have to make a change, just for the fact that you want your crowd to cheer your hockey club on and be supportive and behind you. If they're booing your hometown goaltender, that's going to affect your whole hockey club. I remember during that year, when we skated onto the ice they always announced the starting lineup. The booing had gotten so bad that they started to announce the staring lineup before we got on the ice. That's when I knew that my days were numbered in Detroit.

Scotty Bowman, having won nine Stanley Cups, has a great feel for things. I think that is what separates a good coach from a great coach, having a "feel" for things that aren't in any manual—whether you should kick a guy in the ass or pat him on the back. Scotty seemed to know that there was enough pressure on the goaltenders here and he didn't have to put any more pressure on us, he tried to deflect the pressure instead. He had a great feel for that situation. Professional athletes do have some intelligence, and you know when a coach is throwing you underneath a bus and making you the martyr or the scapegoat. You also know when a coach is deflecting for you.

I was disappointed with what happened to my career in Detroit because we had a really good hockey club and were right on the cusp. I think it was two years after I got traded when the Wings played in the Stanley Cup Finals and eventually won a Stanley Cup.

I was part of a team that finished last in the regular season and within three to four years was getting over 100 points and winning the division. We were an extremely close team. When you get to the NHL, everyone's goal is to win a Stanley Cup. Everyone in the Red Wings organization felt that we were very close and very capable, so to all of a sudden see your career start to fade out was tough.

I have nothing but fond memories of Detroit. My son was actually born in Detroit, so that's a big tie there. Everything about Detroit is a positive—I love the city. In Saskatchewan, they look at you like you have six heads when you say this, but in a perfect world I would have no problem going back and living in Detroit. There were some negatives, but there were way more positives that came out of living and playing in Detroit.

Being a Red Wing meant that you were part of a great family with a large amount of tradition. The only thing that they accept is winning Stanley Cups. If you become a Detroit Red Wing, you can have 50-goal seasons, win Vezina Trophies, have 120 points, you will still be judged on whether you hold that Stanley Cup over your head. If you talk to any player, now or in the past, they will all say that the expectations are very high and that's the way it should be. Red Wings fans are very passionate and they love the game of hockey very much. So when you're a Red Wing you're coming to a very passionate state that expects a lot.

Tim Cheveldae's Career Highlights

* Going from the team that didn't make the playoffs to a team that was considered a Stanley Cup contender.

* Playing in the All-Star Game in 1992.

* Coming back from being down three games to one against Minnesota in the first round of the 1992 playoffs.

* Over a combination of three seasons, having the most victories of any goalie in the NHL. "One year I tied Kirk McLean for the most wins," Cheveldae said.

* Playing more than 60 games a year for three consecutive years.

PAUL MacLEAN

RIGHT WING

1988–1989

Was I hoping to play with Steve Yzerman when I came to Detroit? Yes, but I didn't expect it by any means. I don't recall whether it was the first day of training camp, but somehow I ended up playing with Stevie and Gerard Gallant. Our line ended up being very good.

I knew Yzerman was a good player. That's one reason why I wasn't completely disappointed when I was traded. I played with Dale Hawerchuk in Winnipeg. We had a lot of success in the seven years I was there. We had tremendous chemistry. That was something that I didn't want to voluntarily give up. But having the opportunity to play with Stevie made it easier to accept. Everyone knew that Stevie was a tremendously talented player. Anyone who had the chance to play with him had to make sure that he complemented his style. You had to allow him to become the player he could be.

I was established in the league when I came to Detroit. I wasn't going to change my game. I was a player who played in the front of the net and dug pucks out of the corner. I was able to get open and shoot pucks in the net when people passed to me. Gerard Gallant was also a good shooter. He was a hard-nosed guy to play against. Stevie was blossoming as a playmaker and a dominant player in the middle.

Maybe having me there gave them a little bit more of a chance to relax and play their game. Maybe I took pressure off them. It ended up being a

An Antigonish, Nova Scotia, native, Paul MacLean played one season for the Red Wings, scoring 36 goals and adding 35 assists for 71 points, plus 118 penalty minutes, in the 1988–1989 season. Today, he is a Red Wings assistant coach under Mike Babcock.

good line with a playmaker and a couple of shooters who weren't afraid to get their noses dirty. And Stevie wasn't afraid to get his nose dirty, either.

When you play as a line you tend to talk to one another a lot about who is going to go where. The communication between linemates is important. It goes beyond the coaching staff. The line gets together to talk about what we want to do. I'm not going to say I was the father figure. I was the oldest one out of the bunch. I had the seniority, but Stevie was a very, very gifted player.

Steve Yzerman saw everything. When you start to play with somebody and they find you when you don't expect them to find you, then you say, "Wow, that's a good player. He just knows I'm here." That was Steve.

I didn't know a trade was in the works until Winnipeg general manager John Ferguson was offering me U.S. money on a contract. At the time, players on Canadian teams were paid Canadian money, and when you were on a U.S. team, you were paid U.S. funds.

"What's going on?" I asked. "Why are you offering me U.S. money?"

He told me that he had a trade in place based on me signing a contract. Since the trade was going to be done, I wanted to know what team. I wanted the opportunity to negotiate with that team. He told me it was the Red Wings. I was excited. The Red Wings were an Original Six team and I felt they were as good as the Jets. It was going to be a good situation for me.

I was excited about the trade because the team was up and coming. They had lost to Edmonton in the Campbell Conference Finals. I had played against the Edmonton Oilers for seven years and I had been frustrated against them, and here was a team that was getting them in the conference final. In Winnipeg, I always got them in the first round of the playoffs.

I felt Detroit was a place to continue my career and have more success. Maybe I could move forward playing in the Norris Division with the hope of winning the Stanley Cup. It seemed like the Smythe Division, where Calgary and Edmonton resided, seemed like a more difficult way to go.

Jacques Demers was refreshing. Jacques was all about winning. He wanted to make sure his best players had the opportunity to win that game for him. That's not true of all coaches, even today. He had plenty of energy as a head coach. I didn't always agree with everything he said or all of the decisions he made as the year went on. But at the same time, he was the head coach and I was there to play and play as hard as I could.

Coming out for warm-up in Joe Louis was a totally different atmosphere. As much as you see Winnipeg, Edmonton, Calgary, Toronto, Montreal, and

Ottawa as hockey towns in Canada because they live and breathe hockey, I think they do that here in Detroit, too. Truthfully, Detroit is close enough to Canada to be considered a Canadian franchise. The fans are very rabid; it's really exciting to be a Red Wing and step on the ice for warm-up.

I remember specifically the night Bob Probert came back from one of his mishaps and he was worried the fans were going to boo him going out for warm-up. I said, "Ah, Probie, you'll be okay, you'll be okay. They're going to love you. They're going to love you."

During the warm-up, he got a standing ovation, and there aren't a lot of places where that would happen.

The Red Wings are an Original Six franchise, and the fan-base goes back generations. I think, even through the hard times they had, those generations of fans supported iconic figures such as Gordie Howe, Alex Delvecchio, and Red Kelly. The rink is full of pictures of so many iconic players they had. I think somewhere along the line Bob Probert and Joe Kocur, at a time when the team needed some more iconic figures, were like that.

It meant everything to be a Red Wing. At that time, I appreciated the opportunity to play for an Original Six team and play in the same sweater that Gordie Howe, Ted Lindsay, and Alex Delvecchio wore when I was a kid. It was one of the best years I've had in the NHL.

I think it's the same coming back as a coach, but it's different. The expectation levels were just starting to get high in 1988–1989, and now the expectation levels are very high. This is a good place to be. You're an elite team in the National Hockey League and you're expected to win. That's the situation you want to be in.

Paul MacLean's Career Highlights

* Playing with Steve Yzerman and Gerard Gallant on the highest-scoring line in Detroit history. The trio amassed 140 goals with 319 points to break the Red Wings' line record previously owned by the Production Line.

* Playing in the 1985 NHL All-Star Game.

* Averaging 35 goals per season when he played the full season.

* Scoring 40 goals three times while playing with Dale Hawerchuk in Winnipeg.

* Now serving as an assistant coach for the Detroit Red Wings.

The
NINETIES

MARTIN LAPOINTE
RIGHT WING
1991–2001

ITHOUGHT I WAS GOING TO WINNIPEG. The Jets had told me that if I was available that they were going to pick me, but they switched at the last minute and chose Aaron Ward. I knew I had a good interview with Bryan Murray, and the Red Wings chose me with the number 10 pick overall. Getting the chance to play with Steve Yzerman and all the great names that were on the Red Wings at the time was an honor that I will always remember.

In juniors I was a goal scorer, and after I signed with the Wings and received my signing bonus, I showed up at camp 20 pounds overweight. Even though it was my first training camp, I thought I would make the team without any problems. However, when Bryan Murray looked at my weigh-in and saw that I was 20 pounds overweight, he sat me down for a meeting immediately. He told me, "You fat f*ck, you thought you had it made!" After that first training camp, where I wasn't in the best of shape, I realized that this was not the little leagues anymore. This was the big time, and all the players were good. I needed to get my ass in gear.

After playing in the first four games in Detroit, I was sent back down to my junior team. Back in juniors, I knew I needed to change my style to be able to stay in the big leagues. I decided to go out there and hit everything in sight. If I had to fight, I would fight. That's how it all started—after that meeting with Bryan Murray, I changed my style and became what I am today.

Lapointe was the Detroit Red Wings' first-round pick (10th overall) in the 1991 NHL Entry Draft.

When you make the transition to the NHL, some kids get it and some kids don't. You either think that you can make it playing like you did in juniors or you see that you have to change. Part of changing as a hockey player is ego. You have to let go of thinking you'll score every night. I understood that because I wanted to make the NHL so badly. I had to be gritty and hard-nosed and go all out every night. I couldn't take an easy night because there could be someone else taking my place.

Realistically, with all the great players the Wings had, I knew it would be tough for me to make the team. But it drove me to push harder and challenge myself. I wasn't going to be on the first two lines, but I wanted to try to stick around to play on the fourth line. I needed to be grittier because the team had so much talent.

As a first-round draft pick and number 10 overall, you're going to feel some pressure. I felt that pressure. I felt the need to score goals. But at the same time, we had such a good team that the organization could afford to have some patience with me. They took me aside and told me that I didn't have to score 25 or 30 goals. I just had to be a hard-nosed player and just let things happen. I started on the fourth line and was Scotty Bowman's whipping boy for a long time. Scotty built my character, and that's why I'm the player I am today—because of Scotty Bowman.

I wasn't the only guy that Scotty Bowman was hard on. Scotty knows every player so well, and he knew how much he could put on me. He knew how to push my buttons so that the next game I would play more fired up, I would give more. That's how he made me better. I wouldn't snap back at him, instead, I would try my best in practice to show him I wasn't so bad, that I could do stuff. That's what a whipping boy is to Scotty—a player he pushes to get a response from. That's how he was able to get results from me.

In 1994 it was difficult for me to start the season in Adirondack because I had played 50 games for the Red Wings the year before. You never want to go back to the minors after that. Just before I went back down, I went to go visit my parents and I told my mom that I didn't know if I could do this anymore. It was a pretty low time for me. My dad and I didn't talk that much. He had pushed me a lot in my young career but by this point in my life it was up to me, not up to him. I basically told him, "Thanks for what you did for me before, but I'll find my own wings now." I remember telling my mom, though, "I don't know if I can do this. I'm taking a step back now. I just want to quit and work a 9:00 to 5:00 job." She told me, "You know, Marty, you just have to go down and work hard and you'll be called back up." Sure enough, I did that and was called up.

To play on a line with Igor Larionov and Brendan Shanahan—I couldn't have asked for anything more. Igor loved to pass the puck; he could care less if he scored. And Shanny, if you give him the puck it would wind up in the net. It was an easy job for me on that line. I knew I would go up and down the wing. If I gave it to Igor he would either give it back to me or make a play. Or I would give it to Shanny and he would score. I'll remember playing on that line for the rest of my days. Larionov made that line. They say he's the "Russian Wayne Gretzky," and he is! They don't call him "the Professor" for nothing. Playing with those two players made my career and is the reason I was fortunate enough to make a lot of money in this league.

Shanny has also been a physical presence for quite some time in the league and he still does it now even when he doesn't have to. Playing with him took some pressure off of me and let me play more instead of always thinking, *If somebody hits that guy I have to go.* It was nice to play more relaxed and know that Brendan could take care of himself, and if somebody hit Igor that there would be two of us in there. Then it would be rock-paper-scissors between me and Shanny for who takes care of the situation.

While Shanahan was still in St. Louis, he went to hit Draper, and Draper stood there and challenged him. The problem was that I knew that Drapes wasn't going to do anything, so I had to go in there for him. All I could think of was, *Wow, I'm going to fight Brendan Shanahan right now!* I didn't feel that good about it at the time. We started grabbing each other and he started switching arms on me. I felt my two arms closing in on each other and I knew that I was in deep trouble! I just started throwing punches and it turned out to be a great fight, but Shanahan was really tough back then, and I kept thinking to myself, *I'm in deep shit here!*

Once Shanny became a Red Wing, he was my roommate, and fighting him was something we talked about. I would ask Shanny, "Remember the time I fought you in St. Louis?" He would say, "Yeah." I would tell him how I felt my arms squeeze together and thought I was going to be pummeled. He would just start laughing and say, "I know, you were a feisty little f*cker!" It was funny talking with him about that as teammates.

I'll never forget when we had the great season in 1995 and lost against New Jersey in the Stanley Cup Finals. We had an especially hard time playing in their building because they played the trap. They played so well defensively that we couldn't get anything going. After we got swept in that series, I asked Yzerman what happened. Steve turned to me and said, "Marty, I'm so sick of losing right now. It's sick." He had been in Detroit for over 10 years, so it was mind-boggling to me that Steve Yzerman had a chance to win a Stanley Cup and we got swept! All I could do was wonder if we would ever get back to that point again. We did get back to the Stanley Cup, but I'll still never forget the words of Steve Yzerman after that first chance.

Getting swept in the Stanley Cup Finals, you might as well have lost in the first round. We had no chance in those four games. And the next year, in 1996, we lost to Colorado in the conference finals and I thought, *Wow, what the f*ck is going on here?* We had such a good team that year! Looking back, I think losing made us a better team. We knew what it took to get to the next level. The next year we were able to do it and that felt so good.

Having to deal with the limo accident right after that 1997 Stanley Cup win was devastating. I can still vividly recall that night. It was around 11:00 P.M. and I was getting ready for bed. All of a sudden I got a phone call, and the person on the phone said, "Someone's been in a car accident." I couldn't understand. I asked, "What do you mean a car accident?" They told me there had been a limo accident and when I asked who, they said it was Sergei, Slava, and Vladdy. They also said it was pretty bad, so I went to the hospital. It took a while for what had happened to sink in, until I arrived at the hospital. Vladdy was such a big part of the Red Wings team, as was Slava Fetisov, who was lucky because he didn't get the worst of it like the other two. It was a very sad day. The saddest thing about that is they did the right thing—getting a limo in case they drank too much.

That accident was definitely a motivation point for the next year—we wanted to win it again for Vladdy! When Konstantinov showed up in Washington during the Stanley Cup Finals, he got a standing ovation. The team looked around the arena at that time and knew we had to win it for him. Vladdy had given so much for our team and now he couldn't even walk. I believe that he knew what was going on, but you had to wonder. He was a big inspiration for us to win that second Stanley Cup. What happened to him was terrible, but if it hadn't, I'm not sure that we would have been able to win two Stanley Cups in a row.

In the 1998 Stanley Cup Finals, we were in overtime against the Capitals in Game 2. Our focus was keeping the lines rolling because it was such a long game. Scotty seemed to have a feeling that the young guys would have more energy. I'm not sure if we did or not, but it seemed that all the kids were flying in that game. At the same time, we were all scared of losing so we would do anything not to lose that game. There was a battle at the boards for the puck, and I saw Draper coming from the back of the net to in front of it. I can remember seeing his stick, and his face was all red because it was overtime and we were all so tired. I shot the puck toward the net, and he put his stick down and deflected it in. That was a great, great moment. We came back in that game and won 5–4.

Stanley Cup teams are all about the guys who aren't supposed to score stepping up. You know the first two lines will rack up points, but when the unexpected happens, that's the bonus, that's what hurts the other team.

When I was leaving Detroit, I talked to Ken Holland on the phone. I was crying on my end of the line. I told him, "I have to do this. I have to go to Boston." Holland told me, "You know, Marty, we had great moments together and along the road we may see each other again." I was balling like a kid! I was going to turn the page on 10 years of my life. That was one of the more difficult times in my life, saying good-bye to the Red Wings. Kenny Holland really reassured me that I was doing the right thing because I had a family. He told me that it was just business and I had to think of myself first.

It was hard—I'll always be a Red Wing. Every time I go back to Detroit, I get goose bumps. I remember the first time I had to go back and play against the Red Wings at Joe Louis Arena. It was a preseason game, and I kept thinking that I was on the wrong bench. It was the weirdest feeling, here I was wearing a black jersey and they were wearing white. I didn't feel like I belonged on the opponent's side, I belonged on the Red Wings side. I'll always remember that feeling.

The Detroit Red Wings have always been great to me. From the Ilitches having parties at the end of the year and treating me like one of their sons to Bryan Murray and Ken Holland. As general mangers, they were always honest and fair. Scotty Bowman really made me as a player and he still calls me during the summer. I always marvel that Scotty Bowman takes the time to still call Martin Lapointe—who the heck is Martin Lapointe? But Scotty will just call me to talk about anything and everything; sometimes I think I should record it for prosperity.

Martin Lapointe's Career Highlights
★ Winning his first Stanley Cup.
★ Winning his second Stanley Cup.
★ Sitting beside Steve Yzerman during his first training camp.
★ Steve Yzerman telling him, "I'm sick of losing," after the team lost to New Jersey in its first attempt at a Stanley Cup.
★ Appearing in the starting lineup for a playoff game—his fifth game ever for the Red Wings—against the Chicago Blackhawks. "I was shaking in my skates," Lapointe said.

NICKLAS LIDSTROM

DEFENSEMAN
1991–Present

IT WAS IN THE MID- TO LATE-1980S that you started to see a lot more NHL scouts in Sweden. Back then, the Wings had one scout who covered all of Europe, including the Czech Republic and Russia. Now they have a guy in every country. Christer Rockstrom was that scout for the Red Wings. He worked under Neil Smith, who was the head scout at the time. He was the guy who followed me and talked to me before I was drafted. He told me about the Wings' interest.

No one really noticed me when I was 18 because I was still playing for the junior national team in Sweden, so I didn't get picked that summer in the draft. Because I didn't get picked then, I had to go in the top three rounds the next year to be drafted. I was still developing at 18 and thinking about playing for the big national team in Sweden. I was so young that it didn't really bother me that I wasn't drafted into the NHL. My goal was still to play for the national team.

I was supposed to come to the U.S.A. for the draft. But Christer told me that the Red Wings didn't want me to be at the draft because other teams would see that I was over here and they might take me. He told me to stay home and wait by the phone. I remember getting the phone call on Saturday night over in Sweden that I had been drafted. I talked to Christer and a few of the Red Wings people. At age 19, I had been drafted by the Detroit Red Wings.

When I came to my first training camp with Detroit, Johan Garpenlov was there. Johan was Swedish and helped me out, taking me under his wing. He helped me get an apartment and with everything outside of hockey. I played with Brad McCrimmon as my defensive partner pretty much every game that season, and that helped, too. He was a steady, stay-at-home defenseman but would join the rush and was part of the power play. Having Garpenlov and McCrimmon my first season helped me a lot.

Vladimir Konstantinov and I were drafted the same year, and we came to the Red Wings at the right time. It was a transition from having an older defense to trying to get a little bit younger, so we got the opportunity to play a lot. The organization was also looking at getting more Europeans over here to play. Vladdy didn't speak a lick of English when he first came to the team; so even though it was both of our first years, we didn't really spend much time together. Sergei Fedorov helped take care of Vladdy that year, and I had Garpenlov. Vladdy and I got to know each other better and better as the years went by, even though it took us a few years to gel.

It helped me a lot to be able to come to the Red Wings locker room and know how to speak English. I could pretty much take care of myself. I could order food at restaurants and set up a bank account. I could do all the things that were necessary to do. It took me a while to get used to the on-the-ice play. The tempo was higher, and with the smaller rink everything happened faster. It took a little time to get used to that. That's why playing with Brad McCrimmon and having the same partner my first year helped me so much.

During my second year, Paul Coffey came to the Red Wings, and he and I played together for 3½ to 4 years. I would play with Vladdy off and on, as well; we would kill penalties together or play in the last minute of the game together.

McCrimmon was my first partner and since he was a steady, stay-at-home defenseman, he would let me get up in the rush and would stay back and cover for me. When I played with Paul Coffey, it was a little bit different. I was playing on the right side and he was a great offensive defenseman, so he would join the rush a lot more than I did and I would sit back. I learned a lot from Coffey and the way he would carry the puck up the ice, the way he was skating, the way he saw the ice. Larry Murphy was my next partner, and I thought we were a great fit together. He wasn't the quickest skater out there, but he was for sure one of the smartest. It was fun playing with Murph. He

When Nicklas Lidstrom won the James Norris Trophy as the league's top defenseman three years in a row, from 2001 to 2003, he was the first to accomplish that feat since the great Bobby Orr. In 2002 Lidstrom became the first European player ever to win the Conn Smythe Trophy.

was always very patient with the puck and would hang onto it, waiting for players to get open or for me to get open. We were a great combination.

My mix of defensive partners benefited me a lot because, early on with McCrimmon, I was seen as an offensive-minded defenseman who could join the rush. Then all of the sudden I played with Coffey and he was up the ice most of the night, forcing me to stay back more. That taught me how to play defense better and read different situations when your partner is up the ice. Each of my defensive partners has influenced my game and I'm extremely grateful to them.

Slapshots, taking one-timers, and keeping the puck in on the blue line are skills I have worked on since I was 16 years old as a junior player. I just developed a sense of playing my position the right way. Dave Lewis taught me that my first season with the Red Wings, that you were better off playing your position right, than being out of position and trying to hook or slow a player down. That was something that I picked up on early, that being in the right position was going to help you out a lot. Anticipating plays is a big part of it as well. To be able to see things develop before they really happen is a significant part of my game.

I rely more on instinct and reading the play that's going to develop than studying players. Some of the players, you know what they have a tendency of doing, but most of the time it's more about reading the plays.

Closing the gap is the key to going up against another team's best player. Don't give him time with the puck, force him to do something. He'll have to be creative to make plays. When you're closing the gap, you can't get beaten when you're going at the guy. You have to go up there and then back off at the same speed he's going—so you're closing the gap and staying with him. That comes back to playing your position right. If you're too close to him, he's going to beat you right away. If you give him time, he's going to make a play. That is the fine line of getting up there and closing the gap on a player.

The toughest players to match up against are the guys who are big and strong with speed. Speed is probably the key. Playing against someone with good speed, I find, is always the toughest. Jaromir Jagr is really tough; he has the size, the reach, and he's fast. He's probably one of the toughest players to try and defend. Peter Forsberg is the same way, he's great at protecting the puck and, if you give him time, he's going to make a play. If you go at him, he might make you look like a fool.

Scotty Bowman seemed to embrace the European hockey players. He was the one to put the Russian Five together, and when they were on the ice you saw a different type of hockey. It was more of the European style of hanging onto the puck and making plays. Scotty was probably one of the first coaches to see that develop. When you have the type of team that we had, you could throw out the Grind Line or the Russian Five—that's a big difference having Maltby, Kocur, and Draper out there versus the Russian Five. Scotty had a good sense of seeing the different looks you could put out on a team like we had.

The Stanley Cup that we won in 1997 had a bit to do with the March 26 game against Colorado. We proved to ourselves and to our team, as well, that we would stand up for ourselves—we wouldn't back down. I think that helped us playing them later on that year in the playoffs. That night, March 26, I was on the ice when Forsberg and Larionov started pushing each other and grabbing one another. All of a sudden, all hell breaks loose! I don't even remember who I grabbed, but I remember seeing the goalies coming out and Shanny hitting Roy and them both spinning up in the air. Everything happened so fast with the fights. We were all watching McCarty and Claude Lemieux and then we saw the goalies going at it, too. Winning that game in overtime was tremendous. The way we came back in that game set things up for the playoffs.

We weren't favorites going into the Stanley Cup Finals in 1997 against the Philadelphia Flyers. They had the big Legion of Doom Line with John LeClair, Eric Lindros, and Mikael Renberg. People predicted that they would walk all over us. They were a big team, and people thought they were going to out-muscle us and beat us to the puck. Everyone thought that Vladdy and Fetisov were going to play against that big line, but Scotty Bowman did just the opposite and put Larry Murphy and me against them all the time. Neither Murph nor I were overly physical, but we played our positions just right. We went after the puck and moved it quick, without spending a whole lot of time in our own end.

Winning the two games in Philly and coming back home, Joe Louis Arena was just going nuts. In Game 3 we won 6–1, and they didn't have a chance. Coming out for Game 4, we just felt like something special was going to happen that night, and it did. I got the first goal late in the first period during that game. It was an overwhelming feeling to finally win the Stanley Cup with our fans in the stands screaming after 40-plus years of waiting for this franchise to win the Cup again.

I was close to tears when we finally won the Cup. It was a big relief because we had been battling for two months and had gone through a lot. To be able to finish on top after having all the pressure that we had, it's tough to put into words.

When the limo accident happened, we had done everything right. We were going golfing as a team and would be having a few beers and having dinner afterwards, so limos were set up. We thought we did the right thing. When the accident happened, you just couldn't believe that it was true. We had just seen the guys a couple of hours before, riding in a golf cart, laughing, and having fun like everyone else. All of a sudden you get the call that something terrible has happened. We were in shock for a week. You went home over the summer but you stayed in contact with people in the Wings office, always trying to hear what was going on with Vladdy. Is he improving? We saw Fetisov a few days after the accident when he was still in the hospital. It was tough to see them in that position.

That next season was difficult because Vladdy's locker was right next to mine and they kept his stuff there all year. I was reminded every day of what happened to him. It was always in the back of my mind. I don't know if I was playing for two players, but I realized it every day and especially when the playoffs came around. It was a lot of responsibility that first season. It was hard to go through camp and not have Vladdy there. But I never felt the pressure that I had to take over Vladdy's role. I knew that my role was going to be bigger, but I didn't feel like I was taking over his role on the ice because he was such an exceptional player, really tough to play against.

When we won the second Cup against Washington, there was a sense of relief, but it was tough to see Vladdy. He had been watching up in the stands. It was great to have him there but you wanted him to be more a part of it than he was. You wanted him to be on the bench and on the ice with us playing. It was unsettling to see him on the ice in a wheelchair. I was a lot closer to tears at that time than the year before in 1997.

Winning the Norris Trophy three straight years means a lot to me, but once my career is over and I look back to see what I've accomplished—I think I will appreciate them more. I might not show it to other people, but I'm very proud that I've been recognized as the top defenseman in the NHL.

Being a Red Wing is a great honor. To be a part of the tradition of this organization, looking up at the rafters at Joe Louis Arena, and then meeting Ted Lindsay and Gordie Howe is so gratifying. It's such a classy organization.

I love playing at Joe Louis Arena; I think it's the best rink to play at in the league. I like the ice; I like the fans, even though if we're not playing well we're going to hear it. But when the fans are on you're side, they're the greatest fans in the NHL. They are a lot of fun to play in front of.

Nicklas Lidstrom's Career Highlights

* Winning the Stanley Cup, Norris Trophy, and Conn Smythe all in the same year, in 2002.

* Winning the Stanley Cup in 1997.

* Winning the second Stanley Cup in 1998.

* Playing in his 1,000th game.

* Scoring the winning goal to help Sweden win the 2006 Olympic gold medal against Finland.

MARK HOWE

DEFENSEMAN

1992–1995

I GREW UP AT OLYMPIA, WATCHING MY DAD playing for the Red Wings in the 1960s. I absolutely loved that building. I loved being there for games. I always wore a shirt and tie. Almost everyone wore a shirt and tie to games back then.

After the game, I would stand right at the dressing room door, and the usher would stand there with a hold on me until Dad came in from the ice. If it was a good night for the team, he would tell me to come in right away. If it was a bad night, he knew the boys were going to get yelled at. He would tell the usher, "Hold him here, and I will let you know."

At Olympia, when you came out of the locker room, you went to the left to exit the doors to the parking lot. A little farther along, there were stairs that led up to a balcony that had been added on to the back of the building. I used the rail in between as a net for the hockey games I would have while I was waiting for my dad after games. First I would be in the locker room getting tape balls and cut-off sticks to use in my game.

The longer Dad took signing autographs, the better it was for me. And he never turned down an autograph request. Nowadays there is no access to the players. Back then, it was great. At Olympia, you would come out of the locker room and they would have the little wooden barricades up. You had to walk through the corridor just to walk out to the ice.

I would be in the locker room all the time trying to get sticks. I loved using Nick Libett's sticks. He would give me the sticks he didn't like. I thought I was smart because I would get one of his sticks, and then the next day I would say, "Oh, I left it at home. Can I have another one?" I wanted to have a whole bunch of sticks to play driveway hockey.

When I would be sitting there, fixing my sticks, I would be looking over my shoulder because I knew that if trainer Lefty Wilson saw me with a stick, he would start yelling and chasing me. I'd go running out the door and you could hear all the guys in the room dying laughing. Lefty was just joking around, trying to scare me.

Sometimes I was able to be the stick boy or water boy for the visiting teams. I had good relationship with a few guys. Sometimes Johnny Bower used to let me into the visitors locker room. I remember once I was in there getting autographs, and Eddie Shack was sitting on the training table getting some work done. Eddie, who is a great guy, started singing the song "Gordie Howe Is the Greatest One of All," which was a song that was played at Olympia during the games. I remember turning beet-red. Eddie had a good laugh out of that.

Every time the Chicago Blackhawks came to town, Bobby Hull would bring me half a dozen or a dozen sticks. I liked to watch all of the work the Chicago players did on their sticks, especially the guys with the big curves. I know the goalies on the teams I played for growing up in Detroit cringed every time Chicago came into town. The goalies knew that I would bring all the Hull sticks down to the rinks and let the guys use them in practice. None of us could ever control that big curve.

Dad always sat between Normie Ullman and Alex Delvecchio, and I got to know them well. I got to know the coaches a little bit. Dad was such great friends with the Gadsby family, we did a lot of things with them and Doug Barkley.

These guys were always nice to me, and when I got older, and I could skate well, they would let me practice with the teams. I used to go to training camps, and the Red Wings would let me participate. I remember playing against Dean Prentice in a scrimmage, and he scored three goals and I learned a valuable lesson that day. I had better learn to play defense.

My favorite moment as a youngster came when Dad beat Rocket Richard's goal-scoring record on November 10, 1963. I watched Dad score

As the son of Gordie Howe, Mark Howe's decision to sign with the Detroit Red Wings seemed like a natural fit. He and his brother Marty grew up at Olympia Stadium, and both of them played for the Detroit Junior Red Wings before launching their pro careers. A strong skater, Mark Howe earned the reputation as a superb two-way defender in his lengthy career. Today he serves as a pro scout for the Red Wings.

his 544th and 545th goals. Both games were against Montreal at Olympia. It's something you can't forget. Everyone was hooting and hollering, The standing ovation must have lasted 20 or 25 minutes. It was an absolute roar.

I was sitting there in my seat in Section 7, thinking, *Wow, that's my dad. No one else can say that tonight, but me.* It was really special.

My brother Marty and I played for the Junior Red Wings in Olympia. We used to pack that building as a junior team. I absolutely loved that building. The ice was fast. The boards were fast. Actually, the ice there was superb. You could skate on that ice for 30 minutes before the snow would start showing up. There were less people in arenas back then, so there was less body heat, and that does make a huge difference when you are playing games.

When I left Philadelphia, I wanted to go to a team that had the chance to win, and the Red Wings were one of four teams that I talked to. At the time, I thought Pittsburgh had the best team in the league. But it was a far more natural fit to put on a Red Wings jersey. I was born and raised in Detroit. I liked the city, I knew the city. I had dreams of growing up and playing in the NHL, playing for the Red Wings. It took until I was 37, but I finally got there.

The New York Rangers had made me a really solid offer, and Philadelphia was trying to keep me. The funny thing was that I was interested in Pittsburgh, but the Penguins didn't seem interested. We had an exhibition game at Joe Louis that fall, and I went up to general manager Craig Patrick and said, "I can't believe you didn't make me an offer."

"We knew we couldn't afford you," he said.

"How did you know that?" I asked. "I wasn't looking for money. I was looking to win."

But it was easy for me to come to the Red Wings because you could see that they were a team on the rise, with all the young players they had. I figured I had two seasons to play. Fortunately, I managed to play there.

When I signed with Detroit, I was coming from an organization that was built strictly on team play. If you couldn't be a team player, you couldn't play for the Philadelphia Flyers. I think that was one reason why I was brought there. The Red Wings had more talent than any other team I played for, but they did not play like a team. I tried to bring that into the locker room. But when Scotty Bowman came to Detroit, I think that's when it became about winning.

Scotty Bowman was by far the best coach I had ever seen. He was the only coach I had ever played for where, if we lost, you really felt bad for the coach. He really had the hearts and souls of so many of his players. It's amazing, he would just pick up on the smallest quirky thing, and darn if it didn't work. He found a way to get the best out of his top players. He turned some great individual players into one of the best Red Wings teams of all time.

I missed winning the Cup as a player. We lost to New Jersey in the Stanley Cup Finals in 1995. I wish I had won as a player. I had won championships at other levels—in the World Hockey Association and juniors. When I became a pro scout and we won in 1997, I knew it would not be the same emotion. I could see the joy in the guys in the front office because they had worked hard in that place for so long and so hard. I knew what it meant to win as a player because I had been out there sweating. The guys upstairs are working the pens, and the scouts are providing information. But it's not quite the same.

But I wasn't jealous. I was just so happy for the players I played with. I was really good friends with Nick Lidstrom and Vladdy Konstantiov. My best moment involving the Red Wings was Dad scoring the goals to beat the Rocket's record. My best memory of winning the Cup was how happy I was for my two buddies because they won the Cup.

I think that I can say I was part of the building process. My last season, the team had started to come together. The team was beginning to realize its potential at that time. Even though it was difficult to me because I knew in my heart it was my last year. Anytime your team's enjoying success, that's what the game is all about—winning. We were a good club. We had a lot of success when I was there. Paul Coffey won the Norris Trophy one year. He was just outstanding. Sergei Fedorov won the MVP one year.

Getting to play with Vladdy was special. He was an all-around defenseman. He had the skill to play and, without a doubt, he had the toughness. I think at the time he was injured in the limousine crash, we had him rated probably in the top seven or eight defensemen in the league. And his rating probably would have gone up. We were also licking our chops over knowing that we had Nick and Vladdy for years to comes. My thought was that we were going to have a great team for a minimum of five years. Vladdy had a great work ethic on and off the ice. Even though we all grew up being taught to hate the Russians, just being his roommate and his partner for a year, you got to see what an absolute great guy he is. He was funny as hell. I would be driving down the Lodge from Farmington, and in my rearview mirror I would see a BMW, deking and diving through traffic to catch up. I knew it would be Vladdy.

It meant a lot to me to wear a Red Wings uniform. It probably meant more to me to know how proud my dad was to see me in a Red Wings uniform. It meant an awful lot to him.

Mark Howe's Career Highlights

* At age 16, playing for the U.S. team at the 1972 Olympics.

* In 1985–1986, leading the NHL in plus-minus at plus-85.

* Being named first-team All-Star in 1983, 1986, and 1987.

* Scoring 107 points playing for the New England Whalers in the WHA in 1978–1979.

* Playing on a line with dad Gordie and brother Marty for the Houston Aeros in the WHA when he was 18.

SCOTTY BOWMAN

COACH

1993–2002

AFTER I HAD BEEN OFFERED THE JOB to coach in Detroit, I happened to be in Montreal, and I met up with Kenny Reardon, who was a big player in Montreal [from 1940 to 1950]. He's in the Hall of Fame. I was a good friend of his.

"I'm taking the job in Detroit," I told him.

"You're not," he said. "You can't do that."

"I am," I insisted. "It's a good opportunity."

"You're done with Montreal," he said.

The rivalry between Montreal and Detroit is still pretty strong, especially for those who have been around a while. Being from Montreal, I knew the rivalry from the 1950s. I was a young fan when Detroit finished first seven consecutive times, from 1948 to 1955. When I took the job coaching Detroit, I understood the prestige the franchise once had.

I had seen Gordie Howe when he was a young player. It's difficult to compare eras, but I always say he was the best player I saw pre-1967. If you're going to make a mold of a player, it's hard to make a mold better than Gordie Howe. He had size, strength, and ability. There are not too many players who could play both forward and defense. Gordie was one who could. I remember talking to Wayne Gretzky about what a talented player Sergei Fedorov was, and even Wayne said that he could not have played defense. Mario Lemieux couldn't. Jaromir Jagr couldn't. You have to be a special kind of

Scotty Bowman posted a record of 414–194–88 during his tenure as head coach. Those who know Bowman best say it was his attention to detail that gave him the advantage over other coaches. He was masterful at preparing his team to play, and some say he's the best bench coach in NHL history. That's goalie Chris Osgood with him on the bench.

player. Gordie Howe was just so fantastic. At the time, there was a comparison of Howe and Maurice "Rocket" Richard. Howe was more well-rounded and Richard was spectacular. To have a truce, you would just say, "If you want to win championships or develop a mold of a player, you pick Howe. If want to fill a rink, you pick Richard."

Detroit had plenty of good players in the 1950s. In an era when offense wasn't a big factor for defenseman, except maybe with Red Kelly and Doug Harvey, Bob Goldham was a premier defensive defenseman. He played with Kelly quite a bit, and I've talked to different players on the Red Wings in those years and players from other teams, and they all say Goldham's defensive ability allowed Kelly to play the kind of game that made him effective. Everybody talks about Bobby Orr, but Kelly was the first defenseman that I saw who could skate like a forward. I think Jack Adams was often upset at him for going up the ice. When he played with Detroit, hockey was not an offensive game. If you watch games from the '50s and even the early '60s, there weren't many scoring chances. Goldham was a lot like Al Arbour, who played in Detroit. I had him in St. Louis. Arbour and Goldham had a special knack for blocking shots. There has never been better shot-blockers than those two. And a lot of times they would block those shots on two-on-one plays.

I was at the seventh game of the Stanley Cup Finals at Olympia when Tony Leswick scored the game-winning overtime goal to beat Montreal in 1955. I was coaching an independent junior B team in Montreal. I was 22, I had a really good young player, and everyone was trying to get his release. Detroit had a bird dog named Kenny Brown, and he invited me to the game. I actually went with him by bus from Montreal to Detroit. I was invited up to the Red Wings victory party at the Cadillac Hotel.

That was the championship era of the Red Wings. Detroit did get into the Finals in the mid-1960s, but that was the team's last hurrah until we got into the Finals.

It was good experience for me to win Stanley Cups in both Montreal and then Detroit. When I came to Detroit, I could feel that the fans revered the fact that I had been a winner in Montreal. The people who knew hockey, knew that if you came from Montreal, you were sort of a step above. I was there at the good times, and we had great teams. The people in Montreal had big expectations. I think it kind of spurs you on. In Montreal, people always said, "Geez, there is a lot of pressure on you." But I believed the pressure was good pressure for the team because, if you are a player or a member of the Canadiens organization when they had their good team, it's a pretty miserable time in the summer if you surprisingly get beat in the playoffs. I think that was always a plus and I think it was in Detroit. After you get on a winning streak, players become aware of how important it is to the fans.

227

I enjoy going back to Detroit today. What I found unusual in Detroit was that the other players from other sports, even high profile players, all like hockey. They follow hockey. They're well aware of what the Red Wings mean. That always impressed me. Generally, in other cities, football players are football players, baseball players are baseball players, and basketball players are basketball players. But from a lot of the people I have met through my association with Detroit, I got the feeling they were pulling for us. You meet those guys on the street or at an event, and they are aware of what is going on with the Red Wings. There are different types of fans.

I remember about lots of different games. A favorite memory for me is when we were up 3–0 against Philadelphia. It was two days before the fourth game. I was just driving around the city and I would see all the people with trucks and brooms. At the time, I said, "Oh, my goodness, they're premature." But that was neat to see how excited they were, talking about a sweep. Meanwhile, we were just trying to win the Cup. But I know with a 3–0 lead, it's big.

You certainly remember your first Stanley Cup, but I remember a lot about the last one because I knew all along that that was going to be my last chance. I planned my retirement at the Olympic break. We were training down in Orlando during the 2002 Olympics, and I actually brought my family down for four or five days. I didn't tell them about it. I think the reason I didn't retire before was that I thought, *If I don't come back to coach, what am I going to do? I'm not ready to do nothing.* Then all of the sudden it kind of hit me in that February, this would be a good time for me to try another challenge. That's when I made up my mind. I made my mind up that I was going to make that my last season. I mean, sooner or later, you're going to have to leave this job and do something else. It seemed like the right time.

The Game 7 of the Western Conference Finals in 2002 is one of my favorite games. I had anticipated a tight, tight game, and we had a good start and beat Colorado 7–0. We had been down 3–2 in that series.

There are two other games that I really recall. When we came back to beat Washington and we were down, I think, 4–1, Draper scored in overtime to win the second game of that series. And then there was the long triple-overtime Game 3 in Carolina. I had never been involved in a game that went that long. It was big when Igor Larionov scored because they'd come in and won that first game in Detroit, in overtime. The Hurricanes were on a roll. I had watched that Toronto series pretty closely, and winning the seventh game in Toronto gave the Hurricanes a lot of confidence. The second game of the series had been tight. We won 3–1. Then we were going into their building, with all I had heard about the noise and the excitement in Carolina. That was an important win for us. It was a momentum swing in the series. We did come back in Game 4 and dominated. We played a solid game. But it's tough to rebound when you lose a game like that triple-overtime game. Someone was going to win that game, and the edge was going to go big to the team that won it.

I'm always going to remember the game in Montreal when we knocked Patrick Roy into Colorado, I can't say I have fond memories of it, because I knew after they were going to trade him, Colorado was the worst place he could have gone. We won 11–2 that night. We had the Russian Five rolling. I remember a lot about that. I didn't use them all the time because I wasn't interested in showcasing them, I just wanted to use them in crucial situations. They were a special group the way they played. It just made sense to play them together.

Steve Yzerman's goal against St. Louis to propel us into the Conference Finals in 1996 was a huge goal because it was the seventh game. It wasn't really chopped liver he was playing against. Gretzky was on the ice. In fact, Gretzky actually lost the puck at our blue line.

I see a lot of players now and I have a good rapport with them. I spoke at different times to players when I coached, but I didn't feel comfortable talking to players and then making decisions that could vastly affect them. That was always the tough part of the equation. Maybe if I had just been a coach all the time in my lifetime and never done anything else, it might have been different, but I was a manager in St. Louis for three years, I was a manager in Buffalo for about six years, and I was sort of a manager one year in Detroit because of the trades. It's tough to make decisions that affect people's lives. But I enjoyed being in Detroit. The fans were knowledgeable. We had some good players.

Scotty Bowman's Career Highlights

* Holding the NHL record of nine Stanley Cup championships as a coach. He won three of those with the Red Wings in 1997, 1998, and 2002.

* In 30 years of coaching, having a 1,244–583–314 mark in the regular season and 223–130 in the playoffs. He holds NHL records for wins, winning percentage (.654), playoff games coached, and playoff victories.

* Guiding Montreal to four Stanley Cup titles in a row from 1976 to 1979.

* Winning the Jack Adams Award as coach of the year in 1977 and 1996. He was named NHL executive of the year in 1980.

* Being inducted as a builder into the Hockey Hall of Fame in 1991, the Michigan Sports Hall of Fame in 1999, and the Buffalo Sports Hall of Fame in 2000. He was inducted into the Michigan Jewish Sports Hall of Fame in 2001.

KRIS DRAPER

CENTER
1993–Present

M Y FIRST THOUGHT WAS, *How am I possibly going to make the Detroit Red Wings if I couldn't make the Winnipeg Jets?*

I had played two years in the NHL and only 18 to 20 games with Winnipeg. I spent the majority of my time with their farm team, the Moncton Hawks. Usually when the farm team loses in their playoffs, the NHL team will call players up if they're in the playoffs. I was 21 years old and our season ended in Moncton, but Winnipeg was in the playoffs, yet they didn't call me up. I considered myself a prospect with the organization, and they basically told me to go home and start my summer. I found that pretty weird. I wanted to be an NHL player, but the Jets didn't seem to think that I could do that. I ended up talking to my agent and said, "It doesn't sound like they have any plans for me. What do I do?" That seemed to get the ball rolling, and I got a phone call in the middle of the summer saying that I had been traded from Winnipeg to Detroit for future considerations. I was thrilled to get a new start!

Training camp with the Red Wings went well for me. And even though I started the season with the Adirondack Red Wings, I got called up by Detroit just into the new year. That's how the whole dollar thing happened. Bryan Murray called Mike Smith, or whoever it was with Winnipeg, and said, "We've called up Kris Draper and this was a future consideration deal so

Kris Draper is considered one of the dominant checking centers in Detroit Red Wings' history. Draper is one of the league's swiftest skaters, and he's a relentless penalty killer and forechecker. He had his best offensive campaign in 2003–2004 when he scored a career-best 24 goals.

we have to finalize it. How do you want to do it?" Winnipeg just wanted to make it a financial transaction and told the Red Wings to just give them a dollar and I could play. That was the start of it for me. I didn't even know about it, I just thought it was future considerations. I didn't care what the trade was. All I knew was that I was playing for the Detroit Red Wings. I didn't learn about the dollar exchange until the 1994 playoffs, when somebody asked me if I knew what the trade was. I said I didn't know, and the reporter told me the story about me being traded for a dollar.

It didn't bother me that I was only worth a dollar to the Jets because of the fact of where I was. I didn't care how I was going to get to Detroit; all I wanted to do was get there. Even to this day, people just love to talk about it! To me, it just happened. It wasn't one of the things that I cared about, I just laugh about it. I can joke about it because I'm sitting here still playing for the Detroit Red Wings.

When I came to the Red Wings, the three centers were Steve Yzerman, Sergei Fedorov, and Keith Primeau. That's good company to play with. I just wanted to be in the NHL and was going to do everything I could to keep myself there. That's a big reason why I stuck. I was willing to accept any role given to me. I would kill penalties. I played all three forward positions. Whatever role Scotty was going to put me in, I was going to play hard.

Once Kirk Maltby came to the Red Wings, we started playing together and there needed to be someone else on the right side. When the Red Wings signed Joey Kocur, my first thought was that this "goon" was going to play with myself and Malts. Only after we started playing with him did we realize what a good hockey player Kocur was. We developed good chemistry.

In those days, Maltby and I were very feisty—I was very talkative, and Maltby was a pain in the rump to a lot of people. If Maltby and I had a dollar for every time we were threatened on the ice, both he and I would have a lot of money. Joey would always police the right side for us to make sure events didn't get out of control. It was a line that Scotty Bowman started to have a lot of confidence in. Joey was there most of the time but sometimes Darren McCarty would play with us. It was during the 1997 playoffs that Joey decided that we needed to get a name for our line. We talked about it, and in St. Louis we came up with the name "the Grind Line." The name just stuck, then came the T-shirts and posters. It was just something that caught on. When Kocur left, McCarty came in and the Grind Line continued. It was neat to have the linemates that we've had. The one thing that thrilled all of us was that as a line we scored some big goals during the Stanley Cup play-offs. That was what made it so fun; it was a great line to play on, but it was also a very effective line.

If you look at who we had on our team, we were the fourth line, but we felt like we could play with anybody and play in any situation. Scotty seemed to feel that way, too, and so did Dave Lewis.

If Scotty Bowman didn't like you, you weren't going to be on his hockey club. At times, we had 26 players on our roster and somebody wasn't going to play. There were some nights where I was a healthy scratch, or Maltby was a healthy scratch. As a professional, that doesn't sit well with you. You always want to be in the lineup. You always want to be playing. After winning the two Stanley Cups, we basically solidified ourselves in the line-up as members of the Detroit Red Wings. Once that happened, Scotty knew what he was going to get out of us. There weren't any surprises. That was why Scotty liked our line and liked the way we killed penalties. We took a lot of pride in it and now we've been doing it together for 10 years.

Maltby and I are successful as a penalty killing unit because we have trust in one another. We've played so much hockey together that we let instinct take over. We both like to skate. Maltby is a very underrated skater. If you want to play physical, he can because he's big and strong. But you're not going to out-skate him. What makes Maltby good is that he can run you over and you can't skate away from him. We still feel when we're killing penalties that not only can we out-work a power play—we can chip in with some short-handed goals. It's always been a big part of our identity.

The March 26 game in 1997 wasn't as much about my injury in the 1996 playoffs as it was about how Claude Lemieux handled it. It pissed off our whole team. We had a good team in 1996, we set the record for wins, but we couldn't get over the top against Colorado. We knew that they were defending Stanley Cup champions and, if we were going to win the Stanley Cup, it was going to be through them. Everyone assumed that something was going to happen during that game. You could just feel it. The funniest thing is the two guys who started the whole thing were Larionov and Forsberg. They got into a little bit of a scrum right in front of our bench, and as soon as that happened McCarty made a beeline for Lemieux. The thing that made McCarty such a valuable player for our hockey club was that he was the ultimate team player. He would do anything for his teammates, and that was something that he felt he was going to do. Not only did he go out and pound Lemieux, he then wound up getting the game-winner in overtime. What a night it was for him!

That March 26 game is probably one of the greatest games that has ever been played; not only because of the brawls and fights, but by the way that we won it. We won 6–5 in overtime. It was different coming off the ice after that game. One of my best buddies, Mac [McCarty], had taken care of a situation on the ice that was pretty ugly. To walk off the ice and realize we won the game with the fights and everything—the guys were pretty fired up. We went on from that game to win back-to-back Stanley Cups, so it was definitely a defining moment in our team's identity.

We had just won the Stanley Cup in 1997 and everything was unbelievable with the parade and the rally at Joe Louis Arena, where we thanked the fans. There were twenty thousand people at this rally cheering us on for winning the Cup. Everything about it was incredible. Then all of a sudden there was the limo accident. It was a tragedy that just absolutely rocked all of us. It's something that still hits home every time we see Vladdy. It just puts everything into perspective. All we were hoping for was a recovery by Vladdy, Sergei, and Slava. Then the 1998 season started.

A lot of people ask me about winning three Stanley Cups: how are they different and what's my favorite moment? For me, I will never forget when we won the Stanley Cup in 1998 in Washington. Stevie grabbed the Cup and lifted it over his head like he had done the previous year and then gave it right to Vladdy, who was sitting in a wheelchair. That was the greatest moment that I had with the Stanley Cup, to see Vladdy hold it. To this day, I swear that he knew exactly what he was holding onto and what he was a part of that day.

Steve Yzerman is a great leader because he has always had such a great feel for his hockey club. He knows when something needs to be said. We were down 2–0 to Vancouver in the 2002 playoffs, and all of Canada was cheering for the Canucks. Everyone wanted to get rid of the Detroit Red Wings. Yzerman stood up and had some things to say. We all listened to him. Steve was playing through all these injuries and his knee was really bad. He told us, "We're going to win this series! We're a great team and we have great players!" Stevie said it with such confidence that you believed it—*Yes, we are going to win*. The rest is history; we went on to win the next four games against

Vancouver and then win the Stanley Cup. That's what makes Stevie such a great captain. He knows what to say, when to say it, and it's always at the right time.

For me, everything is about winning as a team. I have never, ever thought about winning an individual award. That's why, when people started talking about me being a candidate for the Selke Trophy, I couldn't imagine being a part of something like that—to have my name on a trophy that Steve Yzerman had won, Bob Gainey had won, and Guy Carbonneau had won. I won the Selke Trophy in my home town of Toronto—it was pretty special. It showed how far I had come. The story of Kris Draper being traded for a dollar was famous, and here I was at the NHL Awards, holding the Selke Trophy as top defensive forward in the game. It was a huge honor for me. The one thing I talked about that night, and every time I talk about it, was this: as much as my name was called that night, the only reason I won it was because I play with a player like Kirk Maltby.

I'm proud to be part of an organization that is committed to winning. That's why you see Stevie playing here as long as he did and Lidstrom playing here as long as he has, as well as me, Maltby, and Shanahan. You want to see guys like Henrik Zetterberg and Pavel Datsyuk do the same thing here. It's such a classy organization, and every year we come into training camp feeling like we can win the Stanley Cup. There are not too many teams that can say that. I think that's why it's so special to be a part of this team. I've been able to play with some great people, make some great friends, and win Stanley Cups. I turned a dollar into a good career in the city of Detroit.

Kris Draper's Career Highlights

* Helping Canada win the World Cup of Hockey in 2004.

* Playing for the Canadian Olympic Team in 2006.

* Scoring the overtime goal in the Stanley Cup Finals versus Washington in 1998.

* Scoring a career-high 24 goals for Detroit in 2003–2004.

* Having played 152 playoff games and winning three Stanley Cups with the Red Wings.

CHRIS OSGOOD

GOALTENDER

1993–2001 ★ 2005–2006

I MET KEN HOLLAND WHEN I WAS 15 or 16 years old while I was playing for Medicine Hat in juniors, which was the team that Ken Holland also played goal for many years before me. He had seen me play in midgets when I was a 14-year-old and followed me up to the junior level until my draft year, and then he drafted me. He never really talked to me about it, but he made sure I was working out and doing all the things I was supposed to do to have a chance at becoming an NHL goalie. I talked to him a couple days before the draft and thought there might be a chance that I was going to get drafted by Detroit. It ended up happening, and I was ecstatic.

After I was drafted, I spent another season in juniors and one full year in Adirondack. I was looking forward to my second season with Adirondack because we had a really good team with Draper, McCarty, Jamie Pushor, Tim Taylor, and Marty Lapointe. I was only with that team for three games, though, before being called up. Detroit had gotten off to a rough start on the road, and Cheveldae had gotten hurt, which left them with Peter Ing and Vincent Riendeau, and then Ing got hurt as well. I didn't expect that I was going to play until Scotty Bowman called me out to the hotel lobby the night before. We were in Toronto to play the Leafs, and he told me that I was in net. I was surprised.

Toronto had started the year out really well and hadn't lost a game yet in the regular season. I was so nervous to play in Maple Leaf Gardens. When you're a Canadian kid and you play your first NHL game in Maple Leaf Gardens, it's a bit overwhelming. But after that game I realized that I could play in the NHL. When I made saves in the game, it was easier than I thought it would be. Nothing seemed as tough to me as I had expected it to be. I knew that I didn't play close to what I could. I didn't play for about a week after that game, but I practiced a lot. That really helped me because when I was called up I hadn't practiced with the team, so in my first game everything seemed quick to me. My first career win was against the L.A. Kings, and I played quite a bit after that. The only problem was that I always needed three pieces of ID on me when I went to the rink because security never wanted to let me in. They didn't believe that I could really be a goaltender for the Red Wings.

It took awhile before I felt comfortable enough to start playing practical jokes on the guys in our locker room because there were so many veterans. I would do stuff without guys knowing and I would never, ever come clean about it over the first three or four years. But then guys began to expect it, so I would have to do something, especially to Draper, McCarty, Pushor, Lapointe, and Kevin Hodson—the guys whom I would hang out with. Norm Maracle was an easy target; I would do all sorts of things to Normie. I would cut his sticks all the time so that they would break as soon as he faced a shot.

Hodson was a classic, the funniest guy that I've ever played with! One of the jokes I played on him was taping pictures of naked women on the back of his helmet in warm-ups. When he was skating around it would look like he had these pictures of naked women painted on the back of his mask. Norm Maracle was a little more fiery and uptight. He hated not playing. Maracle and Hodson would always fight because there were three of us. Hodson would come into the dressing room in the morning and put on all of Maracle's equipment before he got there, so that when Norm came in he would have no equipment to wear at practice. It was one thing after another with those two.

Mike Vernon was awesome to play with. He was very professional because when he came here we switched on and off. We won a Stanley Cup together. I grew a lot playing with Vernon. He was one of the guys who have influenced me quite a bit. He taught me how to play and pushed me to be better. It was disappointing when I wasn't the main guy in the 1997 playoffs. At first I thought I should have been playing, but then I realized that I could learn from this because Vernie had won a Cup before and, in a lot of ways, he

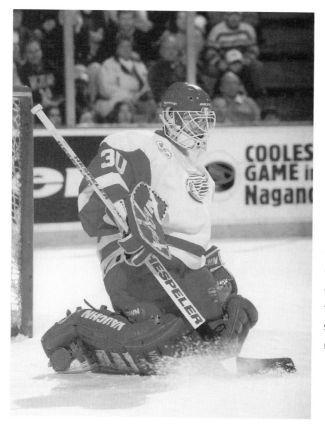

With 241 career wins, Chris Osgood ranks second to Terry Sawchuk on the Detroit Red Wings list for career goaltending victories. In the 1998 playoffs, he posted a 16–6 record with a 2.12 goals-against average to lead the Red Wings to a Stanley Cup championship. He owns the Detroit goaltending record for the longest winning streak with a 17–0–2 run in 1996.

deserved to play, too. You can't be selfish, and that's why the Red Wings were successful—because we didn't have selfish guys.

Everyone thought that we were going to get blown out by Philadelphia in the 1997 Stanley Cup Finals. We heard that we had no chance because Philly was too big. They had the Legion of Doom Line. We went in there and played awesome. We dominated from the drop of the puck and won four straight games. They weren't even in the games. It was great to win the Stanley Cup. It was the thrill of a lifetime in the dressing room at home after we won. The atmosphere driving down to the rink that day was unbelievable.

The next year in 1997–1998, Vernon had left and I was the starting goaltender for the defending Stanley Cup champions, but I really didn't approach it differently because I had played a lot of games. It wasn't like I had never played in the playoffs or any big games and wasn't worthy of being the starting goalie. I had thought I was going to play in the playoffs the year before and I had thought Vernon was still going to be around the next year. Both things were the exact opposite of what I had thought. I just went into the year relaxed and feeling good. There was pressure to win again but I never felt like I had to "replace" Vernon. We had played together and accomplished a lot of things together. I knew I could do it. I just wanted the chance to play all the time.

I didn't feel compelled to fight Patrick Roy, but it was weird because it happened at almost the same time that Vernon had fought him the year before. There was a scrum on the side and it was familiar because Igor Larionov started it, just as he had the year before with Forsberg. There was a tussle at the sideboards, and Roy took his gloves and his helmet off and put them on top of his net and started skating toward the scrum. The minute I came out to the red line, Roy made a beeline for me. I remember that the rink was really loud when I took my helmet off.

We fought at center ice, and it was like we were in a huge ring right in front of everyone. My jersey got all tangled up over my head at first and I was thinking, *Oh, my God, I've got to get my jersey off!* Finally I did, and he would kill me for saying this, but Roy really wasn't as strong as I thought he would be. I could move him around pretty good. Neither of us knew much about fighting. I threw a few soft lefts to try and fake him out and make him think I was a lefty. Then I just started throwing rights to try and protect myself, it became more wrestling than anything else. I wanted to hit him when he was down but I couldn't move my hands anymore. My hands were no longer working. Roy wasn't saying too much during the fight, it was more Scotty yelling. If you ever see the picture that they took of it, the whole bench is laughing and then there's Scotty, who's the only guy on the bench with a serious look on his face.

We both got thrown out of that game, which was good because there was no way I could have played. I got really tired at the end because I wasn't used to fighting at all, let alone for that amount of time. I couldn't even move my arms, but I felt like I won the fight.

I dreaded playing Al MacInnis in his prime on the power play. He was ridiculous to try and stop. His shot was so hard; he broke my hand at Joe Louis Arena once on a shot from the blue line on my blocker. That guy used to terrorize goalies. There would be times on a broken play where the puck would roll out and he would come in and his stick would be like John Daly teeing off. His stick would be behind his shoulder, he had an absolute rocket for a shot. You didn't see it, you just tried to get your body in front of it and

239

hope it doesn't kill you. He was impossible because his shot was much too hard and way too fast.

In the '98 playoffs, everybody remembers that long Al MacInnis goal I gave up in St. Louis late in the third period. It happened because when you have a guy that shoots as hard as he does, you can never just block the shot. So when I tried to block it, it went right through me. After it went in, I didn't really think about it because I was playing well up until that point. I wasn't going to let one play ruin my game or the series. What people don't understand about me is that when something happens, it's over for me. Good goalies can't dwell on things like that. I always believed that we were going to win that game. I said to myself, "It's no big deal; we'll just beat them in overtime." It took two overtimes, but we did beat them. I played like it never happened. I didn't think, *Oh, my God, I'm going to get scored on from the red line again,* or *I could get scored on from the blue line,* or *I better not let in another bad goal.* I never thought any of that, I just played.

During the Western Conference Final, another gem of mine was the Jamie Langenbrunner overtime goal when we played Dallas. The puck seemed to skip and go up my stick, hit my hand, and then go into the net. Up until that point, I was probably having my best game of the playoffs and my best series of the playoffs. Somehow, Dallas had tied the game up with just over a minute left, and then Langenbrunner's goal happened right away in overtime. When I was walking off the ice I was more mad than anything else because I was that close to getting to the Stanley Cup Finals. The goal in regulation made me more upset than the overtime goal. But then I said to myself that we would just get the chance go back to Joe Louis Arena and win it in front of our fans. Nothing ever came easy. The next game I got a shut-out and we moved on to play Washington in the Stanley Cup Finals.

Playing in the Stanley Cup Finals, in games of that magnitude, was awesome. There is nothing better than standing on the ice during the Stanley Cup Finals. It was my dream, since I was playing street hockey out in the snow as a little kid, to be in a Game 4 at the Stanley Cup with the chance to win it. And here I was, up 3–0 in the Finals with the chance to win the Cup. It was an unbelievable feeling. You knew if you won that game that the Stanley Cup was waiting for you at the end of the tunnel.

The Red Wings teams have always been so good because it isn't about one player. Winning the Cup for Vladdy was a big part of that. When we lost Vladimir Konstantinov, it was a devastating loss. He should still be playing today; he was one of the best defensemen in the league. He was an irreplaceable talent. To lose him in the fashion that we did was heartbreaking and it never left our minds that year. That is what we were playing for—for him and to put that cup in his hands again. We wanted to give Vladdy the opportunity to celebrate for a second time. That's why the Red Wings have been so good; they're different than other teams. It is always about being a Red Wing, it's not about being superstars. It's about the entire team and everybody who is involved in the organization.

When I think about scoring my goal against Hartford, I have to laugh because I almost took the head off of the best defenseman on our team and possibly in the history of the franchise in Nick Lidstrom. The puck was dumped in by Glen Wesley from the red line to the side of our net on my left. I stopped it with my stick, and, kind of having an idea where the net was, I fired it down the ice and almost hit Nick right in the head. I nailed it, too, right between the far blue line and the red line. It went right up the middle, and once it hit the ice, there was never any doubt that it was going to go in. The guys came back and they were jumping around. I was more laughing and looking for Drapes because he had told me I couldn't do it. Nick still likes to remind me of the time when I almost hit him in the face with the puck, though. That would have been just perfect!

When I left the Red Wings, I never realized until I was gone for four years what it meant to be a Red Wing. When I put that jersey back on, the sense of pride that I felt was unbelievable. I got a big smile on my face when I looked at myself in the dressing room mirror when I put it on again. I was home playing for my team.

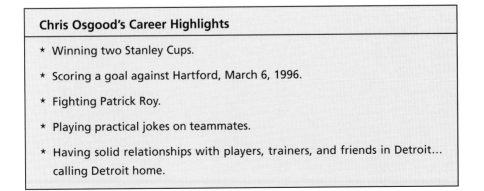

Chris Osgood's Career Highlights

* Winning two Stanley Cups.

* Scoring a goal against Hartford, March 6, 1996.

* Fighting Patrick Roy.

* Playing practical jokes on teammates.

* Having solid relationships with players, trainers, and friends in Detroit... calling Detroit home.

DOUG BROWN
RIGHT WING/LEFT WING
1995–2001

I WAS IN PITTSBURGH DURING THE FIRST LOCKOUT back in 1994, and at the end of the lockout there was the waiver draft. I was protected originally, and then Pittsburgh tried to load up on defensemen and I got a call from the assistant coach to come off the ice the day before the opening game. My brother was also with me in Pittsburgh, Greg Brown, and I knew he wasn't protected. I thought they were calling me over to let me know my brother was picked up by somebody. I went into Craig Patrick's office and he said, "Well, I have good news and I've got bad news for you." I said, "Okay, what's the good news?" He said, "Good news is Ottawa didn't pick you up." I asked him what the bad news was and he told me, "Detroit picked you up." I was confused and asked him if he meant my brother was picked up by Detroit. He said, "No, I mean you," to which my response was, "You've got to be kidding me."

Craig Patrick then tells me, "Scotty Bowman's going to give you a call in a couple minutes or in a couple hours when you get home." I'm thinking, *What, Scotty Bowman?* He told me Scotty really wanted me. I get the phone call from Scotty—and I have three kids, one brand new one—and Scotty's going, "I need you on a plane tonight. We play tomorrow, opening game." I told him, "Oh, no way, Scotty." It was going to take a while for me to get my house together and get out. But Scotty told me, "No, no, no. Come out and play, say hello to everybody, then we'll put you on a plane the next day

Speedy Doug Brown played for Detroit's 1997 and 1998 Stanley Cup championship teams. In 1997–1998 he scored 19 goals, plus four more in the playoffs, to help the Detroit Red Wings repeat as Stanley Cup champions.

and send you back to grab the family and whatever else you need to do." It was very hard, but when I got here everything went great from then on.

When I arrived in Detroit, I saw that Scotty Bowman played a very fast, intelligent game, and discipline was a big part of it—understanding your role out there on the ice as well as being smart enough to create. It's very much a discipline in your own zone, and it's wide open. There were an awful lot of talented players in Detroit, so you had to be able to move that puck fast and move your feet fast. That fit into my skill set. That's how I learned to play the game as a youngster.

Unique is a good word for Scotty Bowman because he is so focused on every possible angle that can help the team win. He's not just playing the lineup: he's playing the refs, he's playing the stands, and he's playing the players against each other on the team. Scotty's playing an awful lot of chess matches to see what his best combination is, as well as setting up his best combination for whom he's going to play later in the playoffs. He's constantly working it so that the odds are in his favor. He knows what group of players will play against what group of players on the other team. He's matching lines in December for March. That's looking pretty deep into the crystal ball, but that's what he's thinking.

I'd like to think that I appreciated, and still appreciate, Sergei Fedorov for who he is and not try to make him someone he's not. He was a 17-year-old boy when he first came over here. He came from a country that was falling apart. His upbringing was done on airplanes and buses and hotel rooms. He had tremendous talent and a tremendous focus on winning, but he had to come to a new country, where he didn't speak the language, and learn on his own. It was almost a mismatch because his flashy style and flashy cars were very bold in the public eye, but in the locker room and in his private life he was extremely quiet and guarded.

We have this attitude in the U.S. that on the ice you pound it out. We learn to respect grinding it out shift after shift after shift. When you look at other sports, like soccer, you have players that are magnificent talents and they're playing the game the way they learned how to play it. But it's much more a style of "wait for that ball to go into your area and then you sprint like crazy on the net." It's much less of a grinding mentality and more like a cat and mouse. You wait for your time to strike and you go.

Sergei was that type of athlete, where he'd be in a circle waiting for his opportunity to pounce. I think Paul Kariya, Teemu Selanne, and Mario Lemieux all played that way at times, too. By no means do I want to put all of these players into the same boat, but what I'm saying is, they're opportunists. Mario and Wayne Gretzky, we love them dearly and they're the greatest players ever, but they pick their moments when to jump at the play so they don't waste their energy doing something that someone else can do.

That wasn't our attitude in Detroit. It was much more of a "blue collar, grind it out, everybody do their job on both sides of the ice," and so sometimes Sergei got rubbed a little bit for it. I have to be real careful here because

I loved the way he played the game. You had to accept it for what it was: he was going to do his job and, boy, was he going to capitalize when that puck got turned over! He wasn't cheating to the offensive side, but I think a cat is a good example of how he's ready to pounce on a situation, so he's not always caught up in the shuffle.

In those big games—all playoff games—Sergei came and he came hard. And people would say, "Why doesn't he do that all the time?" My opinion was, he's like a racehorse—just put him in the big races. Why make him a plow-horse? He has so much talent and was so exciting. We're still going to win our 55 to 60 games, let that horse run when we need it. That's just my thoughts, and Scotty Bowman understood that, too. When we played Colorado, all of a sudden you'd see Scotty whisper to Sergei, "Who's the best player on the ice? Is it Fedorov or is it Peter Forsberg?" Or if Stevie's out hurt and Sergei was going up against Joe Sakic, you'd never know which one Scotty would match him up with, but he'd just say, "Sergei, who's the best one?" And watch him go. It was exciting.

As players, Steve Yzerman and Sergei Fedorov were very good together out on the ice. There was professional jealousy, in a good way. They both were so talented. Just think of a couple great tennis players eyeballing each other across the net going, "What do you got?" Imagine if those two tennis players were doubles partners and needed to go win a doubles match. Together, they'd be unstoppable.

I'm not sure if they had a professional respect for one another, I used "professional jealousy," but I don't know if that's the right term. There was admiration because they're both centermen and they're both two of the best players to play the game in that era. It was Stevie's town, but Sergei at times was electrifying. Certainly Stevie's personality fits the city. Maybe Sergei has got a little more of that L.A. flash, and that doesn't quite fit Detroit, but at times it was magnificent.

They played awesome together, and the atmosphere in the locker room was always outstanding. Steve and Sergei were just from two different cultures. There was never, ever, and this is important to know, any bad blood. Everyone has people they work with that they'll say hello to in the office, but if they're sitting at home watching a game they wouldn't be the first one they would call. But Yzerman and Fedorov really did get along well. I was with both of them seven years. There was nothing negative there. They were just cut from different cloth.

I had played with Slava Fetisov in New Jersey, so he and I were and are the closest of friends. He's the godfather of my oldest son, Patrick. When he came over back in 1989, we were roommates and I had nothing but the utmost respect for him and for his international career. So it seemed logical that I played with the Russian players before Igor Larionov got traded to the team. That's how I got the name "Brownov." I played with Kozlov, Fedorov, Konstantinov, and Fetisov before Igor's trade, before they became the Russian Five. Once Igor came in, he took my spot, and rightfully so, but I would still go back and play with them a lot. Igor would center a line with Brendan Shanahan. During those Stanley Cup years, I would play with Sergei and Kozzie a lot in the playoffs.

The Stanley Cup years were pretty special. Once Scotty brought me in, I understood strictly from a talent standpoint there was at least a half a team, some would say three-quarters of a team, and probably some people could argue a whole team of players out there more talented than I was. But I understood my role was to be supportive and a glue between these multitalented players.

When we won the Cup in 1997, it was validation of the type of team and organization that was put together over the last few years. Winning in 1997 was off the charts, and in hindsight it made me wish we had won it in 1995 and 1996. I kept thinking, "Gosh, those were even better teams on paper than maybe we had in 1997." But we learned how to win, or tweaked it enough, or were in the right place at the right time, been through the battle—you can come up with a thousand different reasons why we won at that time and not sooner.

It took all of the pieces of the puzzle to win in 1998. We knew we had to really fight to become better players. Sergei had his contract issue that year, so we had to learn how to play without Sergei Fedorov up front and without Vladdy in the back. We became a more structured team than the previous years because we didn't have as much speed coming up the ice with all of that talent. Once we got Sergei back, it was a shot in the arm as well as all of those wonderful sentimental reasons with Vladdy; we learned to fight for one another. Really, the team concept was huge.

We had all of that Vladimir emotion and Fetisov was banged up, he couldn't even feel his legs, but he continued to play for us after that car accident. Sergei Mnatsakanov, the team masseur, was in that state as well as Vladdy. It obviously touched us from a human standpoint. How fragile life is, don't take things for granted; and that went right down to don't take any shifts for granted, don't take your life for granted.

All those trivial things in the hockey world became something that we appreciated more. Our team experienced humility, respect, and were more aware of the opportunity we had to be playing for the Red Wings and having a shot at repeating as Stanley Cup champions with Scotty Bowman in charge. That's what the accident did for us, made us appreciate our own health and opportunity.

Respect is the word that comes to mind when I think about my Red Wings career. The respect that was given to me from Scotty Bowman and Mr. Ilitch gave me so much inner strength. When someone you respect so much has confidence in you—especially from those two gentlemen—that meant the world to me. It's like when you're dad gives you the nod that he's proud of you. For Scotty Bowman to give me that type of nod to be one of his players through those championships, as well as Mr. Ilitch supporting me through those seasons and bringing me back, that's what made me grow as a person as well as a player.

Being a Detroit Red Wing is a badge of honor. You're part of something that demands the most of yourself where you do the best you can, keep your mouth closed, and your legs moving. It's understanding what it is to pay the price to help others so that we can all be successful. For me to be a Red Wing, it's tremendous pride.

Doug Brown's Career Highlights

* Scoring the tying goal against the Washington Capitals in Game 2 of the Stanley Cup Finals in 1998.

* Having a five-point night against the New Jersey Devils. "When you play against your old team," Brown said, "you want to prove that you can play the game."

* Helping beat Anaheim en route to the Stanley Cup in 1997. One of their kids pulled me down on a breakaway; we scored on the power play and won the game. Ronnie Wilson, the coach of Anaheim said, "That's a marginal call on a marginal player."

"The next year he was in Washington," Brown recalled, "and we played them in the Finals. I had four goals in that series and two in the final game to win the Cup. Brendan Shanahan just kept whispering to me, "That's a marginal call on a marginal player." He knew how that irked me.

* Having his wife and two children down on the ice after winning the Stanley Cup. "It was my goal to be all I could be in hockey and not my wife's goal," Brown said. "When it's all said and done and you've won a Stanley Cup, you feel like we've done it."

* Playing for Bowman, Ilitch, and "the respect I had for them and what they gave me."

KEVIN HODSON

GOALTENDER

1995–1999

I HAVE A GOOD SENSE OF HUMOR and I love people. I love life. I knew my role in Detroit and I knew my time was limited there. I respected the game and tried to fit in. I tried to complement the goalies who were ahead of me that I knew I would never surpass. That could be a knock, or that could be a positive for me. I knew my role, and I tried to do the best I could in that role to make my team successful. I tried to joke a bit when it was tight in the dressing room, or compliment Chris Osgood. I did what I had to do. I love a good joke. I love practical jokes. I still try to have fun in my life even though I'm 34 years old now and not 25 anymore. I don't know if I'm off-center, but I do have some serious moments in my life, as well.

I would pick my times for joking. If we were on a winning streak, I would want to keep it a little looser. Before a road trip or long flight, I would do something funny so that the guys could talk about it on the flight. Back then I thought that jokes were my role on the team, how was I going to keep the guys loose and deflect some of the pressure? I got that, I wasn't one of the guys who didn't get it or see how the league worked. I understood the politics involved inside a dressing room because I understood people.

We stayed in really nice hotels, and there were a few times where I had my own room on a road trip and I would try and mess with a few guys on the team. I would set my alarm for 1:00 A.M.—I never played, so sleep wasn't a concern for me. I would get up, walk down the hall, and put the breakfast menu order forms on their doors for early in the morning. I got Mike Vernon with this a few times when he was carving me up a bit in practice—I would order room service for him for five days straight. He was convinced for about a year that it was Bob Rouse doing it. He never thought that I or Ozzie would ever do something like that to him. He was riding Bob Rouse for three months, saying, "You bastard, Rouser! Thank God you're in the union because you'd never have any clothes!" Vernon would get on Rouse because he was always wearing NHLPA clothing. I just sat in my stall and watched!

I would get wake-up calls for guys at 5:30 and 6:00 in the morning. I would take the batteries out of the remote controls for their TV, and come to their room with my remote control in my pocket and start changing the channels with it. They would sit there shaking the thing and yelling and then call down to the desk to say that the remote wasn't working and the TV was randomly changing channels. I played in the NHL, but I was more like a big kid.

There were a few jokes that backfired on me. We were in Dallas during the playoffs and there was a morning breakfast. I had wanted to put peanut butter on the ladle of the syrup for the guys eating pancakes and waffles. I thought I would get down there early and put a nice, smooth layer of peanut butter underneath the ladle because, once you get peanut butter on you fingers, it's like grease. I was sitting there by myself, and Scotty Bowman and Dave Lewis walk in! It was around 8:30 A.M., and breakfast didn't start until 9:00 or 9:15 A.M. I also wanted to get down there early and undo the tops of the salt and pepper shakers. I always enjoyed watching these starving guys, after practice or whatever, pour a whole shaker of salt on their food and then blame Ozzie or someone else. But on this day, sure enough, Scotty wanted to eat pancakes; he grabbed the ladle and got peanut butter all over his hand. He started blaming the maître d', saying, "Jesus Christ, these things are dirty! Look at my hands!" I was just sitting there, thinking, "Holy crap!" but I wasn't going to tell him. I just sat there and laughed.

I tried to shoe shine a table once by hiding underneath it. The joke was that Sergei Fedorov had just gotten these new Louis Vuitton shoes from Rodeo Drive. I snuck under the table and put a concoction together of barbecue sauce, ketchup, and Worcestershire sauce—it was a real nice stinky thing. The problem was that I couldn't see anything underneath the tablecloth, but I had a guy working with me who was going to get Sergei to sit with him at that table. When Sergei got up to get more food, that's when I

Kevin Hodson was the backup goalie on the Red Wings' 1998 Stanley Cup championship team. In 21 games that season, the affable netminder posted a 9–3–3 record with a 2.67 goals-against average. It turned out to be his best season as an NHL player.

was going to do it, the guy would tell me to leave, and Sergei would have all this stuff on his shoe. Something went wrong and I ended up shoe shining Steve Yzerman! I got head shots in practice for around two weeks for that. High and hard shots every day! You don't do anything to Stevie; he's untouchable, like the head of the mafia! He pretended that he didn't know, but everyone knew that I did it and it was a joke. He knew, before I knew, that I did it to him by mistake.

The first game I played, I was sitting downstairs eating breakfast at the Pontchartrain Hotel when my wife came down and said some guy named Louie called me. I was confused and asked, "Louie?" She said that some guy named Louie had called me to tell me that I was playing that night against Chicago. We had just played Pittsburgh the night before, and Ozzie had gotten pulled and I had played half the game and let one goal in. I asked her if it was Dave Lewis? She said, "Yeah that was it. Dave Lewis called." I couldn't believe it!

The auto show was going on at the time, and I was so nervous that I had to walk around. So I walked around the auto show for about an hour and a half. I threw up at around 3:00 P.M. in the afternoon. I had thrown up before every game that I played in Adirondack and every game in juniors. I was more petrified of throwing up in front of these guys than anything because it was just something that I did, I didn't know why. It was like Gump Worsley. I was walking through the auto show and it was a surreal moment; I had called my mom the week before and told her I was called up but probably wouldn't play. But luck had it that she had come into town for this game; my sister and my wife were also there. I remember walking to the arena by myself and walking past the big Joe Louis sculpture in Cobo Hall before going into the Joe Louis Arena. I was all psyched up and tried to walk past security, who stopped me and asked, "Can I help you?" I tried to tell them that I played for the Red Wings and my name was Kevin Hodson. They responded by laughing and saying, "No, you don't." Being stopped by security pulled me right out of that mood. John Wharton, our trainer, had to call down and tell them that I was the back-up goalie.

Scotty Bowman then pulled me into his office and sat me down. He said, "This is your night. You made it to the National Hockey League and this is your first game. I just want you to enjoy the game. I'm going to let you play the whole game, so enjoy it and play hard. We know what you can do from Adirondack." It was a really nice thing from Scotty because it was the last time that I ever spoke to him.

I remember the crowd. I remember the smell. I remember walking out for warm-up. Steve Yzerman would skate by me, followed by Paul Coffey, Sergei Fedorov, Larry Murphy, Igor Larionov, Dino Ciccarelli, Kris Draper, and then Ozzie. I was blown away and thought, "I can't do this! This is crazy!" I threw up before the game, and Paul Coffey made a joke about Ozzie needing to be ready. In the first period Coffey came up to me and said, "Stay in the net, stop the puck. Don't come out of your net, don't try to play the puck, just stay in the net!" It was a neat thing.

When we scored our first goal in the second period, it was the loudest noise I've ever heard in my entire life! I still remember it. It was deafening. I had goose bumps. We scored again, then went up 3–0 with seven minutes left, and Chicago took a four-minute penalty. I knew at that time that the game was over. I could smell the popcorn and see people's faces. I knew that people hated Chicago because it was a heated rivalry. When I won the game,

I pointed up to the sky to my grandmother and said, "We did it!" She was a huge fan of mine and had just passed away. It was probably the greatest memory I have of playing in the National Hockey League, other than winning the Stanley Cup my second year.

My heart problem just started one day. We were going to play a game that night in Adirondack, and Kris Draper had just made the worst pasta and meat sauce dinner with stale buns. We were eating at the table, and all of a sudden my heart started racing. I couldn't breathe and I started sweating. This had never happened to me before. Draper put me in his car and drove across town to the arena and called our trainer, Piet Van Zant, who is now with the Red Wings. Piet put me on a heart monitor and had me ride the bike—my heart rate was at 212. Piet tried to be calm but he was freaking out, knowing that I needed to get to a hospital. I got to the hospital and they gave me some drugs to stop it, but it was pretty scary. It also affected me in a game against San Jose once, it just started racing. I was fortunate enough to have surgery at the Cleveland Clinic. I had two surgeries because the first one didn't work.

If not for the second surgery, I probably would have had to retire. The heart medication was making me very lethargic and my whole mood changed. In the first procedure, they went through my arteries. The second time, they went through my veins and arteries, up through my groin using catheters, through the stomach and poked a hole in one of the chambers of my heart and burned the excess pathway off. I've had some reoccurrences a couple of times, the last time about a year ago, so I'm always watching for that.

It's always in the back of my mind if I'm training—will I have a heart attack? Will I have to go back on medication? It's funny when you have something like that happen; how surreal it makes you feel about your life and taking every moment in. After my heart surgery, I said to myself, if I ever had the chance to play again, I would really try to make a difference and not just play. I wanted to volunteer my time in the community and have an impact on people's lives who hold me in high esteem because I played in the NHL. I have become active in Sault Ste. Marie, and I do speak across the country to different charities and businesses about my life and my career and how some of the struggles I've had have affected the way I live my life today.

Draper gave me the nickname "Ticker," and it stuck. The first game I played with the nickname "Ticker" I got a shut-out. It was all over the TV, and everyone kept calling me "Ticker." I think I was more famous for my heart surgery than for my play, but it worked out okay.

Mr. and Mrs. Ilitch really treated the players like family. They love the city of Detroit and made us feel like we were playing for the city of Detroit. They made us think of the fans who were working hard for their money and spending it to come and watch us play. The Ilitches really wanted us to represent the city of Detroit well. Marian was very kind-hearted. When I had heart surgery she wrote me a card and a letter saying, "If there is anything the Ilitches can do for you or your family, please let me know." I was the starting goaltender in Adirondack at the time, I had been called up for three months, and they made this gesture toward me. They are phenomenal people, and the players playing for them appreciate that they are playing for people who don't treat them like meat. The Ilitches always cared about who you were, who your wife was, who your kids were. I have the utmost respect for the Ilitches because they changed my life. They helped me get the proper care for my heart.

Being a Detroit Red Wing was a like a dream to me. It meant that you made it not only in the NHL, but you played on the best franchise in the history of the game of hockey. It was a privilege and an honor to play for them. I'm proud and honored that I had the opportunity to put the jersey on and have my name on the back be associated with the Red Wings. I can always tell my kids that Daddy played for the Detroit Red Wings—the best organization in professional sports!

Kevin Hodson's Career Highlights

* Shutting out Chicago in his first NHL game.

* Spending $6,000 on rookie dinner. "There were three of us, and I only had a Blockbuster Visa card with a $1,000 limit," Hodson said. "So everyone kidded me that I had to share my Blockbuster points with them. Yzerman had to pay, and we all paid him back."

* Having a 9–3–3 record during the 1997–1998 Stanley Cup season.

* Winning the Hap Emms Memorial Trophy in 1993 as the top goaltender in the Memorial Cup.

* Ending his career with a 2.79 career goals-against average.

KIRK MALTBY
LEFT WING
1995–Present

I WAS TOLD I WAS TRADED TO DETROIT because there was a game where I absolutely steamrolled Paul Coffey. Apparently, Scotty Bowman liked that so much that he figured, "Hell, I'll just bring him here." I know Scotty and Paul butted heads quite a bit, I don't think that's top secret. I don't want to say he didn't like Paul because I don't think that was it. But Scotty's a little different with things like that. The story could be totally false, but that's one scenario that I heard.

The year I got traded I had my eye injury. It was during practice in Edmonton. We were doing a drill, and I was chasing Louie DeBrusk from behind to play him with the puck. He decided to get the puck, turn around, and shoot it. His follow through came up and caught me right in the eye and cut me for about three or four stitches on the eyelid. It scratched my cornea and the major damage was ripping my retina. I guess I was within millimeters of possibly losing my eye and ending my career. I was pretty fortunate that the bone around my eye took a good portion of the blow. It could've been a lot worse. It was a total accident, and I know Louie—for a big tough guy—felt terrible.

It was a pretty scary situation. Earlier in the year, we had a guy who took a puck in the eye and he ended up having to retire because of it. On the drive to the hospital I remember wondering, "What's going to happen to me?" I ended up spending three days in the hospital and then having a

Kirk Maltby has played with the Red Wings for the past 10 years. In the 2006 playoffs, he scored the game-winner in overtime of Game 1 versus Edmonton on April 21.

week's bed rest without doing anything more than walking to the bathroom and back to bed.

As far as recovery, I'd say I'm at 95 percent today. I get some burners, I call them "hot flashes," where you're sitting there and you think you see something out of the corner of your eye crawling down the wall. But it's nothing crazy or major. It's still a little sensitive to bright light, but aside from that I'm very, very fortunate.

When guys separate their shoulder, blow their knees out, or lose their teeth—those are things that you can fix. You can put a brace on or get your teeth fixed at the end of your career. After that day, I decided that my eyes are too important to lose. I wasn't going to put myself in position to take a blow to the eye again. I don't know if I'm more susceptible to losing my eye or receiving more damage easier than anyone else, but I really don't want to take that chance. I decided I was going to wear a visor.

A lot of people don't know, or realize, why I actually put the visor on. I can talk on and on about the heat that I've taken over it, but I don't feel I need to explain myself to anyone. If I had a nickel for every time someone said, "Pull your visor down" or anything to do with a visor—I don't think I would need to sign another contract. Obviously, it doesn't help being a physical player and an agitator. People don't like the fact that a guy can be physical and still wear a visor.

When I was ready to return, Edmonton sent me down for a four-game conditioning stint since I missed a couple of months because of my eye. The day I got called up was the trade deadline, and we were in Pittsburgh. When I arrived at the rink from the airport, I found out that I had been dealt. Ron Low, the Oilers coach, called me over and I thought he was going to ask me how the conditioning stint went and how I felt. Instead, he came from left field and told me I had been traded. I just went silent. I think I asked him, "For whom?" He told me and I was stunned. As much of a surprise as it was to be traded, it was a bigger surprise to be traded to the Detroit Red Wings, who were in the midst of setting the record for most wins in a season. I was in disarray.

I knew who was going to be in that locker room before I entered it: Steve Yzerman, Sergei Fedorov, Paul Coffey, Dino Ciccarelli, Slava Fetisov, and on and on. Normally, there would have been someone on the team that you had played with before, but not for me. I had never met one person in the Red

Wings dressing room until the day that I arrived there. I was a little intimidated and a quiet guy to begin with.

Scotty Bowman talked to me for maybe 30 seconds, but I was basically on my own. He knew that I had the eye injury and asked me how it felt. I gravitated to the younger guys on the team like Darren McCarty, Tim Taylor, and Kris Draper. They invited me out to dinner, or lunch after practice, and we got to know each other. Looking at the team, it was hard for me to believe that these guys really needed anyone or anything. They were pretty much a shoe-in to go to the Stanley Cup Finals that year. I had no idea where I was going to fit into this organization.

At the end of 1995–1996 season, we lost to Colorado and ended the season on a really bitter note. For me, I had one year left on my contract but had no idea where I stood with the team. I went through the off-season and training camp and made the team, but I was in and out of the line-up and not playing on a regular basis. Soon I started to hear the rumbling of the Wings looking to sign Joey Kocur from the beer leagues. I really believed that was going to be the icing on the cake for me. If they needed to make room for Joey, I thought for sure that I could be the one to go.

It wasn't that I thought Joey was a better player than me, but they were getting him for a specific reason—toughness. I had no clue what was going to happen, but to my surprise, Joey came in and they put him on a line with me! I played on the left wing and Joey on the right with Draper in between us. It snowballed from there, and the Grind Line was formed at a time when I thought I was going to be the odd man out.

From day one, the Grind Line just clicked. Whoever it was that played on the right side with Draper and I always fit. We're good skaters and we always know what the other one is going to do. Draper is a little quicker. He can get to the puck and create things, and he knows that I'll always be there. When we had Joey, McCarty, or Lapointe with us on the line, we had no worries about playing a physical game. The popularity of the Grind Line was amazing; the fact that we had a T-shirt and a commercial boggled my mind. I never expected anything like that. We were a big part of winning the Stanley Cups, but it still really leaves me a bit dumbfounded to think of it.

Is trash-talking a part of my game? Yes and no. Kris Draper is a fireball. He gets fired up, and when he decides he's going to say something, whether it's to me or anyone else, you're not going to change his mind. Most of my trash-talking doesn't come out until the end of a play or if someone takes a cheap shot or retaliates. I try not to say too much, but when you're out there in the heat of battle, it almost comes naturally. Our mouths have gotten us all into trouble a few times, but to say it's a big part of the way we play—no. For me, I think sometimes not saying anything when a guy is trying to get my attention by cursing at me—ignoring him—pisses him off even more. Sometimes silence is golden.

A guy whom I always knew I would have a run-in with would be Peter Forsberg. Every time it would be something, and that's just because he's such a competitor. He can give it as much as anybody. He wasn't afraid to give you a little cheap shot here or there, and that was part of the fun of the whole deal. As long as you know that a guy's going to take it and give it—that makes it a little more enjoyable. It motivates me and gets the engines revved up a little bit more.

Jaromir Jagr is next to impossible to check. He's so strong and yet so skilled. He can pass as well as anybody. He can shoot, he can stick-handle, and he can skate. I haven't had to play as much against Sergei Fedorov, yet, but he's a guy who can do things with the puck at such a high level and a high speed that most guys can't. He's so strong on his skates that you just try to minimize his chances, not try to stop him.

Every time you win a Stanley Cup, there is something that the team has to go through to achieve that. Winning the first Stanley Cup was about ending the drought for the Red Wings. The second Stanley Cup was all about Vladdy being on the ice after the limo accident. It was hard to feel good about winning the Cup, even though it was a good situation having Vladdy there to be a part of it. You remember what happened, and the emotions were a rollercoaster. I don't want to say you felt bad, but it brought you back to the moment in time when the accident occurred. I know there wasn't one guy involved with the team and the organization who wasn't happy to have Vladdy on the ice, and see that Cup on his lap, but you wish he would have been able to do that under his own power.

For some reason there's a special relationship between Kris Draper and me on the ice. I don't know if we just think alike, but we're always on the same page; we're trying to accomplish the same things. Whether it's the penalty killing or five-on-five, whatever it might be, we always work well together.

We feel like we kill a penalty better when we're not trying to do something structured. If we just do what Kris likes to call "controlled chaos," we just go, go, go. Usually he's the first one down there and I just kind of hover around and wait for something to try and pounce on. I know that he's going to come into the space or the area where he needs to be. I also know that if it gets by me, he's going to be in the position to help our defense and allow me to get back in the play. I wish I could pinpoint something specific, but it's just a chemistry that is there, and we've been able to have some longevity with it.

Kris Draper has always stood by me throughout my hockey career, both on the ice and off the ice as a friend. It doesn't matter if things are going good or bad, one thing I try to take pride in is I don't feel like I need to be told that I'm playing crappy. I know it, for the most part, and I'm trying to turn it around, but Kris is always there to tell me to keep going, keep plugging away, or with advice to try different things. If I were to have a best friend from the hockey standpoint in my life, it would have to be Kris Draper.

Being a Red Wing is really an honor. When I was traded here, I didn't know why I was coming, what I was going to be doing, or how long it was going to be for. The journey that it has been for me in Detroit, from day one, has been incredible. If I quit playing hockey tomorrow, I would have nothing but fond memories of putting on the Red Wings jersey.

I still remember the year after winning back-to-back cups; we got knocked out by Colorado. We were losing the game, but the Red Wings fans were still chanting, "Let's go Red Wings!" Even though they knew we weren't going to win that game, we were getting knocked out and our playoffs were over. For reasons like that, it's just a pure honor, nothing short of it, to be a Detroit Red Wing.

Kirk Maltby's Career Highlights

* Winning the first Stanley Cup against Philadelphia.

* Scoring the first goal of the 1997 Stanley Finals short-handed. "Drapes and I went in on a 2-on-1 against Ron Hextall," Maltby said.

* Winning the Cup in 1998 and again in 2002.

* Netting a hat trick against the Toronto Maple Leafs in Maple Leaf Gardens in 1997.

* Helping Canada win the World Championship in 2003.

TOMAS HOLMSTROM

LEFT WING

1996–Present

I TOOK IT STEP BY STEP.
I was playing in the league under the Swedish Elite League, and in 1992–1993 I got the chance to move up to a better team in that league. There was a scout for Washington who saw me play with that team and told me that I was going to be drafted. I thought I was going to be a Washington Capital, but it ended up that the Detroit Red Wings took me in the 10th round. My goal at that time was to first play in the Swedish Elite League and maybe even break into the Swedish National Team before I would get the chance to go to the NHL.

Until they drafted me, I had no idea that the Red Wings were interested in me. I didn't know that much about the team except for a few of the players like Steve Yzerman, Dino Ciccarelli, and Keith Primeau, who was a tough boy. I knew that they were a good hockey club and one of the Original Six teams. I didn't know much more than that. Nick Lidstrom had just come to the Red Wings a few years before I got drafted in 1994.

In 1996, when I came to Detroit, the team had won 62 games the year before. I was coming into one of the best hockey clubs in the National Hockey League. It was a big step for me. There were a lot of big names on the team then, and I knew that it was going to be tough for me. My first year, I was sent down for two weeks to Adirondack, and that was tough. I saw how hard the guys worked down there. Every guy down there was working out really hard, lifting weights and trying to take your spot on the NHL team. It was a good eye-opener for me to see all the guys in the minor leagues working so hard to try and make it up to Detroit. Those two weeks were the only time that I ever spent in the minor leagues in my NHL career.

I'm not the best skater, but I get there sooner or later. I just have to force myself more than others. I like the smaller rinks in the NHL better because the net is closer—I like it when it's a little more crowded and you're battling for the puck. That is my kind of game. It was a big adjustment for me to play eight years over here in Detroit and then try to go play in Sweden during the lock-out year on the big ice. It took some time to get used to that again. I still prefer the smaller rinks in the NHL.

When people watch what I do on the ice, they probably think that I have to be crazy. But I don't think anything about it. I go in front of the net and I do my job, I want to set screens so my teammates can score goals or I can get a tip. If I can provide a screen and my teammate can score, I feed off that. I feel like I deserve a lot of the credit when that happens, because you can't really score a goal from the blue line if you don't have that screen.

I consider myself a role player, especially on the power play. I don't go up to the point and I don't set up the play. I'm there around the net and I dig out the puck for Henrik Zetterberg and Pavel Datsyuk, or I get it out to the defenseman and then I go to the net. They know my role and I know their role. It's a good fit.

The referees in the league know that it's me in front of the net, so players are allowed to give me a couple more hits than the regular guy because of my style. It was supposed to be better in the "New NHL" but it's still there. I know that defensemen playing against me want to clear the net and they get frustrated with me. The goalies and defensemen talk about me, but they know that I'm coming back for more. You hate the defenseman whom you battle against, like Rob Blake, but you would love him if he were on your team.

My first fight in the NHL was against Rob Blake. It was a bloodbath for me. I had cross-checked him around the net and, once the puck moved out, I heard someone screaming behind me, saying, "You chicken!" He had no gloves on and he just grabbed me and started punching me. I ended up on my knees; it didn't turn out that well for me.

Patrick Roy was a pretty active goaltender with his stick; he didn't like me very much. Marty Turco in Dallas, he jabs and slashes and spears me. Eddie

Most NHL goaltenders would select Tomas Holmstrom as the league's most annoying pest. His modus operandi is to station himself in front of the net to act as a screen for the goalie. Then he takes advantage of being one of the NHL's best deflection artists to score. In 2005–2006 Holmstrom scored a career-best 29 goals.

Belfour went after me a lot with his stick, too. The goalies have the advantage; I can't really do anything to them. They can hack and whack and punch me a little bit with their blocker in my back. The refs say, "Stop doing that!" but, in the next shift, it happens all over again. Once in a while a ref will call it on the goaltender, but that doesn't happen very often.

I got a lot of help from Barry Smith when I came to the Red Wings; he worked with me a lot after practice and in one-on-one drills. Scotty Bowman picked the team and decided who was going to play and he helped me a lot, too, through the years. He was pretty tough on me for the first year or two and made me work for every opportunity I got. I became a better hockey player because of that. If I made a stupid mistake, I knew that Scotty would bench me for a period. And sometimes if someone else made the same mistake, he wouldn't say anything. There were a lot of mind games that would go on. I just worked hard and he started to play me after that.

With all three Red Wings coaches that I've played under, Scotty Bowman, Dave Lewis, and Mike Babcock, I just try to do my best. When I'm disappointed, I try not to bitch, but every once in awhile you have to speak up and talk to the coaches. At the end of the day, the coach decides who's going to play and what you're going to do out there. If you don't do it for him, you probably don't play. I try to do my best and do what they tell me to do out there.

Nick Lidstrom was the first of the Swedes to come to the Red Wings, so when I came, he helped me a lot to get settled in. He helped me get an apartment, a car, and with all the day-to-day things. He is a good friend; I owe a lot to him. Igor Larionov was my roommate for two years and a linemate for two years with Luc Robitaille. Igor taught me not to panic on the ice and to hold on to the puck. He would tell me, "When you have the puck, Homer, hold on to it! You dictate the game. When you have the puck, you decide what's going to happen." I try to remember his advice when my confidence is not really there.

One time, Igor and I were going to order late night snacks. I said I wanted hot chocolate and sandwiches. He said, "Homer, you see this body? I didn't get this body from hot chocolate and sandwiches." So we ordered a fruit plate instead.

Steve Yzerman had a big impact on me, especially my first season. I remember my first training camp, we would have short nights and have to work out before getting on the ice, and Steve would go back and work out more after practice. I couldn't believe it. I was so tired, but when I saw Stevie doing it, I thought, "I need to go and do that, too!" I still get impressed by Yzerman; he's always at his machine in the locker room. He always wants to be in shape, he never lets anything pass him by. He's been in the league 23 years and he still has the same work ethic as when he entered the league.

When I am a little bit tense, I like to talk more than having too much quiet. I don't like it when it's too quiet in the locker room, so I like to talk to my teammates. It gets me going, too, and we loosen up, especially when it's getting close to game time. It fires me up. Life is too short to be miserable; you have to take care of your time here on earth.

Pretty much every game I bug Chris Chelios. He always says to me, "Homer, shut up! Don't talk to me!" I can't help myself, I still talk to him. I talk to Mathieu Schneider a lot, too, about shooting the puck. I like to talk to the defense and tell them to shoot the puck. When they're coming up on the left side they know I'm there, I yell, "Give me the puck! Give me the puck!" I try to imprint it in their head—Homer is there! I'm open all the time! Then they will shoot the puck, but they often tell me to shut up. I pause for a little bit, but then get right back at it. Telling them, "You've got to shoot the puck!"

I don't know why I've been able to excel in the playoffs, maybe it's because more pucks come toward the net then. You have people shooting from everywhere. You don't pass up a shot in the playoffs; everyone is throwing pucks at the net even on the worst play. There are more pucks on the net because everyone is shooting rather than doing all the fancy plays that happen during the regular season. In the regular season, there is more passing back and forth and the shooting on the net becomes more about the rebounds.

Scoring goals in the playoffs is something I've been able to do. They are three games that I recall where I scored some big goals. The first one was against St. Louis when Grant Fuhr was in net; I was able to stick-handle and score a goal top shelf on the backhand. I remember scoring two goals in a 7–0 win against Colorado, and scoring in Game 5 at home versus Carolina in the Stanley Cup Finals; I was diving toward the goal and scored. It's difficult to describe how great it feels to score a meaningful goal in the playoffs.

You can't really compare any of the Stanley Cups. My first year, we won the first Stanley Cup in 42 years and everything was centered around winning it. When Vladdy stepped out onto the ice when we won our second Cup; that was very emotional because of everything that had happened with him. I was fortunate to get the chance to come to the Red Wings during the right time. Borje Salming played 17 years and I don't think he even played in a Stanley Cup Finals. You have to come to a team at the right time, and I've been with the Wings for 10 years and won three Stanley Cups, but it would still be great to have at least one more.

People always ask me how I came up with "Let's Party!" during our first Stanley Cup parade. This is the story. There were so many people, 1.5 million, that when I got up to speak there already had been so much talking. I just thought enough was enough, let's not speak—let's party!

It's really impressive that the Red Wings have had so many different players from different countries. For a time, there were five Russian guys, two Swedes, one American, and Canadians. We've had good team spirit through the years and great team leadership at the top, especially Steve Yzerman and the way he leads the team. Everything comes from there.

I don't think anyone would have ever guessed that the Red Wings would have seven Swedish players play a role on the team. It's remarkable the way the team finds the guys and they produce and become a big part of the team.

Right after I was drafted, I still remember telling my soon-to-be wife that I would give it two years in the NHL and if it didn't work we'd be going home. Ten years later, I have three Cups and three Yankee kids, two boys and a girl, and lots of friends. I can't complain. The Detroit Red Wings have treated me well.

Every time I put on the Red Wings jersey and see the wheel and the wing, I know I'm ready to go. It goes right through you. It's a great honor to be a Red Wing.

Tomas Holmstrom's Career Highlights

* Cracking the 20-goal mark for the second time in his career in 2005–2006.

* Being coached by Scotty Bowman.

* Playing with one of his idols, Igor Larionov.

* Lifting the Stanley Cup at the parade in 1998.

* Helping Sweden win the Olympic gold medal in 2006.

LARRY MURPHY

DEFENSEMAN

1996–2001

WHEN I GOT THE CALL FROM CLIFF FLETCHER saying that he could move me to Detroit, it didn't take me very long to say, "Yes." I had a no-trade clause in my contract with the Leafs, but the chance to come to Detroit was a no-brainer for me and for my career. I knew the Wings had a good opportunity to win it all, plus I had been with Scotty Bowman in Pittsburgh. It was a perfect situation for me to come into.

The Red Wings room was an easy one to walk into because the team worked hard and was committed. You get into some situations where players feel they have to walk around this way or that way, or say this or say that, just to give the impression that they really care—and that's the most important thing to them. In the Wings locker room, the play was the most important thing. It was all about how you went out and played.

Everybody got themselves ready for the game. It was a very comfortable situation. No one was looking at you thinking you laughed at the wrong time or getting upset if the game's in 15 minutes and you said something. On some teams, they're all hung up on that crap—the things that you don't really care about it. With the Wings, the proof was in the pudding. All that mattered was what you brought to games and what you brought to practice. How you got there didn't really matter. No one was trying to sell you anything. That professionalism comes with a mature team.

NHL.com writer John McGourty once called Larry Murphy "the most underrated star of the past 25 years in a major North American sport, a player whose on-ice skills dwarfed his need to be recognized." When Murphy retired in 2001, only Gordie Howe had played in more NHL games than he had. Others have passed him since.

When I started out with the Wings, I played with different partners on defense. As time went on, I played more and more minutes, but I kind of eased into it. I first started to play with Nick Lidstrom on a consistent basis the last few games of the regular season and into the playoffs. At that point I started playing with him exclusively.

The thing about Nick was that I had never played with a defenseman who was always in the right position. He never makes a wrong decision. He's a great skater, he's got a great head for the game, and he's got great hands.

When you mix all of that in with his natural ability, you've probably got one of the greatest defenseman to have ever played the game, and he does it as quietly as possible.

Nick has that subtle approach, so it took some time for people to realize how good he was. He caught my interest even before I got to Detroit. I wasn't surprised with anything I saw from Nick because I knew he was great before I got here. My approach was somewhat the same on defense, so when I watched him, I thought, *Boy, this guy is something!* You watch him and you can't help but learn something.

One thing that did surprise me about Lidstrom was how much he played and how it didn't seem to affect him. You could probably play him 50 minutes a game and in that last minute, you're going to get the same quality of play that you got the first minute of play. I already knew he was a great player, but his endurance was incredible—how well his play holds up day in and day out playing those types of minutes.

For me, the benefit to play with Nick was that he utilized his partner. If you made yourself available, the puck was going to come to you and it was going to come right on your tape. He was the perfect player to play with because our philosophy was the same. We're both better off with the puck, making the smart plays. I always wanted to play with a guy who looked at his partner as a viable option versus a guy that all he wanted to do was bang it off the boards. I knew that when he had the puck, I gave him another option; and if it was the best option, he was going to give it to me. I like playing that way. It's frustrating, at times, when you play with players who don't do that; players who just want to fire it off into the neutral zone or dump it out. I just felt I could be more effective with a player like Nick, and it worked out well.

I had known Scotty for a few years, so there really wasn't anything he could do that would surprise me. I never really gave it a second thought when he put Sergei Fedorov back on defense. I'll admit, I wasn't sure what his motivation was. I found out later, almost after the fact, that he wasn't happy with Sergei and he was trying to send him a message. I thought Scotty had this brainstorm about winning games and that's why he was putting Sergei back on the point. With Scotty Bowman, I learned to expect the unexpected.

I thought having Sergei on defense was a great idea. It was something I had never seen. I loved it! Of course, I had to be on my toes; but I didn't mind playing with Sergei at all. I could've played with him all year! It was a lot of fun. Sergei brought a dimension to that position that teams didn't see too often. The guy could skate with the puck through the whole opposition and he took advantage of that. He was strong enough and smart enough to do it well. We would talk a lot on the bench about doing this and doing that. You couldn't really tell whether he was happy or not with what was going on. He didn't share that with me, he just tried to make the best of it. I got along fine with Sergei, it was an enjoyable experiment. I knew it wasn't going to last that long, but I'm glad I was the one who got the opportunity to be his partner.

Pound for pound, I've never seen a tougher player in the National Hockey League than Vladimir Konstantinov. He wasn't a fighter, he wasn't a goon, but when he hit somebody—he hit them with every ounce of his being. He was tough as nails! He took some licks himself, but I guarantee you it wasn't going to slow him down. It was just going to make him more determined. He was tough, tough, tough! I never saw him fight, but to me toughness is a guy who is mentally tough and basically strikes fear in the opposition. When he was on the ice, everybody was well aware of it on the opposition. That's the one guy I was probably more impressed with than anybody else on the Red Wings. I didn't really know him that well until I saw him game in and game out and just how committed and hard-nosed he was. He was just an "impact guy" in the true sense of the word.

As tough as Vladdy was, and I did play some time with him, he was still strong with the puck. All you have to do is look at the Russian Five when they were out there. He was right in the mix in terms of puck control.

I remember the two years we won the Stanley Cup, the knock was on the defense—that the defense wasn't tough enough. There's a lot of different ways to succeed and, yeah, okay, we didn't have the toughest defensemen. But we ended up winning the Stanley Cup twice in a row, so was toughness that big of a deal? I think management had tremendous focus on putting together a group of guys who would win.

When I look back on playing Philadelphia in the '97 Finals, the Flyers had their Legion of Doom Line. The media thought that we were going to try to match that line physically and they were going to run us over. I give credit to Scotty because his approach to playing that line was, "Well, we're just not going to give them the puck."

Philadelphia thought the Legion of Doom was going to run up against Vladimir Konstantinov. Their plan was to run Vladdy over and bull us over. Scotty just stayed away from that and played Nick and I against them, and they never had the puck. They went through the game and they never got hit, but they also never got a shot on goal because they never got the puck. They wondered what the hell happened! They had this "run us over" mentality and they never got near anybody. That just shows that there are a number of ways to succeed, and they didn't know what hit them. I guess the lack of being hit was a surprise to the Legion of Doom.

Steve Yzerman's approach with the players in the dressing room was that he identified with everyone and gave the kind of encouragement or direction they needed to be successful. Stevie is bright enough to realize how different guys needed to be dealt with in different situations. One of his biggest strengths as a captain was he knew what buttons needed to be pushed in order for a player to be the best he could be. He wasn't a rah-rah type of guy, but when he said something, he had so much respect in the dressing room that everybody hung on every word he had to say. He would pick his spots carefully, which is smart because it makes it much more effective. If you get a captain and all he does is babble all the time, then a lot of what he says gets missed because you just get tired of hearing it game in and game out.

During the 1997 playoffs, we lost at St. Louis 4–0 to tie up our series against the Blues at two games each. Yzerman realized that was a critical time in the playoff run where something needed to be said. I'm not sure how important it was to the rest of our playoff run, but it seems to have taken on a life of its own. The legend has kind of grown to the point where people say, "There wasn't a dry eye in the room," and I feel like I should say that it was one of the greatest days in my life or something. The truth is, Yzerman just said something to all of us that needed to be said—and we responded.

The celebration of winning the Stanley Cup came crashing to a halt as soon as the limo accident happened. The old saying is true—it puts all priorities and what's important into perspective. It was just devastating. To this day, you just shake your head about how it all happened. These are guys who are doing the responsible thing and it turns out, in Vladdy's case, to destroy him; and same with Sergei Mnatsakanov, he'll never be the same.

It hurt on a number of different levels. They're people you knew well personally and you've just gone through this experience of winning the Stanley Cup with them. I wasn't with the team that long, but because of what we went through—the marathon of the playoffs—you felt close to these guys. When something as tragic as that happens, obviously winning the Cup didn't really mean that much from that point on. There was no reason to celebrate. Everything was taken away from you; two friends were fighting for their lives and it was just a horrible, horrible, shocking event.

Without a doubt that accident was a huge factor for the team the next season; it was something to rally around. Win it for Sergei and Vladdy! It was amazing how far that carried us through that season and right into the 1998 playoffs. That was our purpose. Often, when you win the Cup, that next season it's that much tougher to repeat for a number of reasons—everyone's gunning for you and there's no longer that sense of urgency. The team used that terrible situation and tried to make the best out of it by winning the Cup for our two friends. There isn't a greater motivating factor than that!

Being a Detroit Red Wing is being a part of a franchise with a long storied history. The winged wheel—putting that on is special when you think about all the players who played in it and the tradition. The one thing I love about the Red Wings is they stay true to their path, especially in terms of their uniform. You feel the history of being an Original Six team. That's an honor. There are two types of teams in the National Hockey League—there's an Original Six team and there's not. You're either get to experience it or you don't. The Red Wings had that great uniform, and I always liked pulling on the sweater.

Larry Murphy's Career Highlights

* Being the only NHL player to win four Stanley Cups in the 1990s. He won two with Detroit (1997 and 1998) and two with Pittsburgh (1991 and 1992).

* Making the NHL Second All-Star team three times.

* Passing Tim Horton (in February 1999) for most games played by a defenseman.

* Being the fifth highest-scoring defenseman in NHL history, with 1,216 points.

* Getting elected to Hockey Hall of Fame in 2004.

BRENDAN SHANAHAN

LEFT WING

1996–2006

MY DAD STARTED TO GET ALZHEIMER'S disease when I was 14 or 15 years old. He was alive when I was in the NHL, but I don't think he really knew it. He died in 1990 after my third year in the league.

After we won the Cup in 1997, the players had to put in requests for days to get the Stanley Cup. I got it on a Friday and Saturday. We had a whole bunch of things planned for Saturday, but in the middle of the afternoon, I grabbed the Cup and put it in the car without telling anybody where I was going. It was in the middle of August and just a beautiful day. I thought to myself, "I really want to do this. I want to take the Stanley Cup to my father's grave."

I just didn't want it to be inappropriate. I was hoping there wouldn't be a whole bunch of people there who would come over. This was in Toronto; so if people see the Stanley Cup, even in a cemetery, it was going to cause a stir. Amazingly, when I got there, there wasn't a single person in the entire cemetery. I was relieved that we were alone, but afterwards I thought that it was pretty eerie. I've gone to visit him many times since then and on a weekend the graveyards have a lot of visitors.

I took the Stanley Cup out of my car, without anyone seeing it, walked over, and put it on my dad's grave. I just sat there with the Cup and thought about him and growing up with him. I said some prayers and talked to him. As quietly as I had put it down, I picked up the Cup, took it back to my car, and left.

It was show-and-tell for me, and that was my dad's time to see it up close and one-on-one. It was my time to tell him, "Hey, Dad, look what we did!"

Scotty Bowman and I never had any real confrontations. You would have thought that we had this relationship where we would fight and yell at one another, but we really hardly ever spoke. We would always jaw in the press a bit, but I would like to think that I was always respectful of who he was. I never disrespected him in the press. He was Scotty Bowman and he was my coach. I wasn't always happy with him, but I don't feel its right to disrespect your coach, no matter what he's doing to you. I have no problem with having a face-to-face meeting with the guy, but I don't think it's ever right to air your dirty laundry through the press.

I think Scotty Bowman liked me mad and there was nothing wrong with me, as a hockey player, with a little bit of anger. Scotty knew that and he would pick the right time to get to me. As mad as Scotty used to make me, he used me on the ice. He gave me my ice time. When we were down a goal with a minute to go—I was on the ice. When we were up a goal with a minute to go—I was on the ice. As much as people say to me, "It must have been really hard to play for Scotty Bowman!" I just tell them, "We won three Stanley Cups, and when the clock ticked down to zero—I was on the ice." I'd rather have a coach who liked to crap on me but always played me in key situations than a guy who put his arm around me but was afraid to play me.

Bowman liked to test people to see what they were made of. Were they going to turn on the team? Were they going to turn on him? Scotty was all about seeing mental toughness. But then again, I might be totally wrong and he might just like messing with people's heads. I think he wants to see what people are made of because he thought that to go the distance in the playoffs you have to be mentally strong. He had a lot of great players in Detroit who put up good numbers whom he unloaded.

The funny thing is that when Scotty left, the players had arguments about who was hated most by him. Holmstrom thought he was hated most by Scotty. I thought I was. Draper thought he was hated most by Scotty. We all laughed at one another and said, "Oh, no—he loved you! He hated me!" I think he liked Nick Lidstrom and Steve Yzerman, and that was it. But Steve told me that when Scotty first came to the team, he was really tough on him for years! So who knows?

I'm not sure if the March 26 game against the Avalanche was the real turning point for our team, but it certainly seemed to signify it. Who knows if

Brendan Shanahan led the Detroit Red Wings with 46 goals during their 1996–1997 Stanley Cup season and was the team's leading scorer the following season when it won again. Shanahan said he understood the Hockeytown aura as soon as he was dealt to the Red Wings by Hartford. "You quickly get a sense of the passion here," Shanahan said. "There's a mandate from the fans to win a Stanley Cup. I like that." *Photo courtesy of AP/Wide World Photos.*

that was really the day, but a lot of things came together that night for us. We had to do what we had to do that night to turn the page on the previous season. One of the reasons that Scotty brought me in was for games like March 26. It wasn't just about going out and getting into fights, it was about winning the game in the end. The fights are what everyone remembers, but the game doesn't hold the same significance if we don't erase that 2–0 deficit and win in overtime.

Any time we played the Colorado Avalanche, at that point in time, we were ready. I was still a new guy on the team, so I didn't feel like it was my place to start it. But I was glad that I was on the ice when it happened! Darren McCarty, myself, and Igor Larionov were a very successful line at the time. We really had no plan for anything happening going into the March 26 game. And if we did, Darren didn't tell me anything about it. But we had been in enough fights over the year that you knew that guys would watch your back. Little did we know that Igor was the one who was going to start the whole thing.

When Igor started things with Forsberg, everything else happened quickly. On TV, it seemed like McCarty was on Claude Lemieux in a second, but really Mac was paired up with Adam Foote first. He yelled to me, "Shanny, come take him!" I came over and grabbed Foote, who tried to hold onto McCarty before he took off but I swatted his arm. McCarty took off and was on Lemieux the next instant. Two seconds later, I see Patrick Roy already at the top of the circle in full stride. At that moment, I broke loose of Foote and started out to get to Roy before he could get to Mac. Now you see the famous picture of me on my way to Roy with Foote chasing me and Mike Vernon chasing Foote, with McCarty and Lemieux in the background. Everything was happening—the fights, the big flying leap, and then the game ending with McCarty scoring in overtime. It was all a great moment for our team, but none of it would have mattered if we didn't come back and win that game.

After the game ended, the dressing room was just rocking! We were all going crazy and running into the coaches' room to watch the replay on TV because we hadn't seen it. McCarty was blown away—he didn't realize that any of this stuff was happening around him! He was so transfixed on Lemieux that Roy and me leaping in the air, Vernie and Roy fighting, and me and Foote fighting never caught his attention. All this action was happening around him and he really believed that it was just him and Lemieux fighting on the ice and that was it! He thought everyone else was just standing around watching.

There was a moment in the McCarty/Lemieux fight when Mac kneed Lemieux right in the head. If you watch the tape, Paul Devorski was the ref, and he was watching Mac as he was punching him. Devorski looked to the right for two seconds and that's right when Mac knees him in the head. I think McCarty was the most surprised guy in the world that he didn't get kicked out of that game!

Patrick Roy told me the next year at the Olympics that the leap with me messed his shoulder up. A few years later at the All-Star Game in L.A., in 2002, Roy came up to me and said, "You know, my shoulder is still messed up from that time when I jumped in the air." I'm not even sure who jumped first. He saw me coming, and I saw him coming, and at the last second we both just lunged in the air. It was *Matrix*-like.

When we were presented the Stanley Cup in 1997, it was the first time I had ever seen a player be told, "Go take a lap by yourself!" It wasn't planned, but everyone just stood back. It used to always be the whole team taking a lap and the Cup being handed off from guy to guy. This was the only time I could remember a guy taking a solo skate and it was great to watch. It was awesome for Steve Yzerman.

Everything about the Stanley Cup celebration came to a screeching halt when the limo accident happened. It had been a week-long love fest and party and all of the sudden it was just over. But it also brought our team closer together; you appreciate the guys more. That is what I took away from that moment—a real appreciation for the guys who I have gotten to play with in Detroit.

I didn't golf at the time, so I planned it that I would arrive and meet the guys as they were finishing their golf games. Before I left my house, I was watching a musical tribute to the team that was shown on TV; the clip it ended with was Vladdy's hit on Dale Hawerchuk and his icy stare. I turned to my wife and said, "I love Vladimir Konstantinov!" I meant it; I just loved him as a player and as a teammate! He never said a word, he just showed up every night. You hear people say that a lot after something happens to a player, but we were saying it before he ever had his accident.

When I arrived at the golf course, those guys were leaving early. They were getting ready to leave in their limo and rolled down the window because I was the one guy missing on some of the things they had signed by the team. I stopped and signed the stuff to complete the set for them and teased them about leaving early. They said that they were tired and had enough; they just wanted to go home. That was it.

The next year, I had no doubt that the team was willing to make the sacrifices to do it again. I thought at the time that Steve Yzerman had taken his game to a new level that year. He won the Conn Smythe in 1998 and really deserved it.

Coming to the Red Wings, you know who Steve Yzerman is and what you get from him, so he didn't surprise me. My first impression of the team was that I couldn't believe how talented our third and fourth lines were with Maltby, Draper, and McCarty. That just doesn't exist in other organizations. The second thing that struck me was how much of a warrior Vladimir Konstantinov was.

During my first practice with the Wings, I met Darren McCarty and Marty Lapointe. I took it upon myself to give them advice on how to be physical and score goals. By the second practice, they were asking me how to get open. They already had the intimidation; they just needed to turn that into space and room so they could score. I used to call those two "my children." It made me feel good to have these guys looking up to me and asking for my help. It was a different atmosphere than other teams; in Detroit you were immediately brought in and welcomed.

Jimmy Devellano was in our room one time talking about the nucleus of the Red Wings team. I had always thought that the nucleus of the team was made up of guys who were draft picks. But he told me, "We consider you part of our nucleus." That made me feel really good! They may talk about the players they drafted like Steve Yzerman and Nick Lidstrom, but now I'm at a point where I'm one of the originals, too. There are certain players whom you identify with certain teams around the league, and I think that I'm now seen as a Detroit Red Wing with guys like Ted Lindsay, Alex Delvecchio, Gordie Howe, Steve Yzerman, Nick Lidstrom, and Vladimir Konstantinov.

When I first came to the team, I met Ted Lindsay and we hit it off because of the style that he played. He was such a champion. To think of 20 or 30 years from now, our group of players being thought of like the Howe-Lindsey Red Wings era when they won Cups—you feel like you're a part of something that is constant and steady.

Brendan Shanahan's Career Highlights

* Winning the first Stanley Cup in 1997 against Philadelphia.

* Winning the second Cup versus Washington.

* Winning the third Cup against Carolina.

* Eating team dinners—all of them—over the years.

* Being in the Red Wings dressing room. "It's the funniest, most cut-throat room I've ever been in!" he said. "You sit in your stall and wait for someone to do something—and then you all pounce!"

KEN HOLLAND

GOALTENDER

1983–1984

GENERAL MANAGER

1997–Present

AFTER MY HOCKEY PRO HOCKEY CAREER was over in 1985, I considered a career in vacuum sales. Jimmy Devellano had called to say that the Detroit Red Wings weren't going to re-sign me. They wanted to go with younger goalies. When I called around the league for the next three or four weeks, it didn't look too promising that I could find a job in hockey.

My wife, Cindy, and I had three kids, age five, three, and one. She was a nurse, and I was working for the Vernon [British Columbia] liquor store. We were golden until Labor Day. I was 29. Cindy had convinced me that she could work full-time at the hospital and for two years we would remain in Vernon and I would go to college because I loved numbers. Then we were going to Vancouver so I could go to the university for a business or finance degree. Cindy would put me through college.

My mom caught wind of this and, when Cindy had the kids at the pool, my mom told me, "You're the breadwinner of the family. You need a job."

She said, "You have the gift of gab. You would be a good salesperson."

"What would I sell?" I asked.

She had been looking through the *Vernon News* and she saw an ad for a vacuum cleaner salesman for the area. She had called the 1-800 number and the job was still open. These vacuums were going for over $320. Ten or 20 percent of all sales went to the salesperson.

"I need a new vacuum and I'll be your first sale," my mom said.

Then she talked to my Grandma Eistbrecht, my mom's mom who lived five doors down, and she said she would buy one from me.

I'm thinking, *This job is great. I haven't even got the job and I've sold two vacuums*. I asked my mom if Auntie Emma might need a new vacuum. She lived two doors down. My mom said we could go talk to her. Now I'm thinking this vacuum sales business is really good. If I could sell one per day, five per week, I would have a decent living. I hadn't got the job and business was booming.

Then it hit me: I had run out of family members. *Who was I going to sell to on Thursday?*

That's when I realized that vacuum cleaner salesman wasn't the career for me, and a week later Jimmy D called, saying the Red Wings were looking for a western Canada scout.

I remember that Jimmy told me on the phone, "If you work hard, you get along with people, and you know your business, you never know how far you can go."

And that's how I went about my business with the Red Wings. I was Neil Smith's protégé, and when he left to join the Rangers, Jimmy D took me under his wing as a young hockey person with executive potential. I owe him for where I'm at today. When I moved to Detroit in 1994 and was in the office daily, working with Jimmy D and Scotty Bowman, I learned much about the business. Behind the scenes we would throw ideas around, compare numbers, and build a hockey team. Those three years for me were like going to Harvard.

Jimmy D's strength is that he loves the game. It's all hockey for Jimmy. He knows when to make a decision and he's comfortable around people. When he walks into a room, it doesn't matter whether he's facing the president of the United States or the owners, he has a comfort level. He can get a conversation going. His ability to build relationships helped him. And Jimmy D taught that me this is an entertainment business. Winning is most important, but if you can win with big names it's even more exciting.

Ken Holland has been Detroit's general manager since 1997, guiding the team to two Stanley Cup championships. Some younger fans don't know that Holland actually played three games for the Red Wings in the 1983–1984 season, posting an 0–1–1 record. Today, he is one of the league's most respected executives.

In 1997 the Florida Panthers had asked for permission to talk to me about an assistant GM job and were turned down. In 1998 the St. Louis Blues' Ron Caron had contacted the Wings about their GM opening. About that time, Jimmy D had talked to Mr. Ilitch about going to a traditional front office model. At the time, we had the three-headed monster—with Bowman, Devellano, and Holland—and we had success with that. Scotty was also the director of player personnel and he could make player moves. My thought was, *How could I become the general manager if Scotty had all the authority?*

I was interested in being general manager, but it wasn't going to be good for my career or for the Red Wings if I had the title of general manager and I was Scotty's puppet. There were a lot of discussions behind the scene. Let's just say relationships were not totally harmonious. There was some stress. It came to a head when Scotty and I agreed to meet in London, Ontario, at Swiss Chalet at 3:00 P.M. on a Friday. Scotty came from Buffalo and I came from Detroit. After that meeting, I felt comfortable that I could be the general manager. He apologized for something that had happened the season before, and I told him that I respected his knowledge and wasn't going to make moves without getting his input.

"We are going to work together as a team," I said.

I think that was important for Scotty because he didn't want someone coming in and trying to make the team younger or cheaper. The meeting took three hours. It was like a marriage. We had to work out our issues.

From that point on, Scotty and I have had an unbelievable relationship. We were both on the same page about getting the right players here to win.

We already had many of those players, like Steve Yzerman, Nick Lidstrom, and many others.

Lidstrom took his game to another level after Vladimir Konstantinov's accident. He knew we needed him to do that. If you came to the rink to watch the Red Wings play for one game, and someone said Nick was a superstar, you might not see it. He is a superstar because he does it every game, every season. When you watch him every day, you appreciate all that he does. He rarely has a bad game. He rarely makes a bad pass. Rarely does he get beat.

To me, Nick is one of the top 10 defensemen to play the game in the history of the NHL. Nick doesn't do a lot of talking. You don't get that good without having a burning desire to be the best.

There is no doubt the Chris Chelios deal was one of the best trades I've made. We tried to bring in Chelios to help us get a three-peat in 1999 and it didn't work out. We gave up two first-round draft picks and Anders Eriksson, who helped us win a Cup the season before. But six years year later Chelios is still an important player on our team. In 2002 he had one of the best years of his career. He was runner-up for the Norris Trophy. And his contributions will last long after he is gone. Seeing the competitor he is has had an impact on players like Pavel Datsyuk and Henrik Zetterberg.

Probably the little move that worked out the best came in 1998. We acquired Dmitri Mironov to play in our top four and we landed Jamie Macoun for our seventh defenseman. The opposite happened. Scotty Bowman liked the pair of Bob Rouse and Macoun, and that pair helped us win a Stanley Cup.

You can't put into words what kind of player Yzerman has been for our organization. He's an incredibly determined athlete. He has great skills, but it's the mental strength that amazes everyone around him. What he went through in 2002 just to play was amazing. He was bone on bone in his knee. He motivated our team. He willed our team through the Vancouver series. We wouldn't have won that series unless Stevie willed us to win in Vancouver in Games 3 and 4. We were down 2–0, and Steve just decided we weren't going to lose.

When Scotty Bowman came to Detroit, there were rumors that he wanted to make changes. Steve wanted to remain a Red Wing. Steve completely transformed his game from being one of the league's greatest offensive players to being the best two-way player in the game. When your best player pays attention to defensive detail, everyone around him does the same.

But Scotty's energy level also was crucial. His energy level is unmatched. His passion is unmatched. During the 2002 season, I remember Detroit pro scout Danny Belisle saying, "Scotty has been here eight years and I've never seen him yawn."

Scotty's whole life was about hockey. No one dissects players and systems like Scotty. Because he was successful, he wasn't afraid to try different coaching moves. If it didn't work, he tried something else. And he had no problems stirring the nest. In fact, even if it didn't need stirring, he stirred it just in case.

His mind is like no mind you have ever been around. Every detail is important to him. He would talk to the cook to see which players were coming in there, or he would talk to the parking lot attendant to see who was arriving with whom and what time they were coming in. His mind is going in one hundred different directions at the same time. He prepares for every different scenario going into a game. He looks at every match-up. He knows who is going good and who is going bad on every team. As soon as the Internet became popular, he figured out how to use it effectively. He wanted every bit of information he could get.

One day during the 1996 playoffs in St. Louis, Danny Belisle and I were out for a walk and we saw Scotty sitting by himself in a coffee shop. We sat down with him and he spent two hours talking about all the different scenarios that could happen that night. Leaving there, I marveled at how prepared he was.

When Scotty was coaching, we always had the same routine. We would look for a sports bar with a bank of TVs. We would order chicken wings and watch every game. We had a blast. Scotty has such great passion for hockey.

Here's a story that shows Scotty's incredible attention to detail: it was the third round of the playoffs in 1998. We were tied 1–1 with Dallas. The series was coming to Detroit. We were to skate at 10:30, and the road team at 11:30. At 12:30 I got a call in my office from Scotty to come down by the bench. He had to show me something. I went flying down there. I got there and he showed me that ESPN had put an overhead camera on the bottom of the score clock. He said that that was against playoff regulations. I hadn't read the entire book, but Scotty said the camera could only be so many feet below the clock. The overhead camera was clearly bothering him.

"What's the difference?" I asked finally.

He explained to me that the Dallas defense, particularly Derian Hatcher and Richard Matvichuk, who would play half the game, liked to clear the puck off the glass and into the neutral zone. When we were under pressure, our defense liked to flip the puck high into the air. He felt that there could be a chance that one of our defensemen could hit that camera. Then the face-off would be in our zone. He thought Dallas was better on the face-off. Dallas would win the face-off and would score a goal. Therefore that camera was an advantage to Dallas. He wanted it removed.

I didn't quite know what to do, but five minutes later we had 15 people looking at it. We had TV people, league people, building people, etc. I figured, if he wanted it handled, it would be handled. I went back to my office.

At 7:15 that night, I went up to watch the game and the overhead camera was gone. In the end, Scotty was right. He thought that camera was a one-in-a-million advantage for Dallas and he didn't want to give the Stars that advantage. He wouldn't take a chance.

He was concerned about everything, whether it was the schedule, travel arrangements, or even whether the benches were too high or too low. Some of it was just for effect, and sometimes he had a legitimate concern. It all came from the experience of doing it for 30 years.

Scotty Bowman is the guy who came in here and put on the finishing touches. We had been working here, drafting young players, bringing in skilled players. He was the guy who taught us how to win. He was a major factor in the Red Wings winning three Stanley Cups.

When he came behind the bench, our organization was still young. We had talent, and we would beat you 5–4 in the regular season and lose to you 3–2 in the playoffs. When teams in the playoffs tightened up, we were still young colts, playing wild run-and-gun hockey. Scotty came in and observed the first year. He had to see what he had. Then, after we lost to San Jose in the playoffs, he got the authority to make the moves. He brought in Mike Vernon, Slava Fetisov, Igor Larionov. He put together the Russian Five. He brought in players we needed to play the kind of hockey he thought we needed to play to be successful. We learned to check better. I think he helped Steve Yzerman transform himself into an even better player.

We've had great success, and Europeans have been a big part of that. When Scotty put together the Russian Five, that was really the start of the Red Wings we see today. I think it even had an impact on how we developed our drafting philosophy and scouting philosophy.

We won the President's Trophy and went to the Finals and lost to New Jersey in 1995. In 1996 we got 131 points and made it to the third round. We won the Stanley Cup in 1997 and again in 1998.

Scotty was all about maxing out the team's potential. Every day there were things he wasn't happy about. One day he would come in and complain about six issues and I would agree with him. The next day he would be complaining about six different issues. The way I approached Scotty is that if he complained about the same player day after day, then I knew, if I liked that player, I had to figure out how to get that player in Scotty's good book or I would have to work the phones to make a move.

Scotty was never going to come into my office and say everything was perfect. He was looking for perfection. He wanted great practices. He always felt that he could push his players a touch more. He pushed and he pushed and he pushed.

But we had three Stanley Cup parades.

Looking back, I think Scotty pushed buttons on players because he thought they had more to give. I think there were players whom Scotty felt he didn't have to push. But my feeling was that Scotty Bowman enjoyed coaching this group of players. He liked their skill level. He liked their commitment, and he liked them as people. I can say this: if Scotty Bowman didn't like you, you weren't in Detroit long. When Scotty was coach, he didn't want to get too close to his players. He didn't want anyone having a comfort level when he came to the rink. Now that he's not coaching, I think he shows he likes the players. I think Scotty was proud to be coach of the Red Wings, and the success we had in his nine years of coaching.

Some days I wake up and pinch myself to make sure I haven't been dreaming about the opportunity I've had as general manager of the Detroit Red Wings. There are only 30 manager jobs, and only six are with Original Six teams. It's an honor to be general manager of the Red Wings. It's also a responsibility. This franchise has been around for many years and has had so many great players, you feel an obligation to keep it strong. Everywhere we go, we play in a sold-out building. There are many passionate Red Wings fans around the world. This franchise means so much to so many people, you don't want to screw it up.

Ken Holland's Career Highlights

* Originally drafted by Toronto, Holland played one NHL game for Hartford and three for the Detroit Red Wings.

* Trading Slava Kozlov and a first-round pick, on July 1, 2001, to Buffalo for Dominik Hasek.

* Being inducted to the Binghamton Hall of Fame, in New York, in February of 1998. He had a strong minor-league career in Binghamton.

* Signing free agents and future Hall of Famers Brett Hull and Luc Robitaille in 2001.

* Being Red Wings GM when they won the Stanley Cup in 1998 and 2002. Was assistant GM when the team won in 1997.

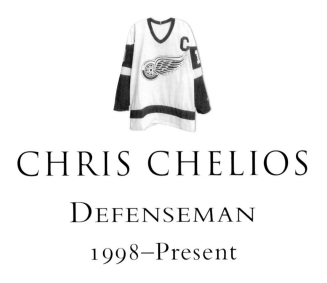

CHRIS CHELIOS

DEFENSEMAN
1998–Present

I HAD A SISTER WHO WAS GOING THROUGH chemotherapy, and that affected my decision to stay in Chicago, probably a year longer than I really wanted to. It got to the point where I wanted to be traded; Detroit was an easy commute where I would still be able to get to her and help her. I told Chicago management that I didn't care where I went; I just wanted out. I was fortunate enough to come to Detroit and to a team of this caliber. It was a second life for me because Chicago's management almost had me convinced that I was done and should retire after the year.

When I was in Chicago, I put my foot in my mouth, telling everyone that I didn't like Detroit. That's the one quote that is always brought up, my saying, "I will never play in Detroit." Obviously, things change. I can honestly say that I didn't dislike Detroit until I came to Chicago, because the Blackhawks and Red Wings had quite a rivalry. That's where the quote came from. It's odd because Detroit and Chicago have the same sort of tradition and history with hockey. You say things. I don't regret saying it because I felt it at the time, but now I've come to Detroit, found a home here, and things have been great.

I can say this now that I've played with him, but as much as I went after him, Steve Yzerman was my favorite player in the NHL all those years. I've never told him that—I've probably never told anybody that up until this point. I just love watching him play. I don't have too many idols, or favorites,

A case can be made that Chelios is the greatest American player of all time. When the Red Wings acquired Chelios, he looked like a short-term fix. But he was 44 in 2005–2006 when he played his seventh season with Detroit. Considered the ultimate warrior, Chelios has played in four Olympic Games, including two while he was playing for the Red Wings. He was plus-15 for the Red Wings in the postseason during the 2002 Stanley Cup championship run. *Photo courtesy of AP/Wide World Photos.*

but he was one of them. I was just happy to be on the same team, and in the same dressing room, as Steve Yzerman. He's everything that I thought he would be. He has such a great work ethic and grit. He's one guy who I went after who, for a skill player, would give it right back to you. He wouldn't shy away from the physical contact, and I respected him a lot for that. In Montreal we didn't see Detroit that often, and their team wasn't very strong back in the 1980s. We really didn't take the Wings too seriously. But to play against Yzerman in all those games with Chicago, and in the playoffs, it was great to get to watch him.

Once Sergei Fedorov came to the Wings, I was glad, because then I didn't have to go after Yzerman anymore because Fedorov was an easy target. I used to get under Sergei's skin and I made him drop the gloves a few times. But that was my job in Chicago. That was the way that Mike Keenan coached, and I didn't have a problem doing it. Guys like Bob Probert and Darren McCarty would watch Fedorov's back, and that made it even tougher for me.

Sergei is really the nicest kid in the world. I see what he goes through now when he comes back to play in Detroit, and that's just a part of the game— the fans boo the other jersey. What Sergei Fedorov did for this franchise, I don't think anyone can forget. He was a great kid when he was on the Red Wings. He lived close to me and was on his own and single, so we spent a lot of time together. We would go to dinner and the movies. I got to know Sergei a lot, and he kind of needed a baby-sitter. He didn't have a lot of friends, and I felt like I should spend time with him. When he was in a good mood, he played better, and that's what we needed on the Red Wings.

Fedorov always did his own thing; he would play video games for hours like a kid. I never really asked what type of person he was or if the guys liked him. He was laid back, which was the total opposite of what I am. I got along well with Sergei. I enjoyed spending time with his family and parents. It's hard to keep in touch with players after they leave because of the long-distance relationships, but I still speak with Sergei all the time.

It takes a bit of everything to get inside an opponent's head. With the new rules now, it's tougher to instigate something. Most of the time, when you go after their top players, you wake up the rest of the team and end up being chased by the whole team. That's just the way it was. I have a little thing going with Todd Bertuzzi and some of the other top players, but now it's different because Nick Lidstrom and Andreas Lilja go against the other team's top lines. I go out there and play now and I'm not that worried. You just have to be smarter in today's game. Back in the day, you could get away with a lot more, whether it was an elbow to the head or a slash—the rules were a lot more lenient.

Whether it's Paul Kariya or Todd Bertuzzi, it's always a challenge because of the competitiveness in me. In the old days with Montreal, it was Peter Stastny and Michel Goulet, and in Chicago it was Yzerman and Fedorov. Kariya has an extra thing going for him because I don't really like the way he plays the game. He goes around the perimeters and floats, and that's basically the way Nashville plays, but they are a skilled, fast team. It's nothing personal, it's on the ice. I talk to Paul Kariya off the ice and he's very nice. I always tell my sons that when they grow up and play the game, they should act like Steve Yzerman or Paul Kariya—nice and classy. But once we get on the ice, I can't stand him!

Jiri Fischer and I had a great relationship, especially in his first year. On the road we would have dinner because I'm so busy with my children when we're at home. It's hard to have the same relationship with players that I used to have because of my obligations to my own kids now. Jiri Fisher was terrific to work with because he had a tremendous work ethic. He was really the first kid I had to take under my wing and help along. I knew that was why I was paired with him. It couldn't have gone any better, and we wound up winning the Stanley Cup that year. Fischer loves hockey as much as I do. The effort that he puts in on the ice and off the ice—it's hard to question a kid like that.

Playing with Fischer probably made me a better defensive hockey player. Instead of leading the charge up the ice, I would back up Jiri and let him carry the puck. It was a safety hatch for him and different for me. I didn't take the chances offensively that I did before. It's the same now with Brett Lebda. I would have felt very selfish if I hadn't done that. It was a sacrifice for me, but at the same time a very rewarding feeling. I would love to be able to play my old game and get going offensively again, but the Wings have made it clear that that's not what they want me to do. I have no problem with that at this point in my career.

Unless you saw Jiri Fischer's face, how his body was reacting, and could see our players standing 10 feet away from him when he collapsed on the bench against Nashville, you can't fully understand it. [Doctors say that Fischer's heart stopped due to cardiac arrest on November 21, 2005. They have not determined why it occurred.] It was the most terrifying event that I've ever had to experience in the game of hockey. I've compared it to when my sister passed away because I was beside her and there was the same sort of breathing. Those tight, last breaths. I was devastated, watching him go down and watching him be taken out of the rink. At that point, I just went to the locker room. I couldn't watch it anymore. I thought Jiri Fischer had passed away. I knew what was going on because of my sister, and it was terrifying.

The NHL league supervisor was there that night and he said that he felt like we should play the game. But you had to be there, we were 10 feet away from Fish, watching him go through that. Our players were falling apart—there's no way we could have played that game! We sat there and talked about it, and the coaches pulled three or four of us aside, no one hesitated—we weren't going to finish that game. You couldn't second-guess that. I know there were a few fans who really didn't understand what actually happened and what a terrible thing it was, but we made the right decision.

Jiri Fischer was all about hockey and working out, no one was in better shape than him. It has to be tough for a 25-year-old to have all of that taken away. It's always great to see him down at the rink. I'm sure it's difficult for him to watch the games, but he seems to be in good spirits. There's always an outside chance, maybe not now, but somewhere down the line—who knows?—maybe he can play again. Maybe modern medicine can come up with something that gives him a second chance. But after watching what Jiri went through, he's lucky to be alive, and I think he realizes that. He'll probably always have that thought in his mind of playing again; you never know what can happen.

Having Scotty Bowman for a coach was amazing. Playing for the greatest coach ever, Scotty Bowman, I was tickled pink. It could not have gone any better for me. Not just with Scotty, but with every coach I've had, I consider myself to be a coach's player. I believe it's my work ethic. When you go out there and do the best you can from an effort standpoint, you earn the respect of the coaches.

Scotty knew what he was getting when he traded for me. I think Scotty is a big fan of veteran players. I'm sure that Scotty okayed the trade. He must have wanted me. He made me feel welcome on the spot. He has a great, dry sense of humor. I always got a kick out of it because you never knew what to expect from him. I'm not saying I could predict what he was going to do, but it was always entertaining coming to the rink. Whether it was ripping the microphones off the glass in practice or pushing a media guy—it was always fun. I've always liked the unexpected, and that was Scotty.

Brett Hull is my best friend, and I think the greatest American hockey player ever. What he provides, as a person and on the ice, you don't find that too often. He's a special person. As much as he whines and complains publicly, and said what he wanted to say, there was no one who loved hockey more then Brett Hull. He always wanted to be the first one at the rink. I don't know if he worked out as much as he should have, but it was always great to see him go into Scotty's office, park his butt on a chair, and start drinking coffee and shooting the bull with Scotty Bowman. I don't think there's another player who could do that, but Hullie didn't think twice about it. It didn't matter if it was Scotty Bowman or anyone else. It was comical. I loved that about him.

I believe in fate and I'm convinced that I was put on this earth to play hockey. There is no reason in the world why I should have made it as a hockey player. I grew up in Chicago on the South Side and no one else had ever made it in the NHL from that part of Chicago because it's not a money area. I moved to San Diego at age 15 and didn't play hockey for three years, except for pick-up and unorganized hockey. There was no way I should have made it to the NHL. I got a break, meeting some kid on the beach to go to Moose Jaw—it was a fluke. At that point, my career was over. Some things happen for a reason.

I've never taken anything for granted with my NHL career, especially with what my sister went through. We didn't have a lot growing up; my father worked 80 to 90 hours a week at a restaurant. I saw what he had to do to support our family. When you don't come from a lot, you learn to appreciate when you do get things. The one thing I probably did take for granted was my education after I went to Wisconsin to play. I wish I would have taken it a little more seriously, but I had my heart set on playing in the NHL. In the end, it is what it is, and I ended up being a hockey player.

My time in Detroit has been great. Every year has been different; we've gone through three coaches since I've been here. I always love coming down to the rink because of the history of Joe Louis Arena, it's one of the older buildings now. Everything about Detroit has been such a great experience for me; I haven't had a bad experience yet.

Being a Detroit Red Wing is being a part of a great tradition and history of a great franchise. I feel fortunate that I've been able to play for three of the

Original Six teams. To win a Stanley Cup in Detroit makes me feel like part of the family. I can honestly say that now and I wouldn't have said that before winning a Cup here. For myself and my family, there's no better feeling then being a Red Wing.

Chris Chelios's Career Highlights

* Being the first NHL player to play 400 games with three different teams.

* Winning the Stanley Cup with both Montreal and Detroit.

* Winning the Norris Trophy in 1989, 1993, and 1996.

* Being the runner-up to Nick Lidstrom for the Norris Trophy in the Stanley Cup year of 2002.

* Playing for the 1984, 1998, 2002, and 2006 Olympic teams.

The
NEW
MILLENNIUM

JIRI FISCHER
DEFENSEMAN
1999–Present

WHEN THE NHL SEASON STARTED UP AGAIN after the lockout in 2005, I was having the best start of my career—and then I woke up in a hospital bed. I had no idea what had happened. My fiancée, Avery, was sitting next to my bed and was absolutely terrified. My first thought was, "Something bad must have happened!" Did I get hit on the ice and lose consciousness? All I could do was wonder what the hell happened to me!

I don't remember anything that happened on the bench that night against Nashville, but I've seen it on video since then. I don't remember any ambulance ride or any doctors working on me. I remember all of my life, except for a half-hour of it. I'm hoping that one day it will come back to me. From what people tell me, I had my eyes open, was breathing, and seemed to understand what people were saying to me. I just wasn't replying back to them because I was fighting for my life.

I've already died once. Every time I say that I feel like the luckiest guy! I was told by several doctors that I won the lottery—the lottery of life. I was so lucky that Dr. Tony Colucci, our head team doctor, was sitting right behind our bench. It could have happened on the road, where so many of the team's doctors are seated in the press box. How long is it going to take for a doctor to recognize what is going on, make his way to the ice level, and then try not to panic and help the player? For the doctors, it's probably the first time in their lives that they've been in this situation and they have to be able

Czech native Jiri Fischer was a regular on the Red Wings defense when Detroit captured the 2002 Stanley Cup championship. He was plus-17 during the regular season and contributed three goals, three assists, and was plus-6 in the playoffs.
Photo courtesy of AP/Wide World Photos.

to manage it. Dr. Colucci happened to be an emergency doctor specialist; he deals with situations like this on a daily basis. When it was happening and he was doing chest compressions on me and trying to shock my heart with the defibrillator—I was not aware of any of it.

The odds of having this happen to me when it did and how it did are very similar to the lottery. I had the doctor sitting right behind me. It didn't happen in the middle of the summer when I would go out running in the extreme heat. In the summer sun, on a track in 100-degree heat, your heart rate is going really fast and you're more dehydrated than you are in the first period of a hockey game. It could have happened during a practice, on a plane, or when I'm out biking. I believe that it was all supposed to happen to me!

It's changed my outlook on life and how I treat every situation. Yes, I get frustrated at things—but a lot less than I used to. There are too many people who get frustrated too easily—their lives are passing them by and they're not enjoying it at all. If you're working, in a bad relationship, or frustrated with your kids—you're not enjoying life. I'm not trying to give people life lessons at age 25, but these are ways that I look at life differently now because of what happened to me. I'm sure that the way I look at things now is similar to people who have survived cancer or a massive heart attack, anyone who has lived through a condition that threatened their life. Not many people can die and come back. And if they do come back, not very many of them can fully remember their past, have a fully functional brain, and be able to have all their limbs working like they did before. For me, that is what it means to really win the lottery.

People go and play the lottery every week to try and win money. They don't care about their health or anything else; all they are thinking about is how cool it would be to win the lottery. Who really cares about that? Money is good when you can enjoy it. When you have someone dying right in from of you—no amount of money is going to help. Even the wealthiest person in the world, I'm willing to bet they would give up all their money just to save their child—if they were watching their child die. I'm not trying to give people ethics lessons or to preach, but what I'm trying to say is that people really need to realize what is important in the world.

Unfortunately, and very painfully, I have to realize that at 25 years old, there are other things in life than hockey. Playing in Detroit, with the way the fans treat you, it may seem like hockey is more important than it really is. Hockey is here to entertain, and people play it to have fun and stay physically fit. On the NHL level, the game gives players an opportunity to make good lives for themselves when they leave the game by doing something they love. I hope no one is going to shoot me for saying this—but it's still only hockey! I've realized a lot of things, and the fact that hockey is not the number one priority of 90 percent of the people on the planet is one of them. This revelation came at a costly price, but on the other hand, it's not costly at all if you consider what could have happened. I feel very grateful.

I'm 25 and, yes, I would like to play hockey again. I don't want my professional dreams of playing hockey to be taken away. That would be very sad for me. I hope by the time this book comes out that I'll be playing hockey again. But I can't take for granted the fact that I'm still alive and there are a lot of people who care about me. I'm sure what happened to me was very tough on my teammates. I know it would have been tough on me if I saw it happen and I had to keep on playing. To chance putting everyone through that again, I feel, would be extremely unwise. It could be very costly, and I realize that.

I really hope that there will soon be more answers in the area of electrophysiology and heart rhythm disorders. From talking with some of the best doctors in the world, I don't think that they've discovered enough for them to say with 99 percent certainty that they can or cannot fix this. Research on this has kept me busy since that night happened. Modern medicine is very advanced in a lot of ways; unfortunately, there are not very many cases that are similar to mine. The cases that are similar often have a different ending to them.

The doctors know the state I was in when everything was happening to me. What they do not know is what triggered it, why it happened at that time, and what the true cause of it was. Was it a previous condition or more immediate? When did it start—on the ice or on the bench? What happened to me is known as ventricular tachycardia, an extremely rapid heart beat, also called ventricular fibrillation. Simply put, there are two ventricles in the heart, left and right. The left ventricle is the bottom part of the heart; this part is a little bigger and stronger because it pumps the blood into the body. The right ventricle pumps the blood with less oxygen and more carbon dioxide into the lungs to refuel them with oxygen. It comes back into the left atrium and left ventricle and pumps the blood into the body.

The ventricular tachycardia or ventricular fibrillation that happened to me started extreme rapid pumping of my heart. The walls of the heart started to shake, as opposed to pump, and my heart rate was up to 250 beats per minute. At that point there was very little, if any, oxygen getting into my body and that is why I collapsed. My body went into shut-down mode. At that moment, the brain starts to shut down before the person dies. I had no heart beat and no breath left in me when Dr. Tony Colucci started working on me. Luckily, he knew exactly how to get my body out of that state, and he did. You don't win that kind of lottery very many times, if at all, in your life.

Hockey has been my life and it still is. It probably always will be. At least I hope it always will be. When you're involved in a sport, you're involved in it forever unless something extreme happens. More than anything, I would love to get back to playing hockey in the NHL! But there are a lot of liability issues that are now involved with playing again; and my goal to play again is not the only thing that it will take to get me back to the NHL. If I can physically prove that my heart functions the way it should, and there won't be any recurrence of anything, then I'm pretty confident that I will be allowed to play in the league again. Of course, that depends on if I'm in shape and if I'm good enough to play in the NHL at that point; which could be a month from now or 10 years from now. Even if all of that happens, and I really, really hope that it will, it will still be extremely hard for me to prove it to the NHL, to the Red Wings, or to any team.

I would love to play for the Red Wings again! I don't know any different; there is no other team that I would love to play for. But there are so many "ifs." I just hope that modern medicine will get more experience with patients like me. I call myself a "patient" now and I will be one until things get resolved. I need to wait for modern medicine to get more information on how to prevent situations like this from happening.

For now, I try to occupy myself with the daily functions of regular life, like doing things around the house. Even my exercising is extremely limited at this point.

A lot of people say, "Once you're a Red Wing, you're always a Red Wing," and to a certain extent, people will always treat you as such. But after time, that persona fades because you're not on TV anymore. You don't have the label "Red Wing Hockey Player" now you're "Ex–Red Wing Hockey Player." Being a Detroit Red Wing is different in different circumstances. It's different being a Detroit Red Wing overseas, or anywhere else in the country, than in Detroit. You have a local celebrity status when you are in Detroit and you are treated differently. It feels really good when you play, so good that it's hard not to get a big ego because of it. That is why it's so much harder for some players to retire than others; because, for their adult lives, they've been treated in this amazingly nice way.

Being a Red Wing is an awareness that I've participated in something that means so much to the people of Detroit. But it still means nothing to people in South Africa. I've been treated so well by the Detroit area. What being a Detroit Red Wing means to me is completely different than what it means to 90 percent of the people in the rest of the world—those who don't know you and don't care.

In Detroit, you can make a kid happy just by signing an autograph for him. This is a little kid who is shaking and can't speak because he's that excited to see you! When I look at these children, I see myself when I was six years old. Being a Detroit Red Wing is an extremely proud feeling when you are here. I realize that to a greater extent now, after my unfortunate heart incident on the bench.

For my parents, to see me happy as a Red Wing and living the life that I have—it's huge. My parents still live in the Czech Republic; and for the last seven years, my dad cries almost every time that we are at the airport saying good-bye, even though he knows he'll see me again soon. Since my incident, obviously we look at that differently, because I came pretty close to never seeing my parents again. As a son, being a Red Wing was a way for me to almost re-pay what my parents had given me: all of their patience over the years. Making my parents proud is the greatest accomplishment I have from being a Detroit Red Wing.

Jiri Fischer's Career Highlights

* Surviving a cardiac arrest on the bench on November 21, 2005, and being fully functional after it. "I won my lottery," he said.

* Helping the Czech Republic win the World Championship in 2005.

* Winning the Stanley Cup in 2002.

* Making his parents proud by being in the NHL. "My dad would never show emotion when I was young, and that was hard on me," Fischer said. "He was the one who took me to practice and to the games. The best aspect about being a Detroit Red Wing is that I made my dad proud! I was given the opportunity by the Ilitch family and the organization, who believed in me, to give my dad something that most sons will never be able to give to their parents, a sense of pride and honor."

* Having Chris Chelios as a partner on defense and a mentor, "and all of the help that I received from every Detroit Red Wing player and coach over the years."

JASON WILLIAMS
CENTER
2000–Present

I'LL ALWAYS REMEMBER THIS, and it just shows what a classy guy Stevie Yzerman is. I had spent a week in Traverse City at the rookie camp and, when the veterans arrived to do their fitness testing, Steve Yzerman met me in the hallway. I didn't want to really say anything, I just wanted to go about my business and focus on somehow trying to get a contract. Steve says to me, "Oh, I haven't introduced myself. My name is Steve Yzerman. You're Jason Williams, right?"

I was stunned and in awe. I was like, "Obviously I know who you are, but how do you know who I am?" He said, "I've heard a lot of good things about you so far that you've done in rookie camp. Keep up the good work, keep playing hard, and do what got you here. Don't try to do anything special."

Why did he come up and say that to me? He doesn't have to do that. I was in shock—I couldn't wait to get back to the hotel so I could call my family and my friends to tell them what he said to me.

That has always stuck in my head—it starts with the captain. It shows the type of organization the Red Wings have; the commitment to winning, and making anybody that comes here feel welcome. It was easy to play my game in Detroit because I felt so comfortable. I didn't feel any pressure. I was going to play hard and not try and do anything special, like Stevie said. I was going to earn a contract.

Not being drafted wasn't a big deal to me. I knew I wasn't going to get drafted because no teams had really talked to me. Guys who are drafted are interviewed by teams. Once you are passed over, you have a slim chance of getting picked the next two years after that. The last two years I played juniors, we didn't have great years as a team; so I think that could've been a factor.

After my junior career was over, I thought I still had a chance to play in the NHL. I decided to dedicate the next five years of my life to making it. With the help of my brother, we made a highlight video of my last year in juniors. I would call the GM or the head scout of an NHL team and introduced myself. I would tell them that I had a highlight tape that I'd like them to take a look at.

Out of the 30 teams, I probably sent out 23 or 24 tapes. Whether they looked at them or not, I have no idea. But I felt I was doing everything on my part to get myself recognized. I was hoping the general manager or whoever I talked to would think, "Maybe we could give this kid a shot." It was a start. At least I was putting my name out there and that's what I wanted to do—get my foot in the door.

It was Joe MacDonald who contacted my agent and said Detroit had some interest and they'd like me to go to their rookie camp in Traverse City. My agent asked me, "What do you think?" My brother and I looked at their depth chart in their minor league system and saw they didn't have a whole lot at right wing or center. Being a right-handed centerman, I could play both positions. I figured obviously I'm not going to make the team, but maybe I could develop in their minor league system and in a few years, hopefully, make the jump then.

People kept asking me, "Why would you pick Detroit? Why would you go there? They're full of talent!" The Red Wings were perfect for a number of reasons. They were an older team, and some guys would be retiring soon, and they didn't have a whole lot draft-wise because of being so good over the past few years. They didn't have a bunch of number-one draft picks, so I thought it'd be a great spot for me and I decided to come to Detroit.

If you look at the core group of guys we have in Detroit, some of them came through the system the same way I did. There's that story about the Red Wings picking up Kris Draper for a dollar and Kirk Maltby has had to battle for everything he's accomplished. So, even though my chances of making the

In 2005–2006, his first full season with the Red Wings, Jason Williams was a 21-goal scorer. On October 22, 2005, Williams netted his first NHL hat trick in a game against the Columbus Blue Jackets.

team were slim in the beginning, I thought about what Drapes and Malts went through. They made the best of their opportunity. I looked to those guys for advice. I also watched how they handle themselves on and off the ice. I have a lot of respect for Kris Draper and Kirk Maltby.

Scotty Bowman is not a players' coach. He's not going to come up to you and ask you how life is going. Sometimes you'll walk by him in the hallway and he doesn't know if you're there or not. I shouldn't have been surprised then when he told me 30 or 40 minutes before Game 3 versus Colorado in the 2002 playoffs that I was going to play with Stevie and Shanny. I didn't know what to think. I was very, very nervous, and both Stevie and Shanny came up to me and said, "Don't worry. Just play hard, play your game and you'll be fine. Just do what you do. Don't worry about us. We'll help you out."

That kind of calmed me down, but I was still nervous because I was going head-to-head with Joe Sakic. I kept thinking that if I make a mistake, this could be the end of my Wings career. As a line, we played well together and had a lot of good scoring chances. When the game went into overtime, we had a shift where we came close to scoring. Once we were back on the bench, I whispered to Stevie, "When we get out there again, I think we're going to get one, we're going to get the winner."

It just so happened that Stevie got out on the ice a little before me. He made the pass to Freddie Olausson, who ended up taking the slap-shot that turned out to be the game-winning goal. I definitely felt that game was a turning point for me. When I called my parents and my brother later that night, they said that was the best game they've ever seen me play and that they were proud of me. I couldn't sleep, I was up 'til 2:00 or 3:00 in the morning because I kept thinking about the game. It was a great experience!

Winning the Stanley Cup was a dream come true and to be able to play in the Stanley Cup playoffs was a rollercoaster ride of mixed emotions. You're really high at one moment after a game, but if you made a bad play you could be really low. I learned during those playoffs to control those emotions. We basically had a Hall of Fame team, and for me to be right up front watching these guys go through the ups and downs of a playoff run made me realize what it took to be a player in the NHL. I learned a lot that year.

I don't feel that I was a huge part of the 2002 Stanley Cup team, but I was part of it, and that is something I felt good about. Now I want to be the go-to guy. I want to be the guy scoring the goals, setting up the plays, taking a key face-off, or making a good defensive play. Whatever it is, I want to be the guy they call upon to go out and do whatever I have to do for us to win.

After we won the Cup, I became frustrated because I thought I was part of the Wings future. But over the next two years, the draft picks came in and we signed other guys who are making $3 or $4 million. I started to wonder if they really wanted to play me or not. I began to believe that the coach was getting pressure from up above to play the guys who were making more money than me. Sitting me on the bench was the easy way out because I didn't make a whole lot of money and I was on a two-way contract, so they could send me down any time they wanted to.

With a different coach, it could've been different, but I don't think I can fault a coach. It's just that after we won the Cup in 2002, I was put aside and I was starting all over again. Mentally, that was hard for me to accept. It was especially difficult the season before the lockout. I sat out I don't know how many consecutive games—it was 20-some odd games where I was a healthy scratch. I became extremely frustrated because I'm watching guys around the league who didn't have near the numbers I had in the minors getting good exposure with good teams and doing very well. I felt that could be me, but it just wasn't happening.

Having Mike Babcock as my coach has really helped me out by giving me a chance to play; I've gotten my foot back into the door again. Every year it comes down to showing what you can do and showing how you're going to get better. Even though I'm having some success under Mike, I feel I could've done this earlier in my career. But if I didn't go through what I've gone through the last couple of years, I wouldn't know how to handle being in a slump or any other types of adversity. Mike has given me the chance to prove myself. He's allowing me to show what I can do.

My brother was like a second dad to me because he's a lot older than me. When he was playing in tournaments or in games, anything that he did, I wanted to do and I wanted to be better than him. That mindset helped me out a lot. When he would come to my games, I never wanted to let him down. He would always tell me if I played a good or bad game. I would try so hard to play well because I wanted to make sure he'd come back to see me play. He's a stubborn guy sometimes. I knew he'd always come back.

Most hockey players will tell you that the support they got from their family played a big role in their careers. When I look back on the sacrifices they had to make, I thank them every day. My parents and my brother made my dream come true. I'm doing something I love because of them. When I have kids, I'm going to do whatever it takes for them to have successful and happy lives.

I'm honored to be a Detroit Red Wing. I'm not sure I can put it into words. You're part of an organization that thrives on winning and has an illustrious history. Every time you put on that jersey, you're representing all the players who have worn the winged wheel. Many of them are Hall of Famers. You're overcome with tremendous pride each time you put on that jersey.

Jason Williams's Career Highlights

* Winning the Stanley Cup in 2002.

* Scoring his first NHL goal against Toronto. "I grew up a Leafs fan," he said.

* Playing in Game 3 against Colorado in the 2002 playoffs.

* Being able to watch Nick Lidstrom play. "All of the years I sat on the bench watching him play are pretty special," he recalled. "I had the best seat in the house."

* Scoring his first NHL hat trick against Columbus.

PAVEL DATSYUK
CENTER
2001–Present

IGOR LARIONOV HAD A BIG INFLUENCE on me my first couple seasons in Detroit. He taught me how to drink wine! My first season we were playing in Los Angeles and we were winning 3–2, but I made a bad play and they scored to send it to overtime. In overtime, I tried to pass to Igor, and Ziggy Palffy stole the puck and scored to win the game. I had just given up two goals! I was so mad on the bus. I wanted someone to tell me it was a bad play and I can't play like that, but no one told me anything. Igor was sitting next to me and I asked him, "Why isn't anyone telling me how bad I was?"

He told me to forget about it and think about tomorrow's game; that was what the other guys were doing.

It was hard to change my mindset from Russia, where I would always think about what happened in the previous game until the next game started. Igor taught me how to move on; that in the NHL, you learn from your past mistakes, but you leave them behind you.

I was surprised when the Detroit Red Wings drafted me. One of my friends on my Russian team told me that I had been drafted and I told him, "Yeah, that's a good joke!" He told me that he was serious, that I had been drafted and I should check the paper. After practice, I went out and bought a paper and saw my name with the other draft picks. I thought, "Wow, I don't know how this happened!"

Russian Pavel Datsyuk's dazzling stickhandling wizardry allowed him to become a dominant player for the Red Wings in recent seasons. He led the Red Wings in scoring in 2005–2006 with 87 points.

I was happy to come to Detroit because they were a good team that won. I also had other Russian players on the Red Wings who could help me. I knew about the Russian Five, but I hadn't seen very many Red Wings games. I saw the Stanley Cup when it came to Moscow but I didn't know much about the Detroit Red Wings organization before I was drafted by them.

Over the summer, I went to Detroit with my agent for the rookie training camp. I practiced with them so they could see how I was on my skates and how I moved the puck. I saw Joe Louis Arena at that time, too, it was very big. Ken Holland was showing myself and Yuri Butsayev around the arena and told us that perhaps we would have a chance to play there some day soon.

After my second rookie training camp, I went up to the team's training camp in Traverse City and that was a bit scary for me. I have never had to wear suits to games before; we would always arrive in whatever we wanted to wear to games, like jeans. Wearing suits to a game was a little weird for me.

In between rookie training camp and regular training camp, I also had my first experience playing golf! I was so good that I sent the ground flying everywhere from all the divots I made. The second time I played, they gave me a bucket of balls to play 18 holes with, and when I came back I only had two balls left. I lost every other ball somewhere out on the course. I didn't really understand how to hit the ball straight, my balls went left, right, and everywhere else.

I didn't believe that I would make the team when I came to that first training camp. When the first regular season game started, I couldn't believe that I was still on the team. I had thought that training camp itself would be a good thing for me and, when I didn't make the team, I would just try again next year. The other Russian guys helped me feel more comfortable, like this was my team, and when the season started everyone else was supportive of me.

When I first came to the team, Steve Yzerman made sure that everyone was nice to me. He knew I didn't speak English, but he tried to help me feel comfortable in the team setting. Still, during my first year, I mostly talked with the other Russians on the team, Igor Larionov, Maxim Kuznetsov, and sometimes Sergei Fedorov, because I didn't know English. After a while, a lot of my other teammates would try and help me. They would talk with me to help my language get better. I was always seen as quiet because I didn't know how to translate what I wanted to say.

Sometimes Scotty Bowman would put me in the first drill at practice, but I didn't know what I was supposed to do if I didn't have the chance to go to one of the Russian guys to translate it for me. Scotty did that a couple of times before he realized it and changed the order to help me. It was hard for anyone, including the coaches, to try to talk to me because I could look them in the face and still not know what they were saying without a translator. Scotty would just stand and stare at me and blink his eyes.

Lots of guys tell me to take more shots, yelling, "Shoot the damn puck!" I think assists are better than scoring a goal. Now, there's more pressure on me to take the shot. For me, first, I need the assist; second, I need to take the shot. I don't know why, maybe I just don't have too good of a shot. But I do have good ears; I hear who yells at me on the ice. It's not my on-ice vision, it's my ears, and I just listen to who is yelling at me and that is who I pass the puck to.

In my first year, Brett Hull believed in me and made me believe that I could play at the NHL level. We didn't play the full year together, but we had a good year. If I was wondering what to do, I would ask, "Where is Brett?" He would be yelling behind me on the right or the left side. He would always be telling me, "I'm here!" Boyd Devereaux and I, we're the same age and we could move the puck well, and Brett would find a good spot for us to pass it to him.

Sometimes on the bench, Brett would tell me how he was open and I would think, "I know, but I couldn't pass you the puck through my legs!" He talked to me a lot in my first year and not as much in my second year. The second year, Zetterberg played with us and he would try to translate for me what Hull was saying, but I didn't need a translator for what Brett was trying to tell me. It wasn't every time that Brett was talking to us that he was pissed off. Sometimes he would try and tell us how he was open and how we could have made a better play.

Henrik Zetterberg is a very good friend of mine. He is a smart, strong, and a good skater. He's a good guy, he could only be better if he spoke Russian. Maybe he would consider changing countries?

Nick Lidstrom is one of the NHL's best defensemen. He's a good skater with a good view of the ice. He's strong, always makes good passes, and he's very hard to beat one-on-one. Players like Lidstrom are why guys who play on the Red Wings get better every year. He plays against the best players every night and the rest of us learn from watching him.

We've also had some of the best face-off men on our team, like Steve Yzerman, Kris Draper, and Sergei Fedorov. I would watch what they did. Every year, I feel like I get stronger because they help me learn how I want to play in the face-off circle. It's not my doing, it's more the fact that I've had good teachers.

During the Stanley Cup Finals against Carolina, there was a moment in Game 3, before Igor Larionov scored in the third overtime, that I had a breakaway chance in the second overtime. In the intermission after the first overtime, we went to the locker room. I am very superstitious and wasn't happy when Larionov told me that I was going to be the one to score. I told him, "No, you're going to score!" Sure enough, I had the breakaway in the second overtime and didn't score, but Iggy did score in the third overtime, just as I told him he would.

In my first year in the NHL, we won the Stanley Cup. It was very exciting for me, but I didn't understand a lot of things. It was amazing because I won the Stanley Cup and went to the Olympic Games in my first year in the NHL. At the same time, it was all a little crazy because my wife and I also had our first baby during that same year. I had a lot of good things happening to me, but everything happened in one year, so it went by fast and I didn't have time to understand everything that was going on.

It wasn't until the next year, when we played Anaheim, that I really understood what the playoffs were all about and what it meant to play for the Stanley Cup; but we lost in the first round. I had been on a good team the year before when we won, and I tried to help the team. But I really had no concept of how hard it was to play for the Stanley Cup that first year. I needed more experience.

I try to talk to fans when I see them out at places, like stores. They know that I don't know the language well. They are patient and they try to help me. Talking with them helps me improve my English. I always appreciate the fans; they believe in me. The fans help to make me feel comfortable, like, "This is my team and I want to play here!"

Being a Detroit Red Wing means playing on a good team, with good players, and having good fun. It's "Hockeytown," and now I believe that my hockey life is meant to be here with the Detroit Red Wings. My life as an NHL hockey player, and as a man, started in Detroit.

Pavel Datsyuk's Career Highlights
★ Playing five seasons in the Russian League before coming the NHL.
★ Winning the Stanley Cup in 2002.
★ Getting to know Igor Larionov not only as a player, but as a person and a friend.
★ Playing on the Russian Olympic team in 2002 and 2006.
★ Helping Russia win bronze medal at 2005 World Championships.

LUC ROBITAILLE
LEFT WING
2001–2003

IN THE SUMMER OF 2001, PEOPLE THOUGHT I had re-signed with the Los Angeles Kings when I really had not. I had told my agent, Pat Brisson, to start calling a few teams. Honestly, I was thinking maybe Dallas, San Jose, or Detroit would be a good fit.

But the night the Red Wings signed Dominik Hasek, that got me thinking about Detroit being the one.

"If you are going to sign somewhere other than Los Angeles, you should sign with a team that has players you can win a Stanley Cup with," my wife, Stacia, said.

After looking at their team again, I can remember thinking that if I could sign there, I would definitely be getting my best chance to win the Cup. But the Red Wings were talking to some other players at the time, and general manager Ken Holland told Pat that he didn't know I was available.

"Are you really going to come here or are you using us to get back to L.A.?" Holland asked me.

"If I'm talking to you, it means I want to be there," I said.

It only took two or three phone calls to get the deal done. My decision to sign there turned out to be the best decision of my career. Winning that Stanley Cup in 2002 was the biggest event of my career.

Playing for that franchise was special. You can be anywhere, even Montreal, and you can't find what they have in Detroit. They don't call Montreal

"Hockeytown." There's just a certain aura that's difficult to describe. I was excited to come to training camp. As a player, I had heard that this franchise was all about winning the Stanley Cup. They had a great owner in Mr. Ilitch, a top general manager in Ken Holland, and a coaching legend in Scotty Bowman.

I remember when the Los Angeles Lakers basketball team had those four future Hall of Fame players, and everyone was talking about how unique that was. That was nothing compared to what the Red Wings had when I came there in 2001–2002.

Steve Yzerman. Nick Lidstrom. Brett Hull. Sergie Fedorov. Brendan Shanahan. Igor Larionov. Hasek. The roster was full of future Hall of Famers.

I was really impressed by how Scotty handled us. He never really talked to us, because he didn't have to. We always knew our role. No matter the situation, we knew Scotty would give us the best opportunity to win. He made us compete for what we were supposed to get. It's a great quality in a coach when you have that many good players.

The coolest thing about that season is just that we pulled it off. Sometimes if you have a lot of great players, it doesn't work. When we were down 2–0 in the series against Vancouver, people were already counting us out. And I think coming back to win Game 6 and Game 7 against Colorado was special. I remember being so pumped before the Game 7. Getting that goal in the first period was one of my career highlights. That was an amazing game for us, especially beating Colorado 7–0. It was a great feeling. It almost felt like we won the Cup right there.

My attitude was, when I went to Detroit, I was going to do whatever it took to win. I was willing to pay any price, cut my ice time, play with different guys, adjust to any situation. I knew that was just really my chance to win. That's what I was willing to do. It paid off.

When we won the Cup, I remember jumping on the ice. You can't describe the moment. My kids shared it with me. Steven was 14 then and Jesse was seven. We took them to the parade. It was amazing to see the red and white everywhere. It was incredible for my kids to be a part of that.

I took the Stanley Cup back to Los Angeles so all of the people who helped me throughout my career could enjoy it. I invited them to a big party. And Chris Chelios had that weekend as well, so we went to his house in Malibu for a big party. Then we took it around L.A. We took the Cup to the Hollywood sign. We took it to the ocean. My kids ate popcorn out of it.

315

Luc Robitaille was a 30-goal scorer for the Red Wings in 2001–2002, and then he contributed four goals and nine points in Detroit's march to the Stanley Cup championship. Although Robitaille played only two seasons in Detroit, his engaging personality made him a lasting fan favorite.
Photo courtesy of AP/Wide World Photos.

What I remember most about my time in Detroit is that everything is special when you are with the Red Wings. Maybe it's because this team is one of the Original Six. But I think it's because Mr. Ilitch appreciated the players so much. That made it special. To this day, winning the Stanley Cup is my greatest memory I've ever had as a player.

Luc Robitaille's Career Highlights

* Scoring at home against Washington, on January 18, 2002—his 611th career goal—to surpass Bobby Hull as the all-time leading goal scorer among left wingers in NHL history. Bobby Hull was in the stands and gave Robitaille a cigar after the game. Robitaille said the milestone was extra special because of Bobby Hull's presence. He added that his first skates were a pair of Bobby Hull–style CCMs.

* Having a goal and an assist in the first 10 minutes of the Game 7 Western Conference Finals against Colorado. The Red Wings eventually won 7–0 and won the Stanley Cup championship that season.

* Scoring his 600th career goal and having it hold up as Detroit beat Anaheim 1–0 in an entertaining hockey game on November 9, 2001.

* Having an assist on March 24, 2004, to reach 1,370 points to pass Johnny Bucyk to become the highest point-producing left wing in NHL history.

* Holding the NHL record of 63 goals and 125 points in one season by a left wing, set while with the L.A. Kings.

HENRIK ZETTERBERG
CENTER/LEFT WING
2002–Present

WHEN I WAS YOUNGER, I was always the smallest guy on the ice. All the guys my age grew a lot quicker than I did. I always had to find a way to play without getting hit. I was always figuring out ways to get out from the corners with the puck when I had all those big guys around me. When I started growing and became almost the same size as those guys, that mindset helped me.

I was a late bloomer, and in 1999 when I was drafted in the seventh round by the Red Wings, I was really happy because I wasn't expecting to get drafted. When Hakan Andersson, the Wings European scout, called me to tell me that I had been drafted by the Wings, I was actually on vacation with my friends. It was a big surprise to me, and it made that vacation a lot better! After the Wings drafted me, they wanted me to come over right away and take part in their summer camp, but I couldn't get a connecting flight from where I was on vacation.

The Red Wings are very smart when they are bringing guys over from another country. They know that the guys are playing pro hockey overseas before they get here, and that the players are pretty much ready to play when they get to the NHL. But if I would have been drafted by another team, they probably would have had me over here a year earlier than I was and I wasn't ready then. The Red Wings let me sharpen my skills and develop in my own surroundings first. They knew that I was going to play in every national

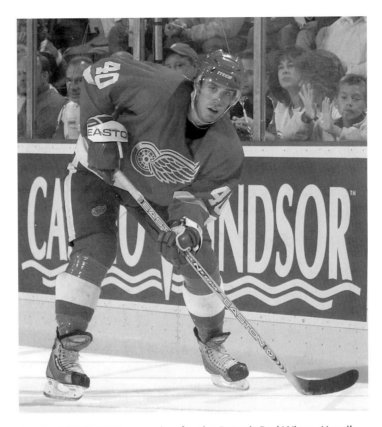

After a standout 2005–2006 campaign for the Detroit Red Wings, Henrik Zetterberg went to Riga, Latvia, in May to help his native Sweden become the first country to win the Olympic and World Hockey Championships in the same year.

tournament and had a chance to play in the Olympics, where I would be playing with the world's best players. I think that helped me a lot.

Coming over from Sweden in 2002, I really hoped that I was going to be able to make the Red Wings. But when I looked at the roster, they had a lot of really good players. I was realistic. I knew that I had to have a really good camp and go from there. It turned out that I never had to play in the minors; I started out and stayed with the Detroit Red Wings from day one.

I was very nervous to meet all the guys on the team. Most of them were really famous; they were my idols when I was younger. Yet, as soon as I got to see the team in the locker room, I realized that they are all really nice guys, and that helped me to relax. I was in awe of Steve Yzerman. The first few times I met him and spoke with him, I couldn't say that much. But he's an unbelievable guy; I think he is the best captain. I've never had a better captain. One of the reasons he is so good is that he's really friendly and always willing to help out.

The biggest adjustment I had to make coming over to the NHL was to go straight to the net. When you're playing in Europe, the ice is so much bigger, so when you would get the puck across the blue line there, you would still have a lot of time to get to the net. In the NHL, when you cross the blue line, you have a scoring chance.

I didn't go and ask teammates for advice as much as I watched guys when they were practicing and in games. I watched how hard they worked after practice, too. I learned by watching. My first week was exhausting—after practice on the ice I would watch these guys go and lift weights for an hour and knew that that was the thing I had to do, too. I just went in there and did it and, after awhile, I got used to it.

Playing for Dave Lewis and Barry Smith my first couple of years was a lucky break. They liked my style of play enough to let me play on the Red Wings right away. If I had a coach who didn't like my style, I wouldn't be here now. Igor Larionov also helped me a lot; he understood the style I wanted to play and encouraged me. Igor was a big help to both myself and Pavel Datsyuk.

When I arrived in Detroit, Pavel Datsyuk was one of the youngest players on the team and so was I. We both played the same style of hockey and we enjoyed playing with each other. When we started playing on the same line, we had to learn how to communicate. I think that we clicked in a good way. Off the ice, Pavel is a really funny guy, and it's true that he can speak more English than he says. We were roommates on the road and have had a lot of good times. When I came to the Red Wings, Pavel helped me a lot my first couple of weeks. He came to me on the ice and we chit-chatted and started passing the puck around from the start. It helped to have someone to talk to and have fun with.

During my first season, I played with Pavel Datsyuk and Brett Hull. Playing with Hull was just awesome. Pavel and I would always work our asses off on the ice because we knew if we could get the puck to Hullie, he would score. But when we didn't see him open, he would tell us about it back on the bench, saying, "How could you not see me!" I never played with a guy who talked that much on the ice and off the ice. It was a great experience.

Brett would never yell to us on the ice because then the other team would know that he was there. But every once in awhile we wouldn't see him there, either. When we got to the bench after he was open, and we didn't give it to him, he let us know! It was always good-hearted and friendly, but the first couple of times it was just like "Oh, my God, I need to pass the puck to him next shift!" The next shift we got on the ice, you could be sure that we would get him the puck. Hull took really good care of me in those first years, too. If something would happen off the ice, he would always make sure that I was okay. That helped me to be more comfortable with the team, knowing that he would be there to help me through.

Both Nicklas Lidstrom and Tomas Holmstrom helped me a lot from the beginning. Everything is so different here from back in Sweden, just getting a phone here takes a week. Having those two guys here so that I could ask them a question in Swedish, instead of English, was a big relief. I had dinner with them before going to camp. They helped make my getting used to the Red Wings a lot easier. They told me just to play my game and not to be so nervous.

I remember Holmstrom from the Swedish Elite League, when he played in Lulea. He didn't go over to the NHL as early as Lidstrom did, so I had the chance to see Homer play more. He was an exciting player to watch back then, too. The thing with Homer is that he never gives up, he always battles. He has a tough job and he does it really well. I don't think there's anyone better than him in front of the net.

Nicklas Lidstrom doesn't get all the credit that he deserves back home in Sweden. He's been over here with the Red Wings for a long time. When you grow up in Sweden, you don't get the NHL games as much. Because the Red Wings are always in the playoffs, Nick doesn't get home as much and doesn't play in the world championships. The young players in Sweden don't get to see him. When you see NHL highlights back home, you see Mats Sundin or Forsberg and not Nick because he is a defenseman. You don't see Nick's good passes as much as some of the other Swedes who are forwards.

Once I got the chance to play with him for a while, I could see that he was an unbelievable player. I didn't know how good Nick was until I started playing with him. I am almost sure that I will never play with a better defenseman than him. I had only seen Lidstrom play a couple of times before I came to Detroit, and I had played with him once before that in the Olympics in Salt Lake. When you practice with him every day, and I've played more than

200 games with him now, you get the chance to watch him and see that he just doesn't make any mistakes. If he makes 100 passes, 95 of them will be on the blade. He does all the little stuff right and always makes it look so easy.

I didn't know much about the history of the Detroit Red Wings franchise, or what it meant to be playing on an Original Six team, when I first came here from Sweden. I started to realize it after I played here for a while. I knew about the Original Six teams and I knew that the Red Wings had won three Stanley Cups in six years. I knew that we had a really good team. It wasn't until I talked to Nicklas Lidstrom and Tomas Holmstrom, and they told me that being in the States was unbelievable, that I really looked forward to coming over here. I feel very lucky to have been drafted by the Red Wings and been fortunate enough to have played my entire career in Detroit without ever having to play in the minors.

Being a Detroit Red Wing is about being around the organization and all the players who play here. It's about getting the chance to meet all the great Red Wings legends, like when Ted Lindsay and Mr. Hockey (Gordie Howe) come down to the rink. To be able to tell my children and grandchildren one day that I was a part of that tradition is unbelievable.

Henrik Zetterberg's Career Highlights

* Starting in his first home game on a line with Shanahan and Fedorov.

* Watching his first Red Wings game against Colorado in the playoffs when he came to sign his contract with the team.

* Developing a friendship with Pavel Datsyuk that will last a lifetime. "He does things with the puck that you think are impossible," Zetterberg said.

* Playing on a line with Brett Hull. "Whenever I return to Sweden, everyone always asks me what it is like to play with Hull," Zetterberg said. "I tell them it could be the best thing in the world but it could be really tough at times, too."

* Starting a game with four other Swedish players. "I didn't realize it was the five of us until Draper yelled, 'Lets go Tre-Kroner!' which is the name of the Swedish national team," he recalled. "Standing with five Swedes on the blue line to start the game gave me chills."

INDSAY · LEO REISE · RED KELLY · MAX MCNAB · MARTY PAVELIC

BENNY WOIT · LARRY ZEIDEL · GLENN HALL · JIMMY SKINNER ·

MAHOVLICH · BRYAN WATSON · RED BERENSON · JIM RUTHERFO

Y · PAUL WOODS · STEVE YZERMAN · GREG STEFAN · JIM DEVELLA

· JIM NILL · TIM CHEVELDAE · PAUL MACLEAN · MARTIN LAPOIN

S OSGOOD · DOUG BROWN · KEVIN HODSON · KIRK MALTBY · T

CHRIS CHELIOS · JIRI FISCHER · JASON WILLIAMS · PAVEL DATS

LLY · MAX MCNAB · MARTY PAVELICH · MARCEL PRONOVOST ·

· GLENN HALL · JIMMY SKINNER · BRUCE MACGREGOR · BILL G

N · RED BERENSON · JIM RUTHERFORD · DANNY GRANT · DEN

YZERMAN · GREG STEFAN · JIM DEVELLANO · EDDIE MIO · SHAW

LDAE · PAUL MACLEAN · MARTIN LAPOINTE · NICKLAS LIDSTRO

BROWN · KEVIN HODSON · KIRK MALTBY · TOMAS HOLMSTROM

IRI FISCHER · JASON WILLIAMS · PAVEL DATSYUK · LUC ROBITA

B · MARTY PAVELICH · MARCEL PRONOVOST · JOHNNY WILSON

JIMMY SKINNER · BRUCE MACGREGOR · BILL GADSBY · DOUG

SON · JIM RUTHERFORD · DANNY GRANT · DENNIS POLONICH

STEFAN · JIM DEVELLANO · EDDIE MIO · SHAWN BURR · HARRY

AN · MARTIN LAPOINTE · NICKLAS LIDSTROM · MARK HOWE · S